Endorsements

Portraying the ceaseless change that is a river, Diana Thomas set herself a challenge that invites us to be inspired and even to challenge ourselves. Be you an historian, a "river rat," an art enthusiast or just a harmless lover of books and beauty, I'm confident that Diana's visual language and soul will speak to you.

—Marilyn Lt Klimcho
Producer and Host of Poets' Pause and Pub Date with an Author,
available on Berks Community Television and YouTube

Current Color on the Susquehanna River is a deeply moving collection that showcases the power of place in daily life, grief, healing and happiness. You'll come back to the art and words again and again.

—Hope Byers
Vice President of Visitor Engagement
Susquehanna National Heritage Area

CURRENT COLOR
on the
SUSQUEHANNA RIVER

*An Artist's Reflection
on Life and Painting*

DIANA THOMAS

Paperback ISBN 978-1-960007-72-8

Published by

Mercy & Moxie

an imprint of

Orison Publishers, Inc.

PO Box 188, Grantham, PA 17027

www.OrisonPublishers.com

Contents

Preface

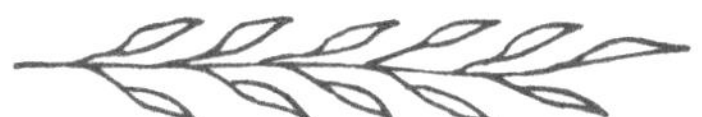

When I set out to paint the Susquehanna River once a week for an entire year, my only goal was to build a new habit of regularly making art just for the sheer joy of it. For at least three decades I'd worked as an illustrator, graphic artist, drawing instructor and needle arts designer, but I rarely made art just to satisfy my artist soul.

The idea for this crazy challenge came from two sources. The first was the echo of my mom's wise words rambling around in my head with greater intensity since her recent passing: "Life is too short to hold a grudge, to *not* say 'I love you,' to put off doing things you need or want to do." The second source—much harder to put into words—felt like a compelling call to action that wouldn't leave me alone. Believing it to be a divine prompt not to be postponed, I picked up my camera and paintbrushes and set happily to work.

Since I had enjoyed journal writing for many years, I thought it would be a good idea to create a weekly notation of what was going on at the river, lessons about the paintings, and the general business of my daily life. There was no particular agenda for the topics; I simply expected that in the course of a year there would be some noteworthy things I'd want to keep. I started on a Tuesday, so my week ran from Tuesday to the following Monday.

At the conclusion of the year's work, it started to become evident that a much bigger plan had been in play all along. This poignant, yearlong journey, full of beautiful colors, also contained a devastating tragedy that would change my life forever. I never could have foreseen how the metaphor of the constantly flowing river and the therapeutic process of painting would comfort and soothe my grieving soul.

A year after finishing the challenge, I was invited to show the series at the beautiful Columbia Crossings building at Riverfront Park in Columbia, Pennsylvania. A friend encouraged me to include the personal weekly journal entries alongside the art. I'd publicly shown my art in the past, but the thought of sharing my private musings, notes and concerns terrified me. It soon became apparent, however, that my artistic and Christian thoughts touched others who not only enjoyed my new river views but who also found common ground in the painful parts of my story while carrying their own losses and tragedies.

After several showings of the series and writings, many people asked if a book was available. This request prompted me to learn how to go about publishing one; hence the book you now hold in your hands was born.

I stand amazed and full of gratitude that the year of saying "yes" to art-making has become so much more. I know now that the work and the story were never meant for me alone. Sharing my beautiful and painful story with others was the intended purpose all along. What's more, the mystery of God's grace in action through His prompt to undertake and follow through with the challenge has been the catalyst that brought additional healing to my own heart.

Thank you for letting me share once more.

Diana

"There is a river whose streams make glad the city of God,
the holy place where the Most High dwells. God is within her,
she will not fall; God will help her at break of day."

(Psalm 46:4–5)

Introduction

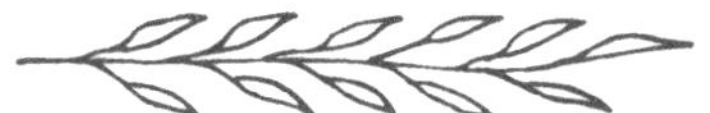

Looking back over 70 years of life, I notice that a number of rivers have played an important part in my personal history, but none more so than the Susquehanna River. The Susquehanna possesses a mysterious power to hold my attention and draw me often to her banks, which I've never tried to resist. I've become so familiar with her moods and currents that she seems like an old friend. Over the years, I've become a Susquehanna nerd who has greatly enjoyed gathering facts about her. While painting the river each week, I traveled to some of my favorite haunts through a 90-mile stretch of the Lower Susquehanna from just north of Harrisburg, Pennsylvania, all the way to Havre de Grace, Maryland.

The Susquehanna River has its humble beginnings at Lake Otsego in Cooperstown, New York. Its North Branch flows 445 miles from there to the Chesapeake Bay. When you include the area of the Susquehanna's West Branch, this huge watershed drains 27,510 square miles of Pennsylvania, New York and Maryland, contributing 50% of the bay's fresh water.

I've lived in the river town of Columbia, Pennsylvania, within walking distance of the Susquehanna, for more than 20 years, giving me ample opportunities to observe, firsthand, powerful floods, ice floes, windswept white caps, stunning sunset reflections and the occasionally calm surface as smooth as glass.

The more I've learned about the river, the more intriguing I've found her to be. Geologists believe it is one of the oldest rivers in the world. In its most southern stretches, the river bottom contains the mysterious "Deeps," where crevasses of 200 feet below the surface have been recorded.

There is a rich store of archaeological evidence of Native American life that flourished in and near the waters, including remarkable ancient carvings, called petroglyphs, chiseled into larger rocks in the riverbed. Most are now submerged by the higher water levels created by dams, but at low water there are some within a few miles drive from Columbia that can be seen when reached by boat.

In the days of the westward expansion of the United States, settlers established ferries at many points on the river to move people and goods across the swift but shallow, rocky waters. Wright's Ferry was one of the first. Built in 1730, it helped establish the city of Columbia as an economic center in Lancaster County, Pennsylvania. Another ferry, in Millersburg, Pennsylvania, was started in the 1750s and has been continuously operated there since 1817. A leisurely ride across the river in this paddle-wheel-driven craft is a favorite summer pastime of my husband and I and our grandchildren.

As the richness of Pennsylvania's natural resources became apparent in the early eighteenth century, the Susquehanna River became a critically important conduit for moving wood, coal and iron to ports like Philadelphia and Baltimore. Since the Susquehanna is the longest commercially non-navigable river in the United States, the Pennsylvania Canal system and the Susquehanna and Tidewater Canal of the early nineteenth century provided safer and more reliable means of moving goods and people along the river's banks before railroads began to be a faster and more efficient means of transportation.

Many bridges have spanned the Susquehanna River at Columbia since 1814. Those who are Civil War buffs will know that the second bridge, built in 1834, was destroyed by fire in 1863 to prevent the Confederate army from moving across the river. In addition, there is a good amount of evidence that Columbia was not only an important connection for moving slaves to freedom, but also likely initiated the use of the term "Underground Railroad." Railroad cars owned by two freed and wealthy business owners, Stephen Smith and William Whipper, were specially fitted with secret compartments for hiding those heading for freedom in Philadelphia.

One last thing I'll mention about why the Susquehanna River intrigues and fascinates me is her importance as another sort of highway. As a bird-watcher, I know this river is a guidepost for what is known as the Atlantic Flyway, an immense migratory pathway for birds flying along the East Coast.

Every fall there are many kinds of migrating waterfowl and songbirds resting along the banks. In February, I am always thrilled to hear the first of the "V"-shaped flocks of swans returning northward, even sometimes flying at night. They bring me a sure sign of hope that spring will be just around the corner. It is rare to walk along the river trails now and not see at least one Bald Eagle. They were nearly extinct in Pennsylvania along the river in the late 1960s, until some pairs from Canada were brought in the 1970s to reestablish them in their natural environment.

These are just a few of my treasured nuggets of information that I think will help you see why I chose to make the amazing Susquehanna River the focus of my yearlong painting challenge. The lines below are by Columbia native Lloyd Mifflin (1846–1921), who was known as an artist and as America's Sonneteer:

How softly round thy clustered rocks of blue

Thou murmurest onward! oh! may we pursue

Our way as calmly to the eternal sea![1]

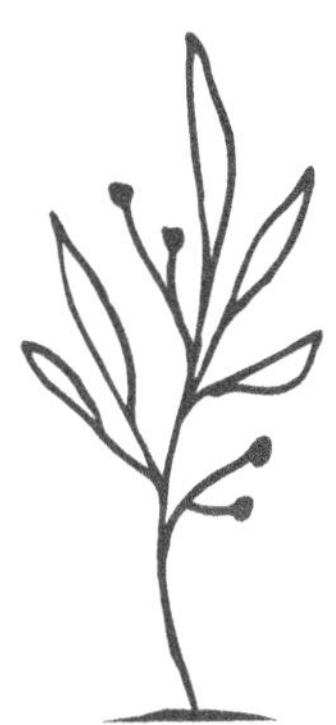

---

1 Lloyd Mifflin, *At the Gates of Song, Sonnets* (Boston: Estes & Lauriat, 1897), 117.

WEEK

1

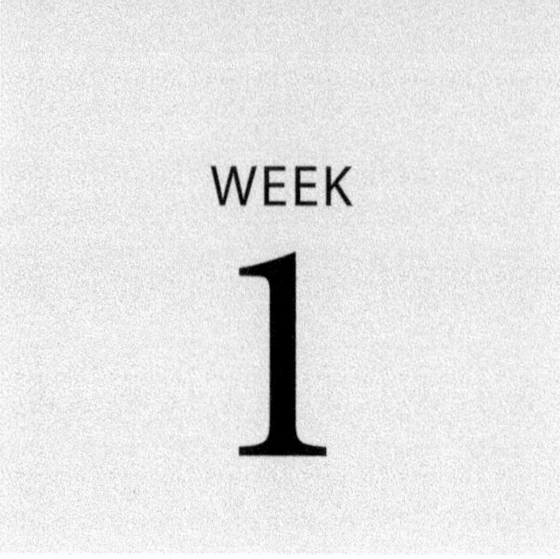

DECEMBER 22–28, 2015

"Veiled"

E. Donegal Riverfront Park, Marietta, PA

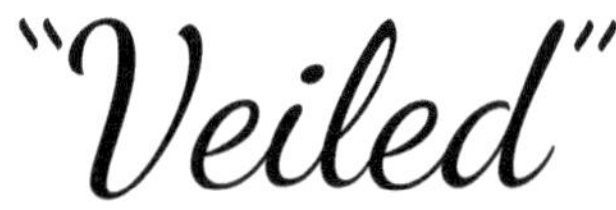

Am I crazy for attempting this project? Yes! I am just crazy enough to think there is a chance I can do a painting a week for a year. I need and want to stretch myself, give "painting time" a bigger space in my life, and get going while I still feel brave.

It's been a wet and cloudy week, keeping the river shrouded and clouded. I'm thinking this is great—mysterious and not revealing too much, too soon.

Standing there on the bank, I thought of this verse:

"There is nothing concealed that will not be disclosed, or hidden that will not be made known."

(Luke 12:2)

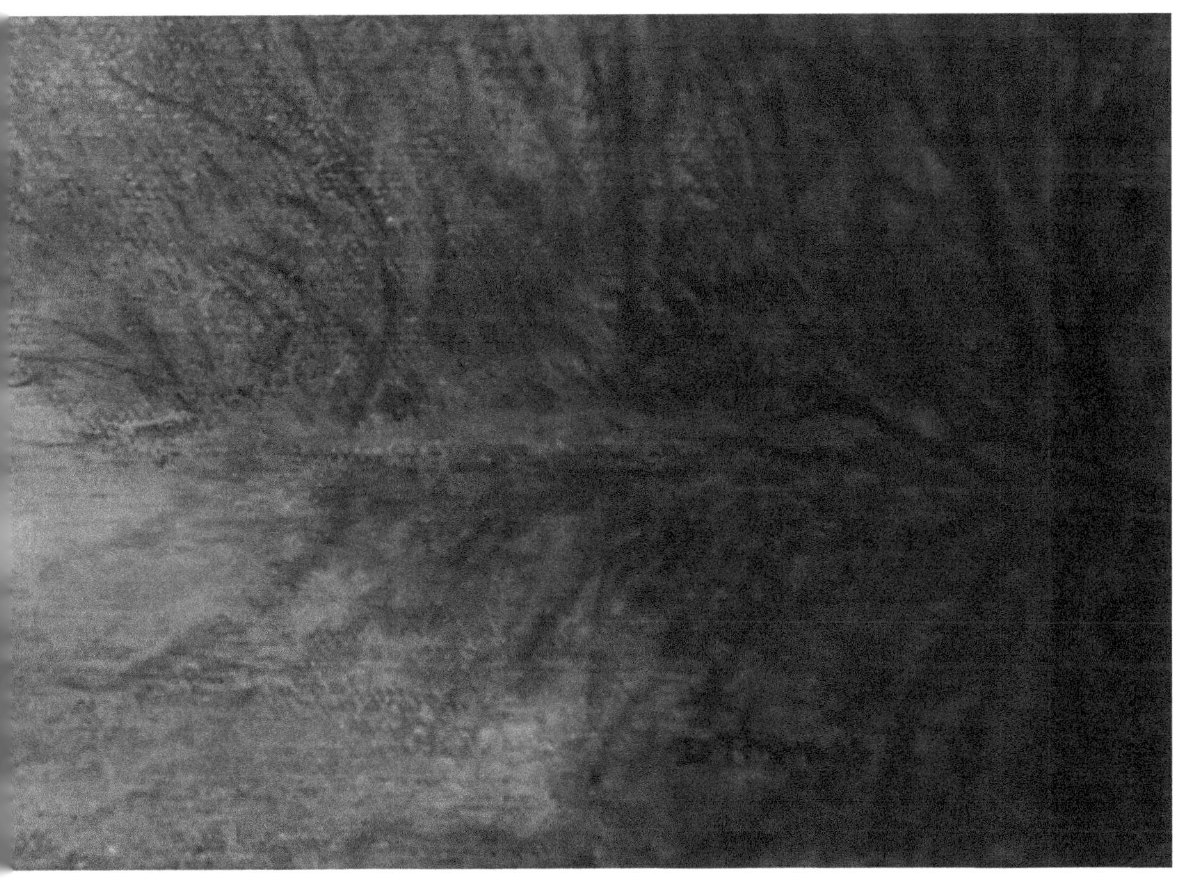

DECEMBER 29, 2015–JANUARY 4, 2016

"Above the Turbulence"

Safe Harbor Dam, Conestoga, PA

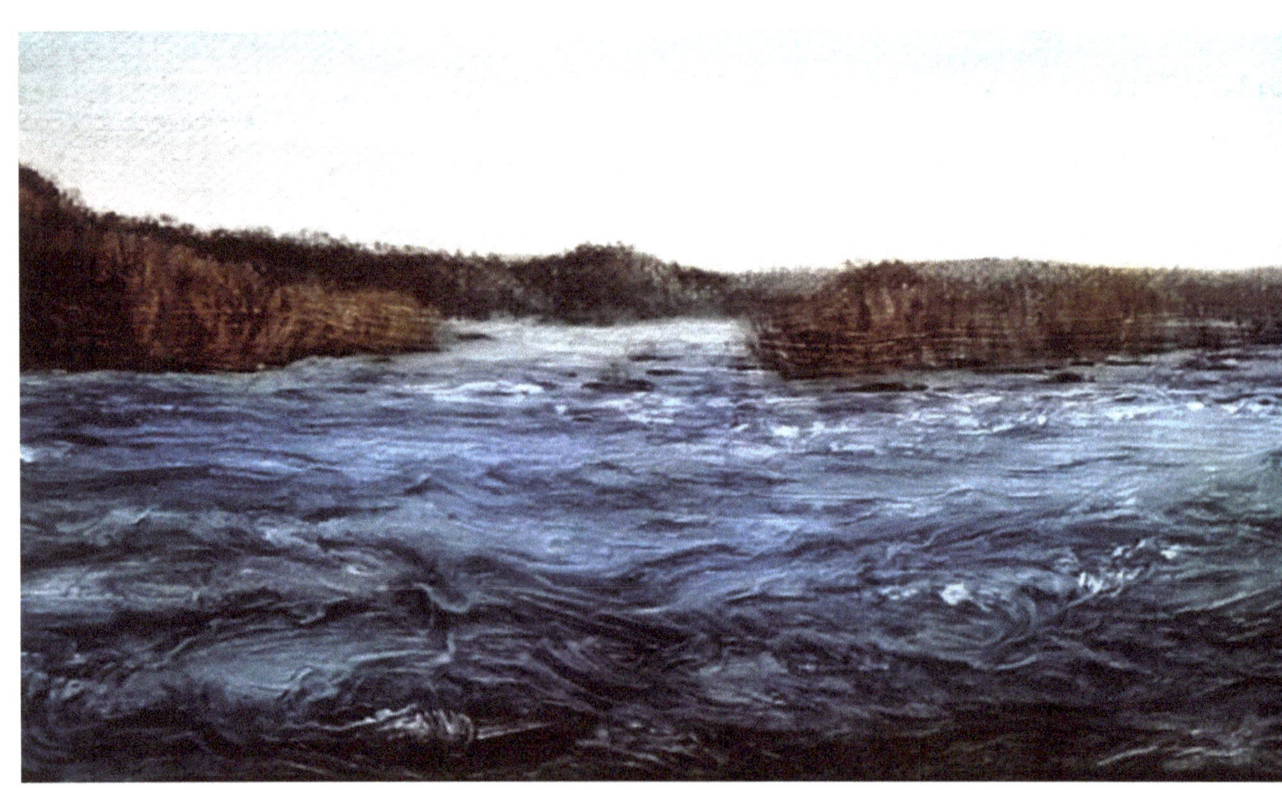

It's a mixed bag of weather as winter seems to be trying to arrive and push out the above-average temps we've had.

Spending time at the river getting photos and thinking about which one to paint and how I want to paint it will be the easy part of this project. I am worried about being overly fussy when I paint, so maybe I will forgo my reading glasses sometimes!

Setting out on this journey feels good. It feels like 2016 is the year for a different kind of journey, a new road to travel.

> "Whether you turn to the right or to the left, your ears will hear a voice behind you, saying, This is the way; walk in it."
>
> (Isaiah 30:21)

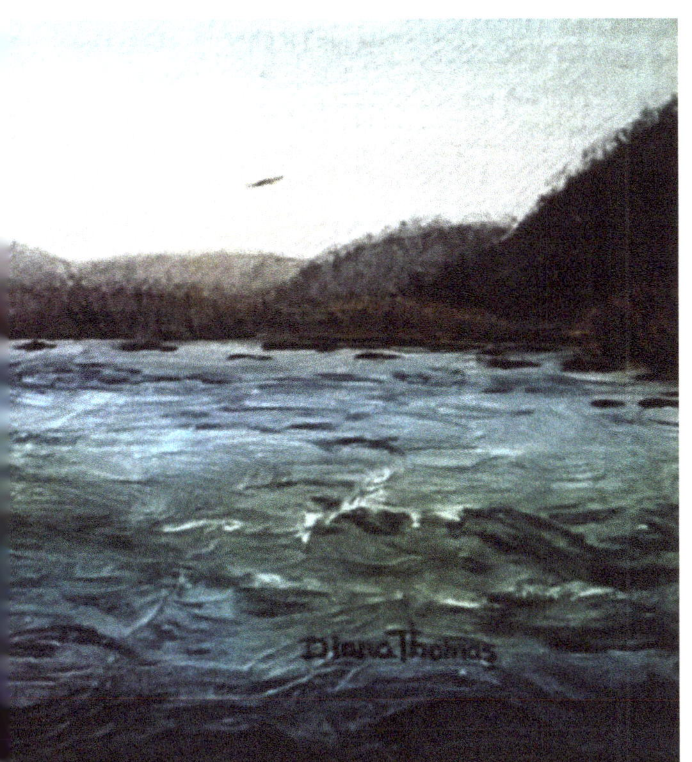

Step 1 – Umber underpainting

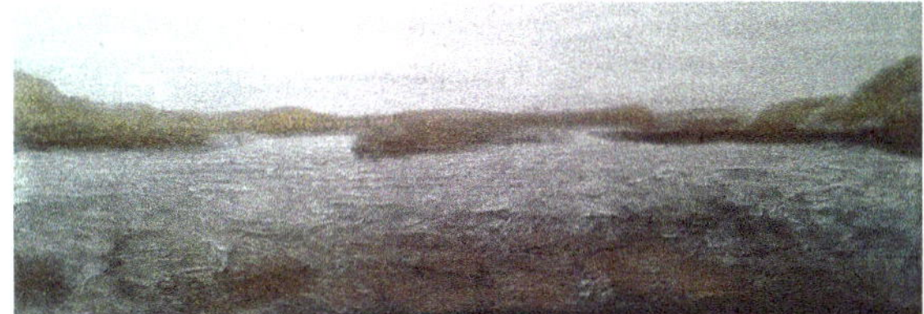

Step 2 – Blocking in

JANUARY 5–11, 2016

"Foggy Bridge"

Wrightsville Boat Ramp at Dusk, Wrightsville, PA

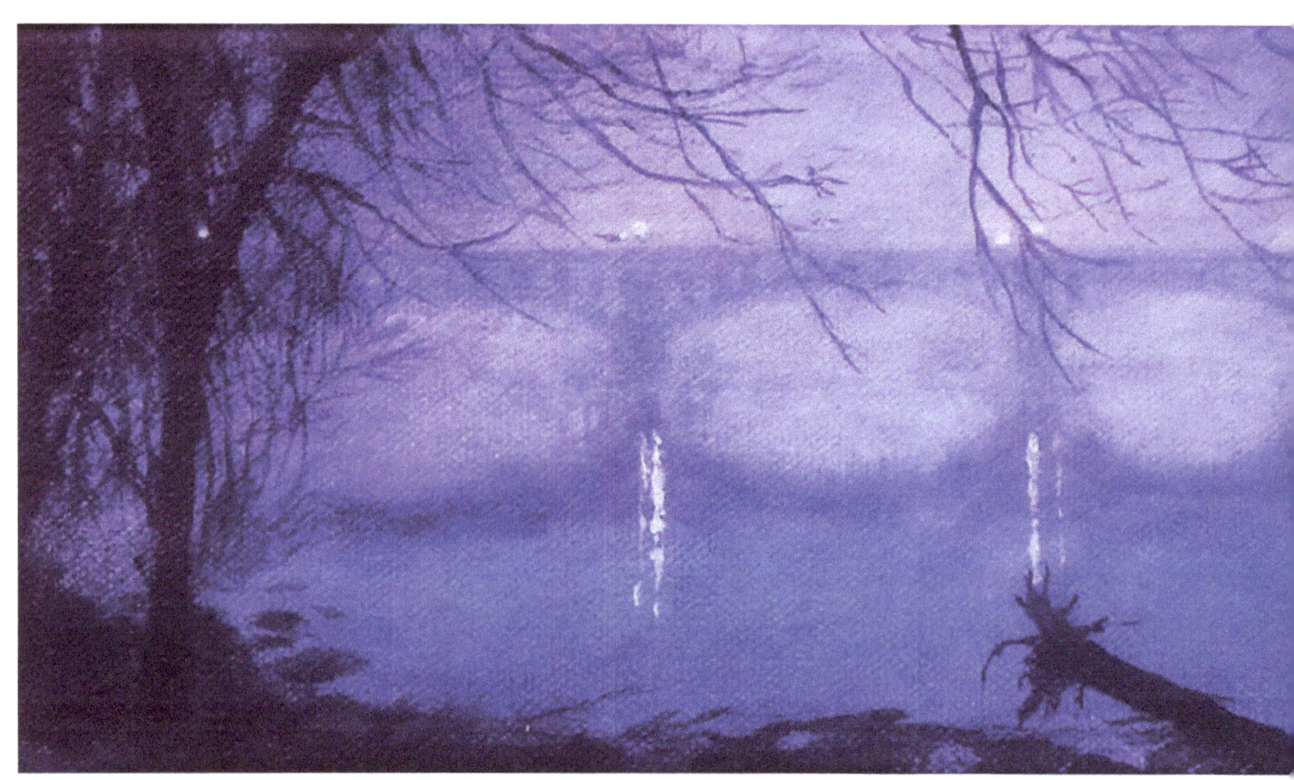

It is very foggy as temps are back up in the mid-30s after being down in the single digits a couple of days ago! I went out about an hour before dark. I almost didn't go out, but I am so glad I did. What beautiful shots! There was a shimmer of various colors in and through the fog. I am not sure if that was part of the sunset trying to come through, or what. How will I capture that?

I am glad this project is getting me off my duff, sending me outdoors and forcing me to paint. This beautiful river has been calling to me for a long time. I am looking forward to what this body of work will look like and what it will say.

It will be interesting to see the variety of colors that represent the water over the course of the year.

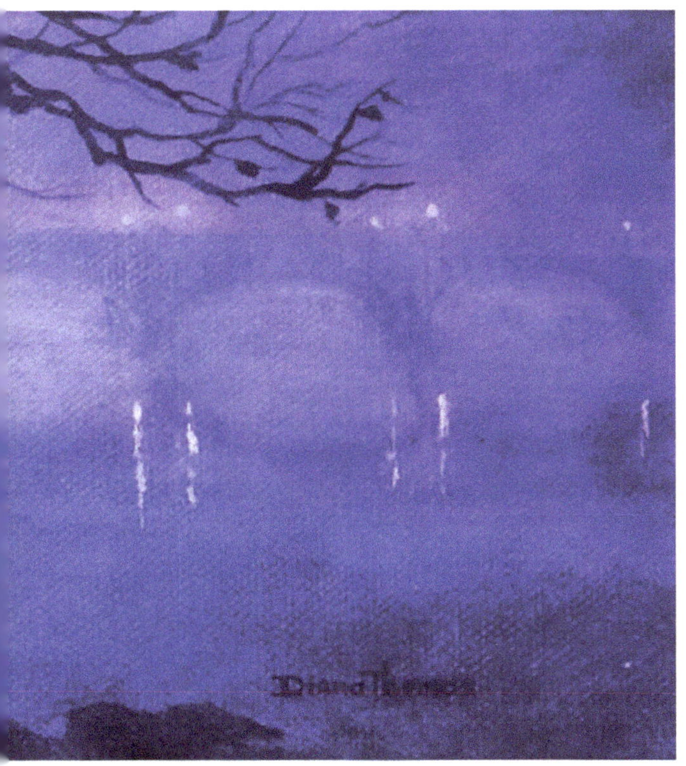

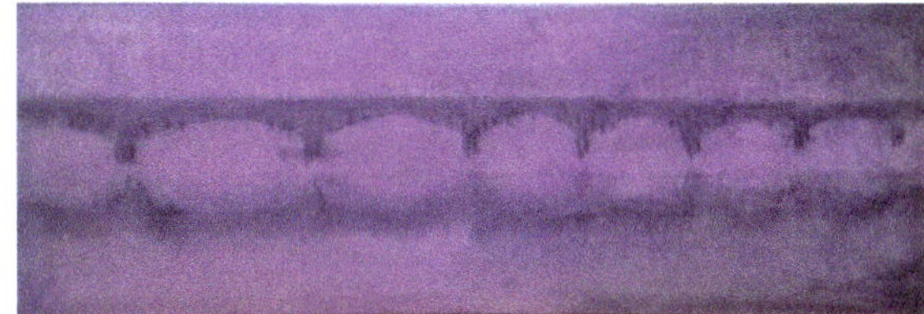

Working very wet on this one…

JANUARY 12–18, 2016

"TMI" and
"Enola Low Grade Trail at Dusk"

Middletown, PA *and* Washington Boro, PA

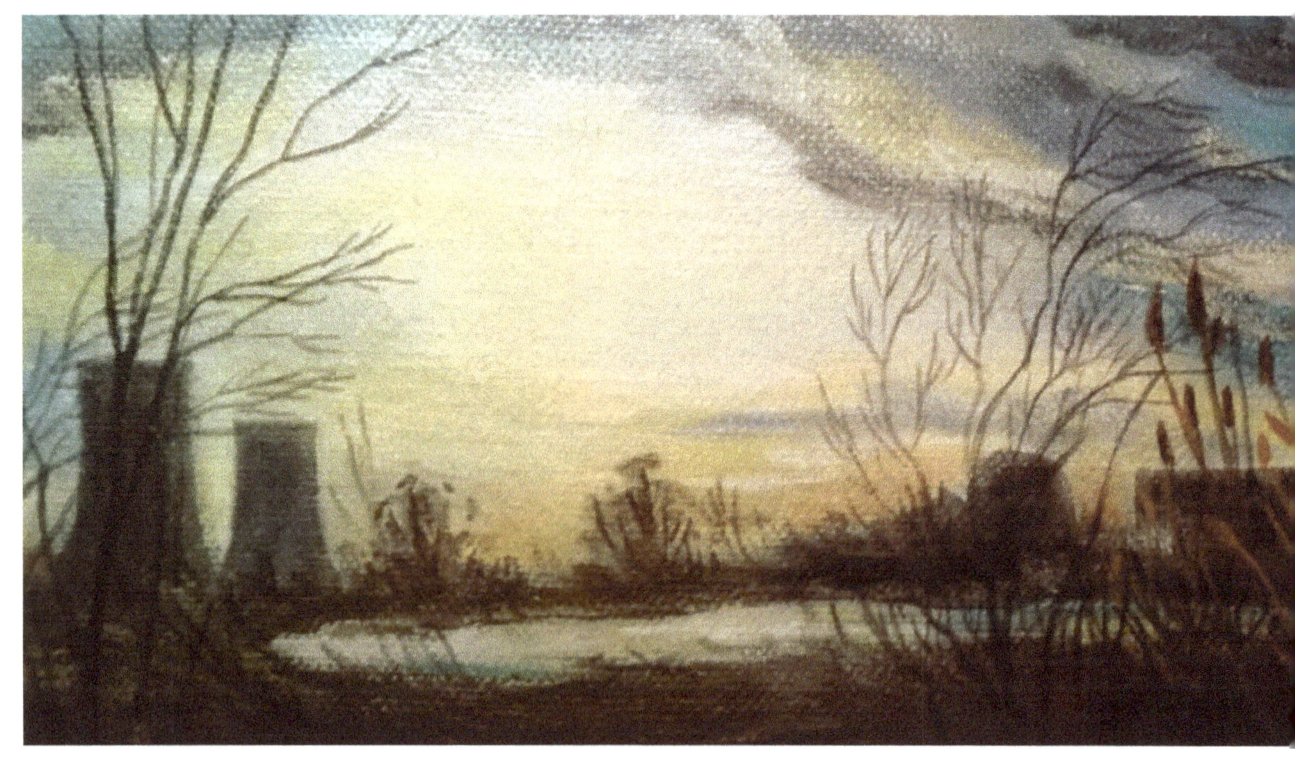

I just realized that the journal entries will actually be a week off since I am painting from the previous week's photos.

I will do the foggy scene from Week 3, but I am dragging my feet on it. What's in my head as far as the colors I want to put in this one is perplexing me. I am not sure how to do it….

"Go! Pick up the brushes and quit stalling! You might like it on the first try, or you might paint over it, or you might even leave it unfinished, but for Pete's sake, go try it and learn something!"

Okay, okay, I'm going. Later….

I mostly like it. Is an artist ever satisfied?

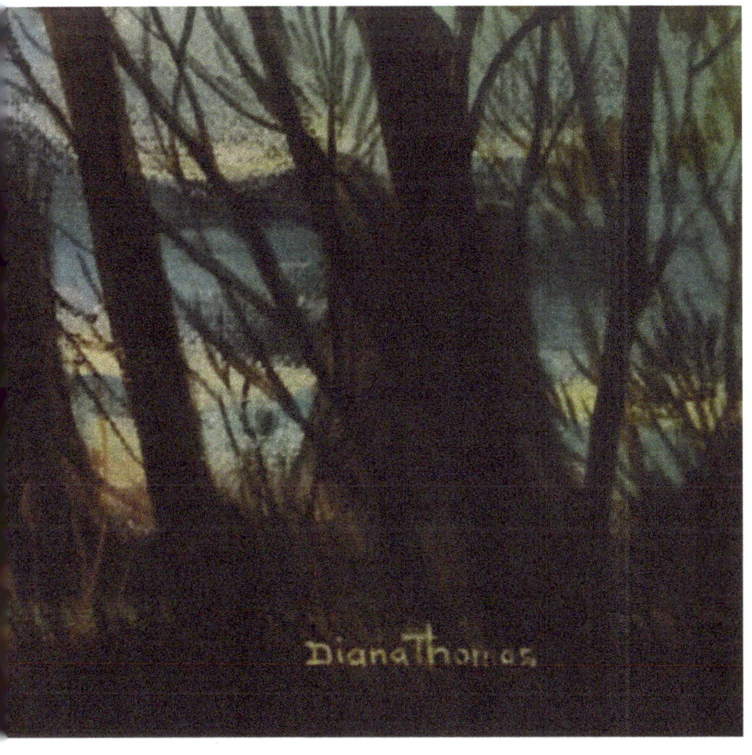

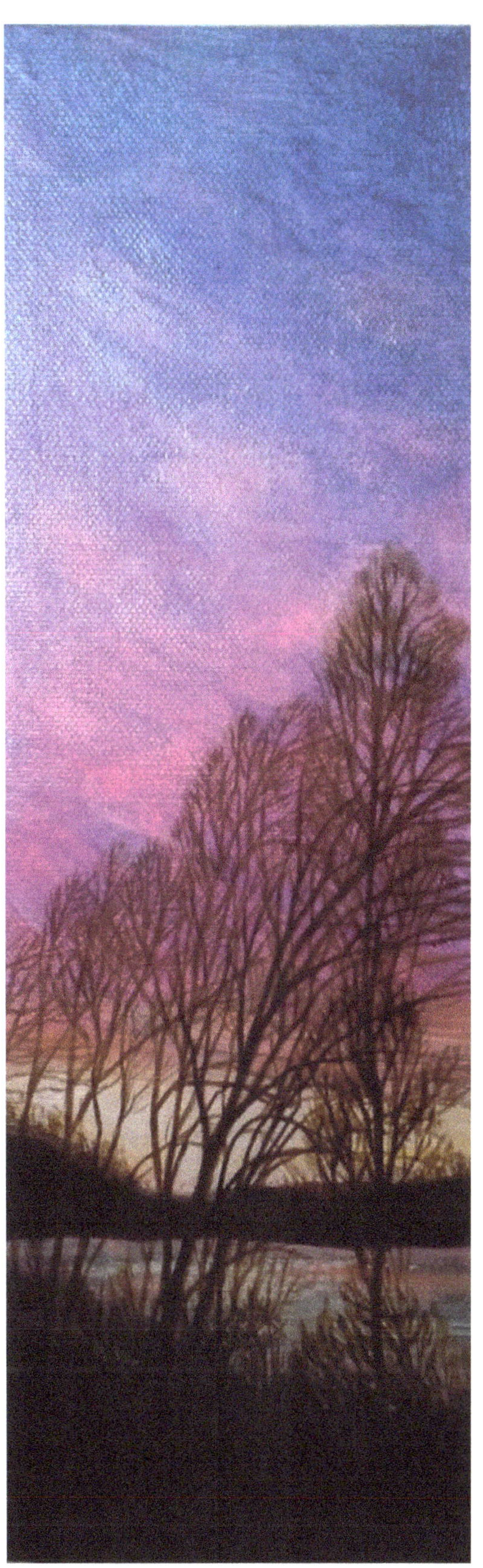

5

JANUARY 19–25, 2016

"Frozen Solid"

From Old Bridge, Columbia, PA

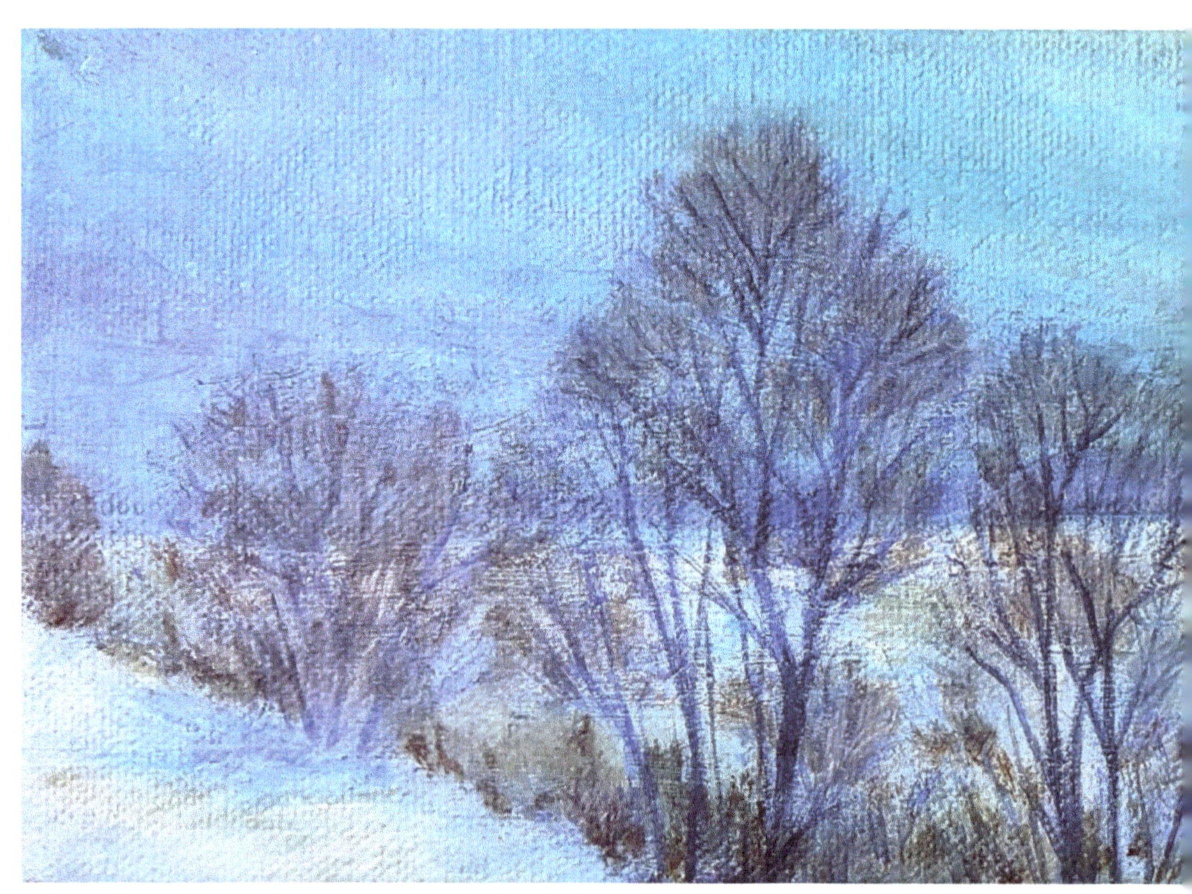

Uh oh, I was afraid of this…. The weeks are starting to get shorter or speed up or something. It is time to pick the one to paint for last week—Week 4—already!

This week will seem short anyway as I get ready to go to Arizona. I will be away for Weeks 6 and 7 and will ask friends if they can get some shots for me as they both love being at the river.

I'm wondering if I can use this finished body of work as a fundraiser somehow? Picturing it finished is a help.

I only got photos on two days so far this week, and the 29 inches of snow we got last night is a bit of a problem. We haven't gotten out the door yet! But that had its advantages since I painted two pieces for Week 4 and I like them both.

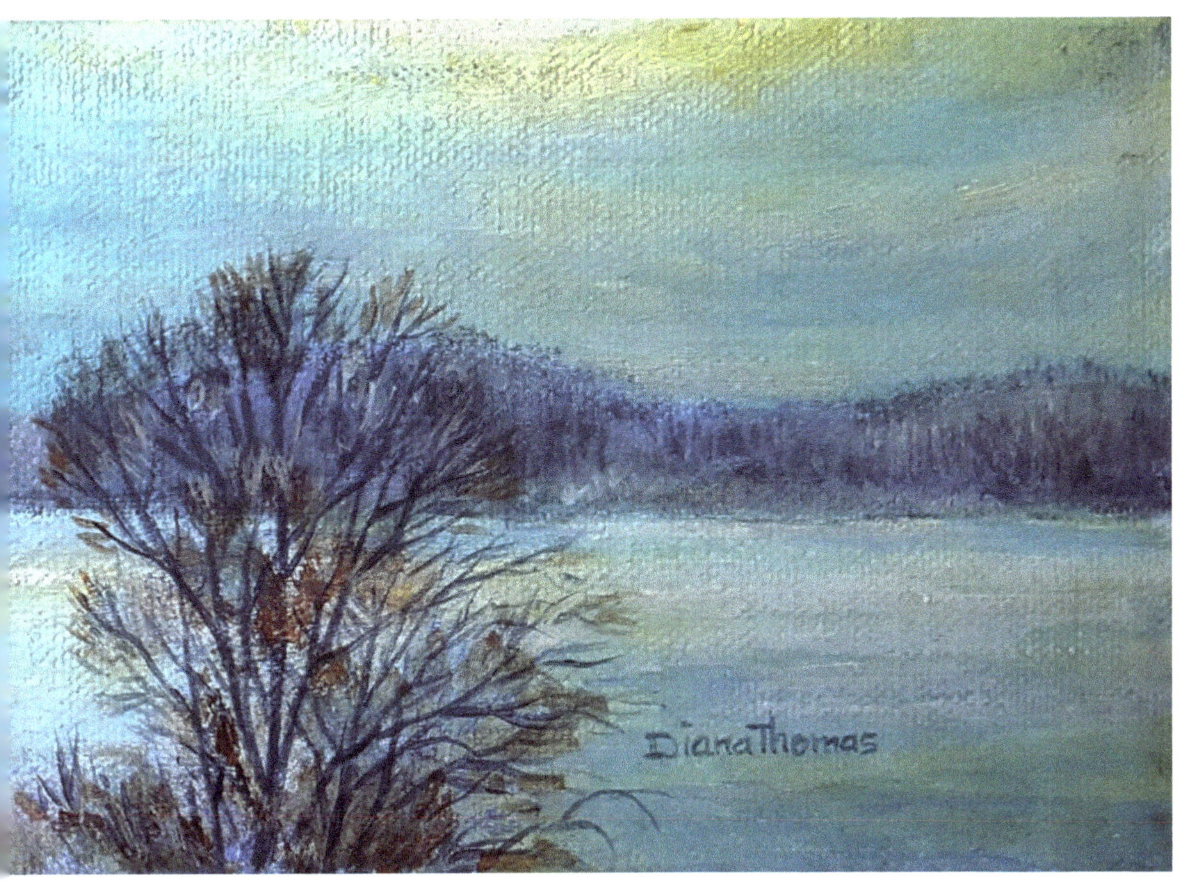

JANUARY 26–FEBRUARY 1, 2016

"Ice Floes" and "Ice Floes 2"

Guest Photographer, Columbia, PA

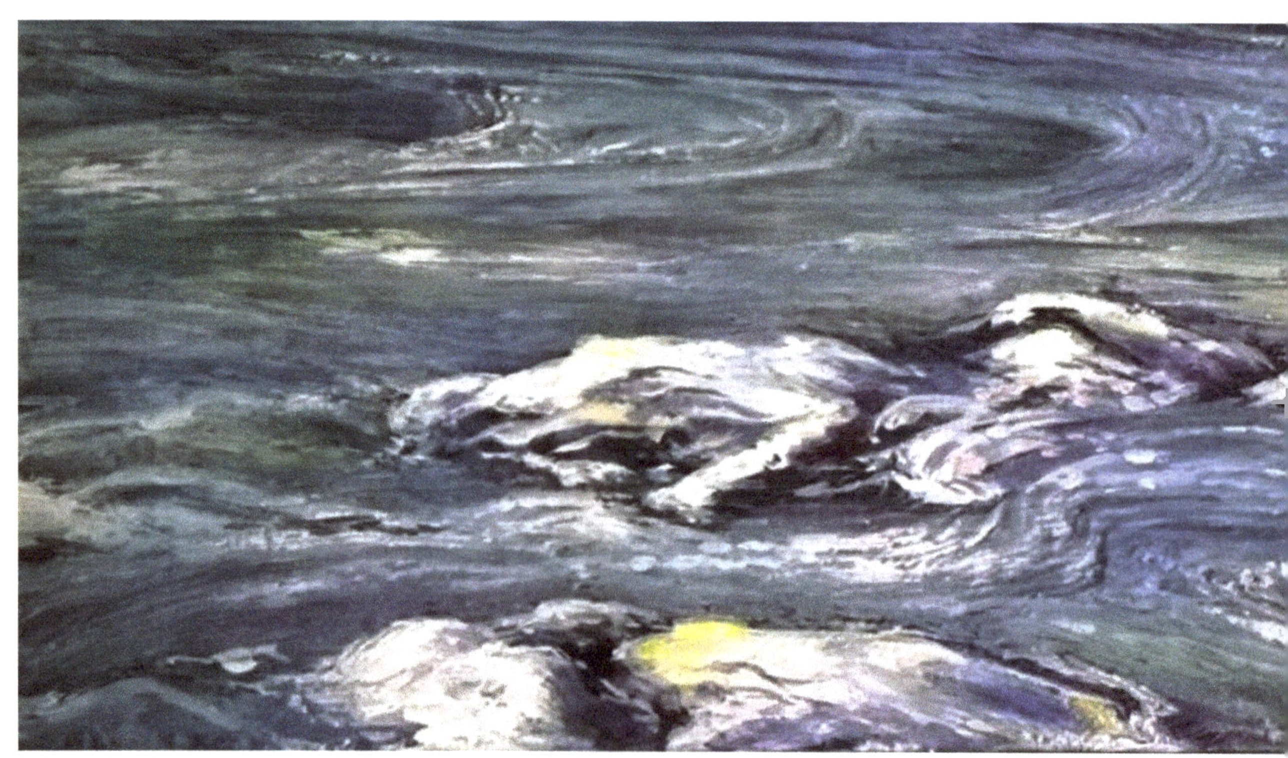

Ahh, resting in Buckeye, Arizona, with my sis—my annual R & R. I am taking time for art and talking about our next stained glass project for the church.

Artsy sisters! Woo-hoo!

Guest photographers Lori and Jeff sent me photos via email so I could try to keep caught up! Thank you.

I'm painting Pennsylvania's frozen scenes out here in sunny Arizona.

I also completed Week 5's piece—I am not too crazy about it.

But, I've got to keep movin'. That's a lesson in itself for a recovering perfectionist: letting well enough alone!

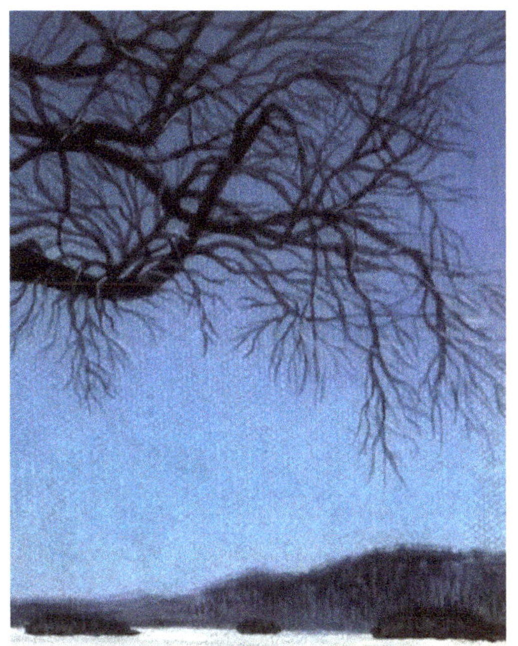

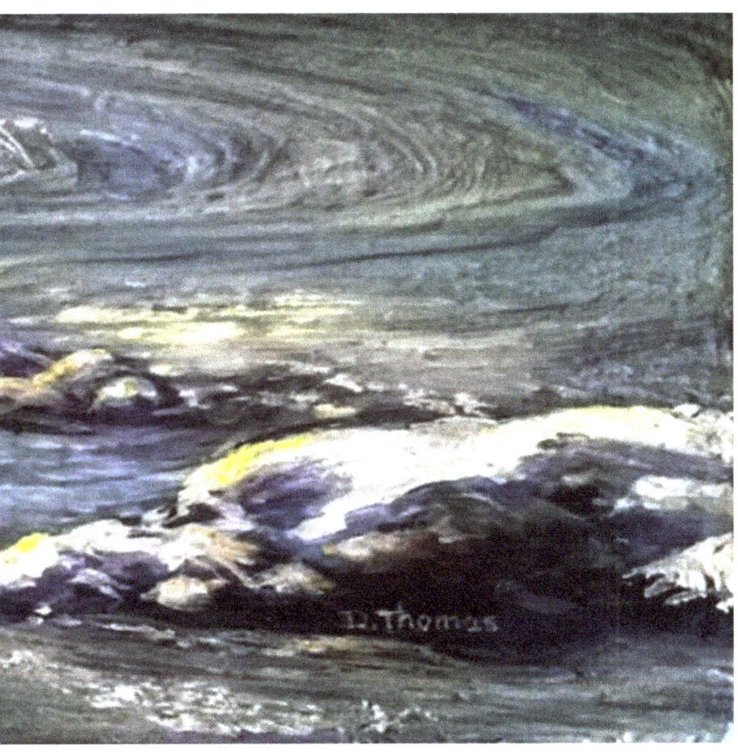

FEBRUARY 2–8, 2016

"Harbingers"

Guest Photographer, Long Level, Wrightsville, PA

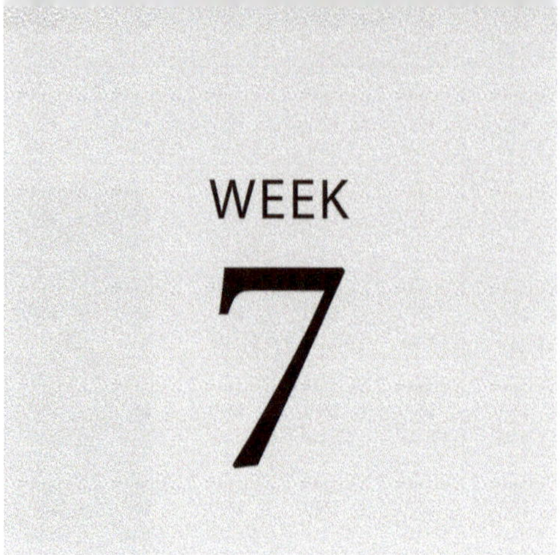

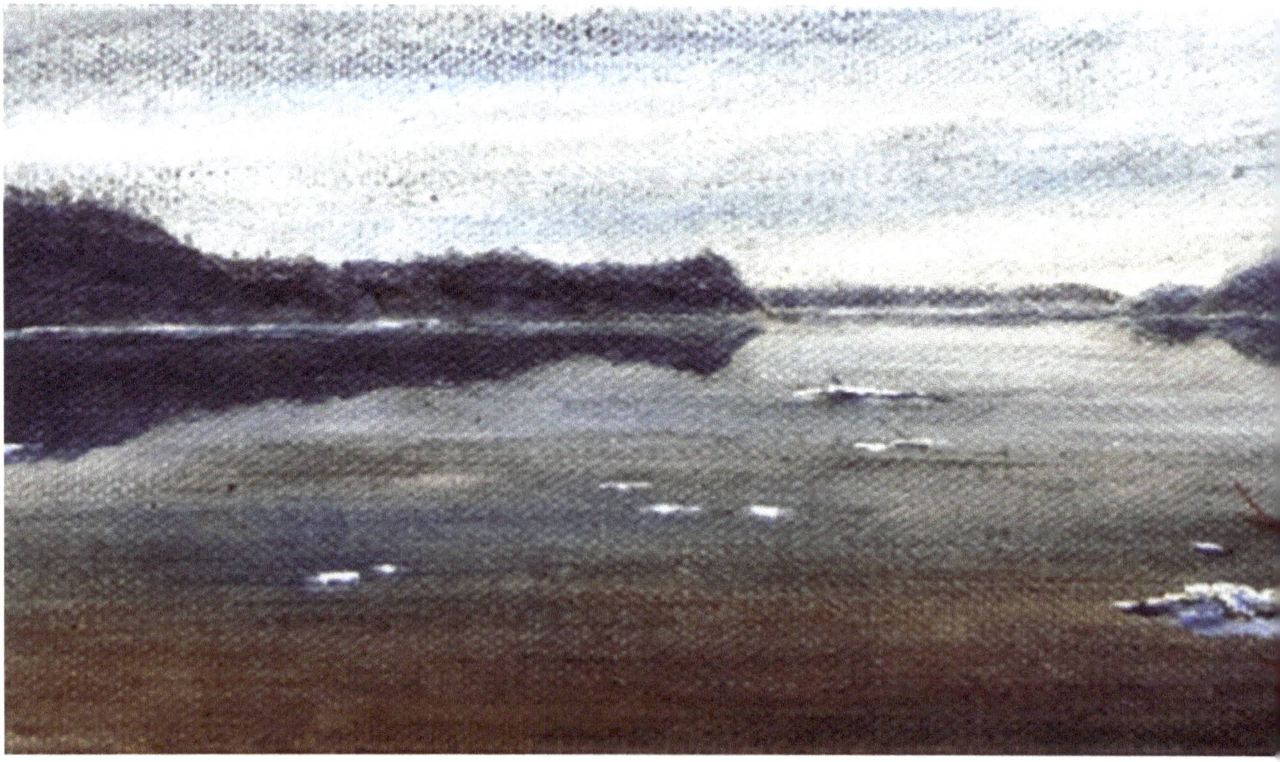

Thank you to my dear friend Lori for her inspiring photos (sans robins) while I was in Arizona—and for the wonderful song you sent: "River God" by Nichole Nordeman. I especially liked how the lyrics illustrated that in the rushing current of life, the friction we undergo rubs away our sharp edges, a process I'm glad is taking place in me.

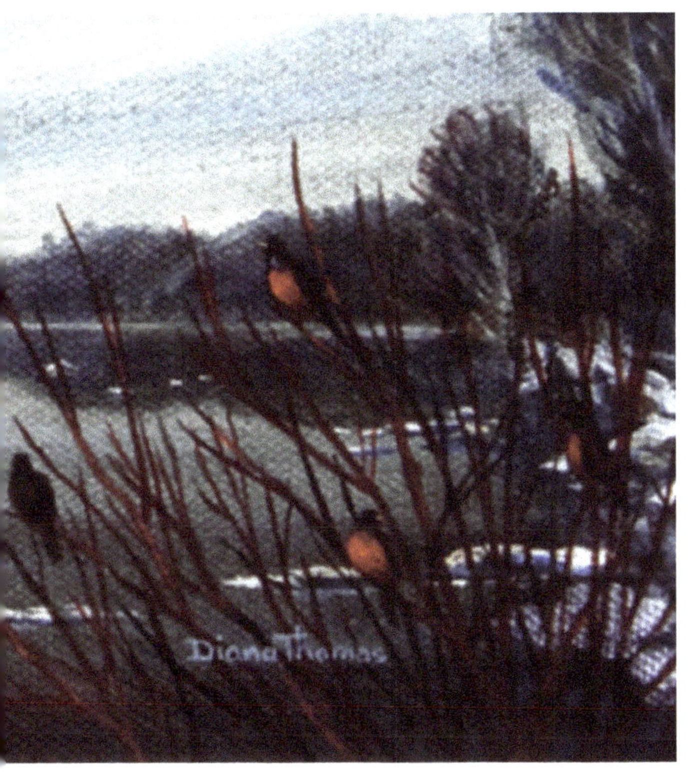

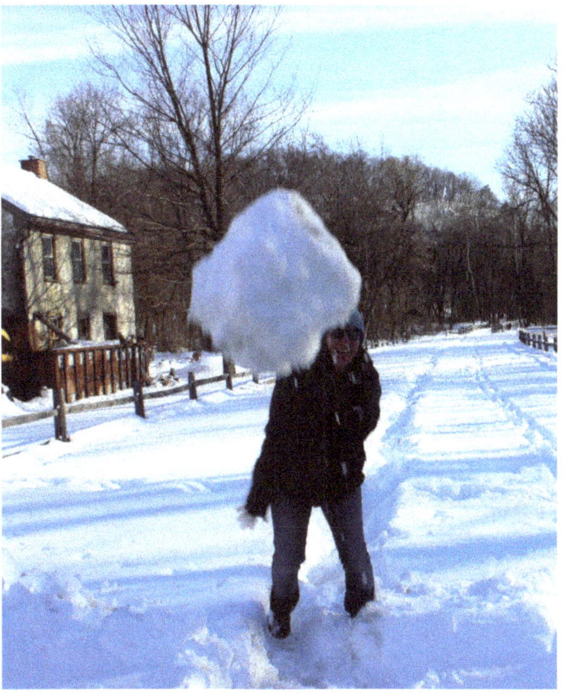

Guest photographer: "Watch out!"

FEBRUARY 9–15, 2016

"Rainbow Sunset"

Columbia, PA

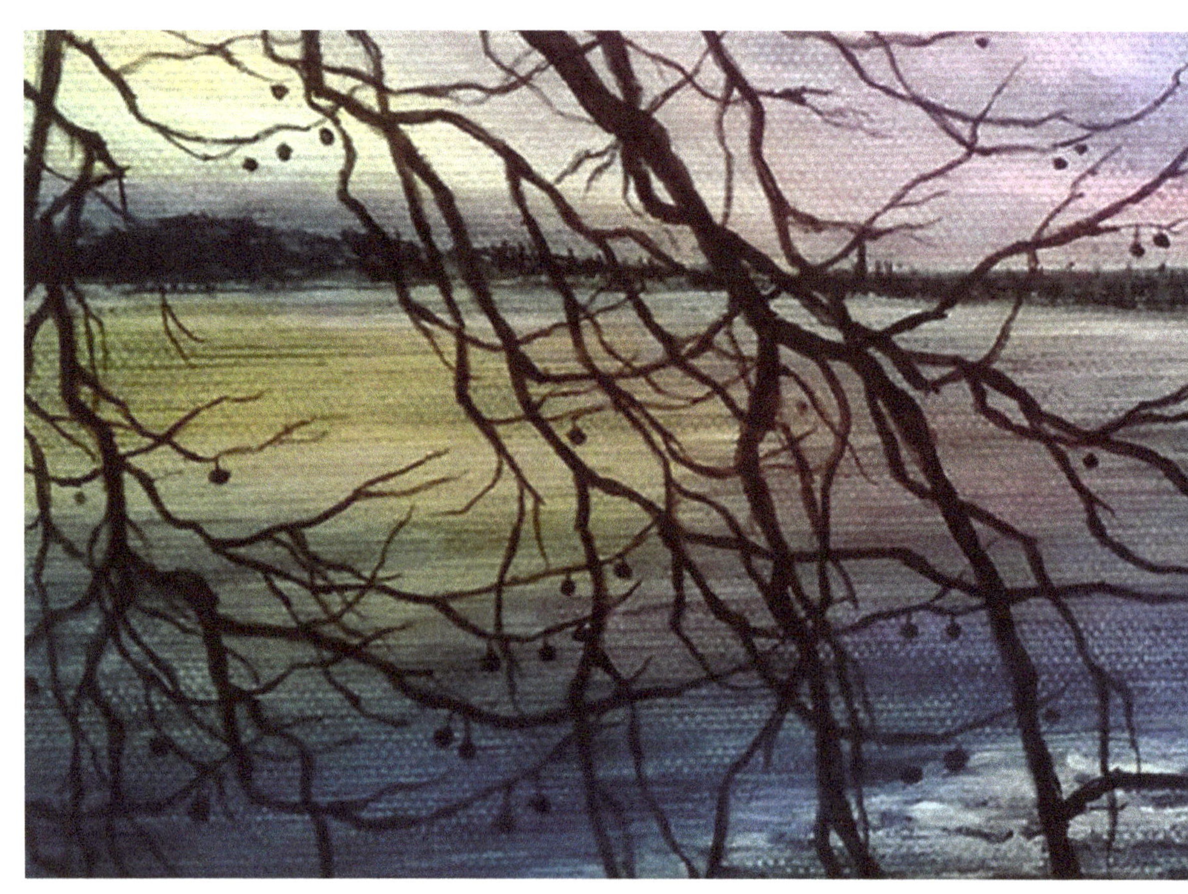

I am home from sunny, warm Arizona to cold, cloudy Pennsylvania. More snow is predicted, but the river was clear of ice.

Later in the week it turned fiercely cold, and the river is freezing again. I went to Safe Harbor and enjoyed a group of immature Bald Eagles and a few mature ones perched in the trees along the bank below the trestle over the Conestoga River. The young ones fought over their catch. I also saw some Common Mergansers.

I didn't paint yet; I must soon get going on Week 7's project. I am looking forward to a change from blues and Payne's grey and adding some burnt umber. Who would have thought that brown paint could be so exciting!

The ever-constant flow of the river seems to quiet my soul while I just sit and gaze at the mesmerizing, shifting patterns on the water's surface.

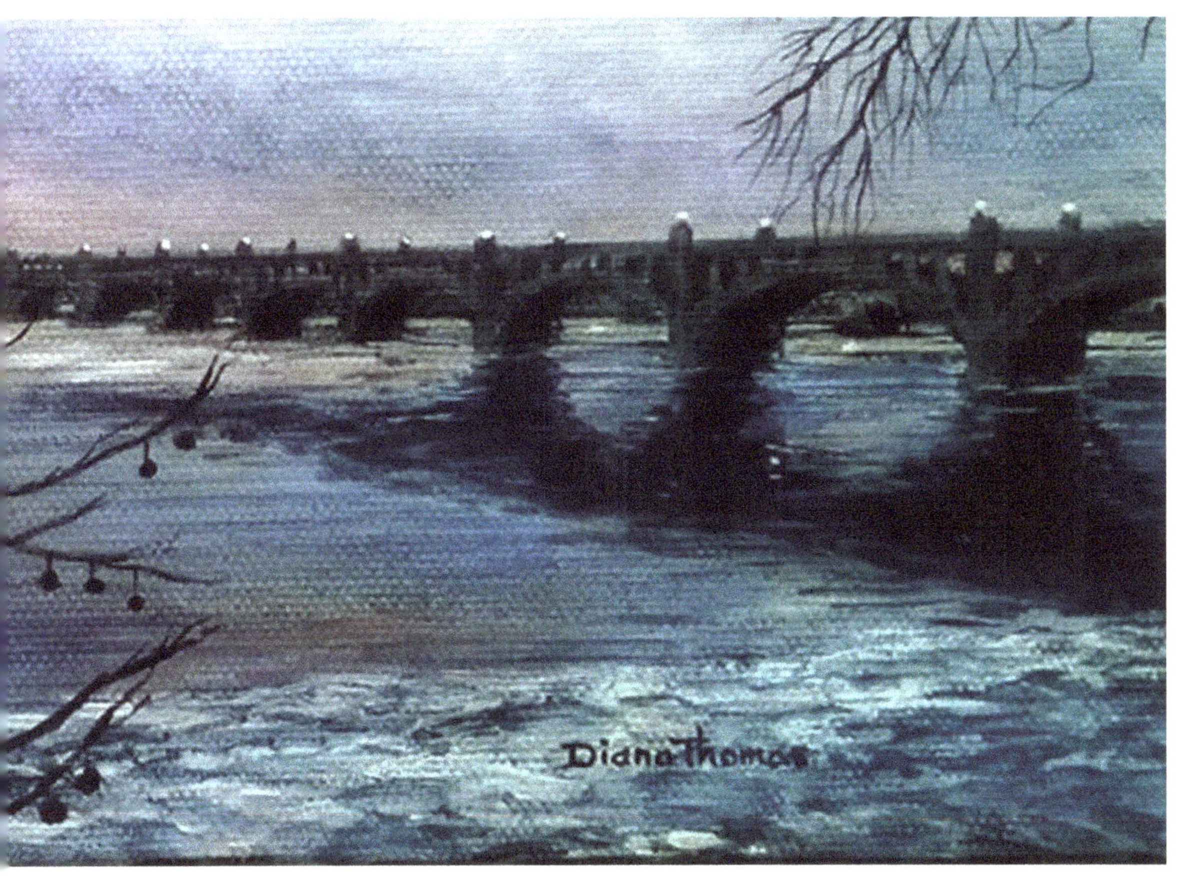

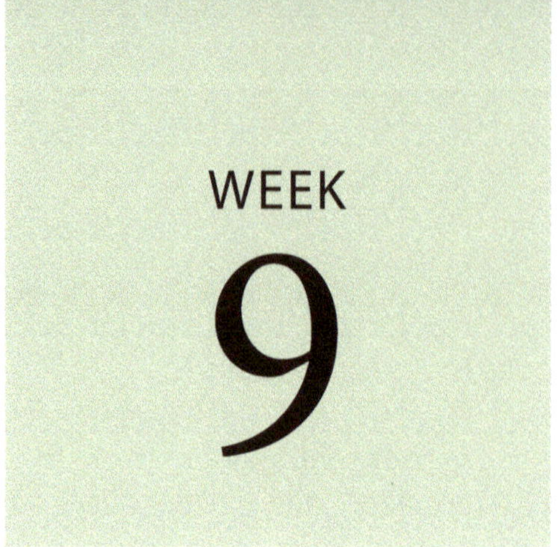

WEEK

9

FEBRUARY 16–22, 2016

"Pequea"

Pequea Boat Ramp Area, Pequea, PA

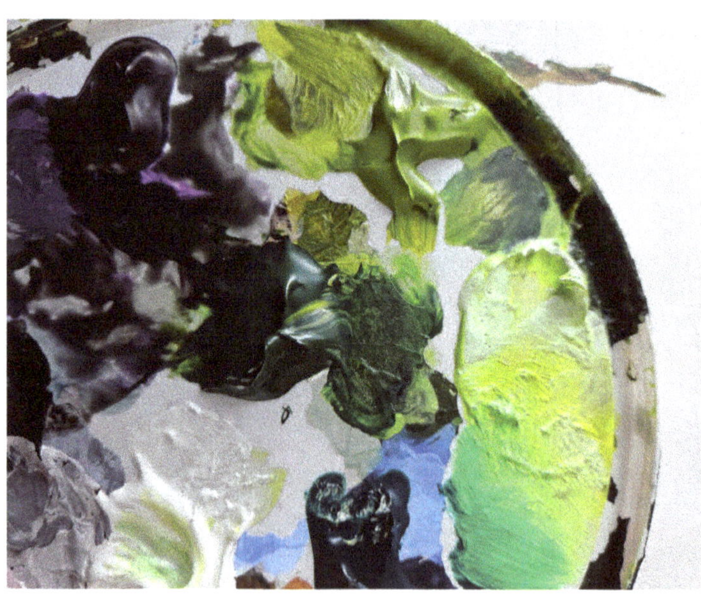

A fresh green palette

For all the 35 years I've lived in
Lancaster County, the Susquehanna
River has had a hypnotic pull on me.

The Susquehanna—sacred, wild,
ancient, wonderful—inspires me
to find peace in her constancy and
comfort in her flow.

I hope I can catch a bit of the river's
mystique and power even on these
tiny canvases.

I just loved this one because of
the green!

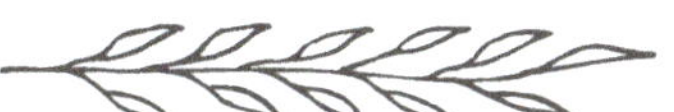

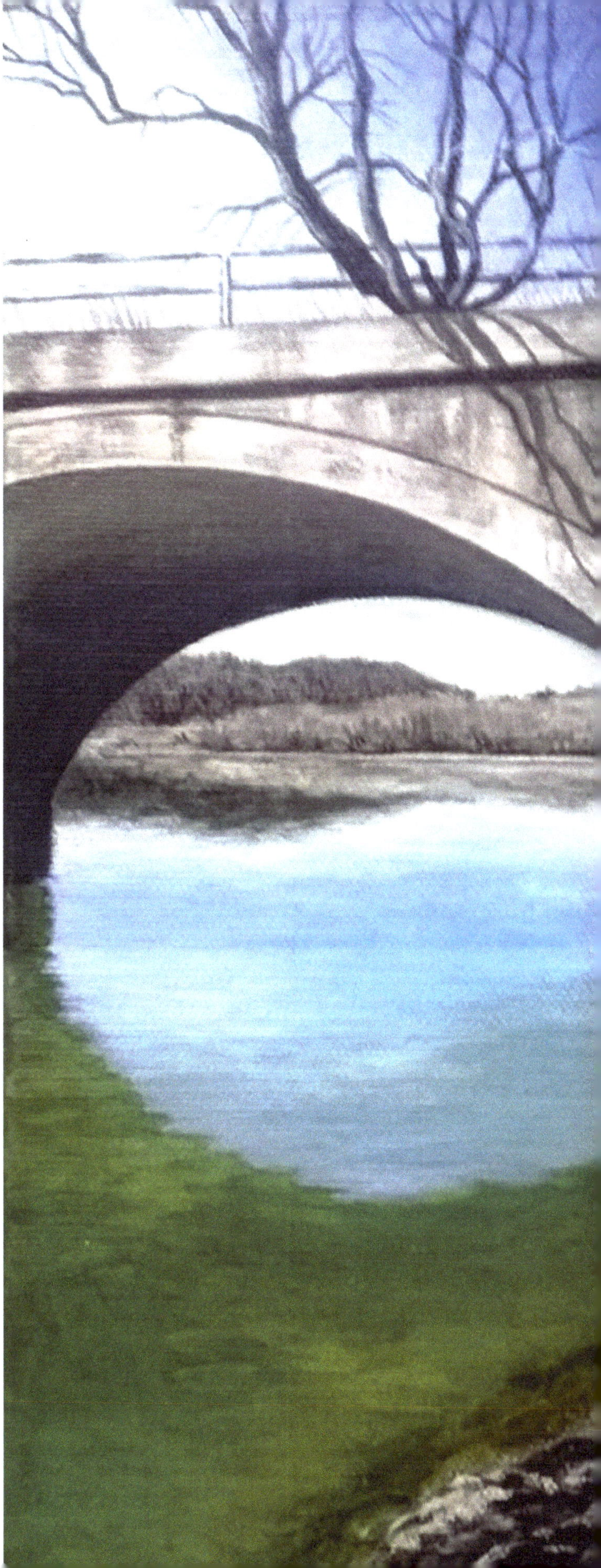

FEBRUARY 23–29, 2016

"Sundance"

E. Donegal Riverfront Park, Marietta, PA

This week I'm hitting the first long, steep climb of this project. I'm still working on Weeks 7 and 8, sometimes painting two at a time. It's already time to take Week 10's photos! I'm not quite a fourth of the way along in this project, and I wonder if I can make it.

The river today (February 25) is muddy and swollen, looking menacing and powerful, a contrast to my thoughts about what power, or lack thereof, I might have. I want this project to stretch me, but not to become some ritual that I dread doing.

I really connected with the excerpt from this morning's reading from *The Forgotten Way of Jesus* by Francis Leeman:

"Two thousand years ago, Jesus stood up in the middle of a crowd and yelled, 'If anyone is thirsty, come to me.' Not thirsty for more religion, or more rules, or more cheap substitutes. What he offers is something more, and it has eluded many people, perhaps religious people most of all. When I was young I was like a parched man crawling through the desert hoping to come across any small water hole. Much to my surprise, I have found a vast river instead."[2]

2 Francis Leeman, *The Forgotten Way of Jesus* (self-published, 2009), 8.

MARCH 1–7, 2016

"Wind and Whitecaps"

Long Level, Wrightsville, PA

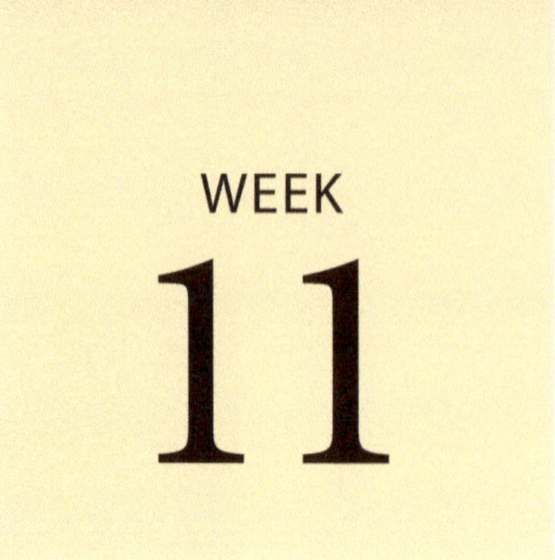

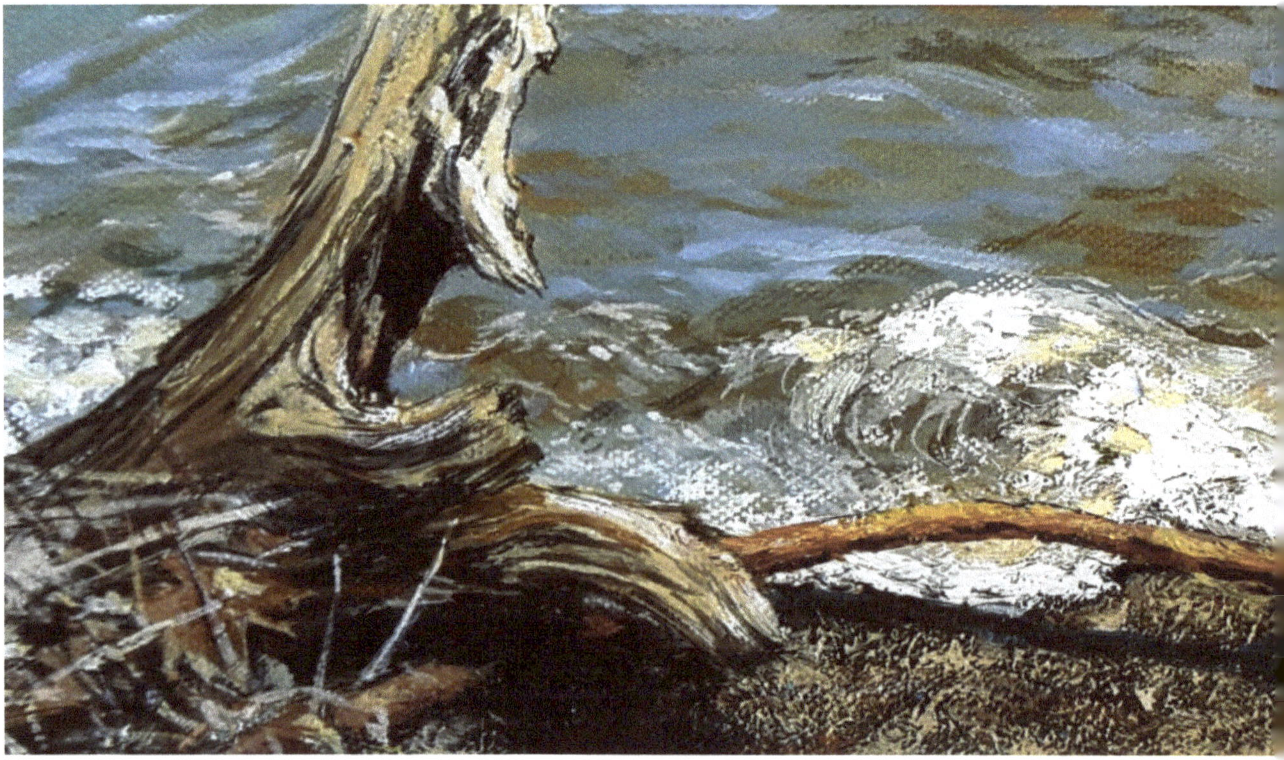

All the weeks are getting shorter! I'm getting ready to paint Week 9 now.

My friend Lori checked in with me today and asked if I am "enjoying" painting. Yes, I am enjoying it when I am painting, but I am not enjoying the feeling of time flying by. (She knows I don't pace myself well.)

I am trying to figure out how to let the time seem to fly without losing the enjoyment of accomplishing a goal I have set. It is a tricky thing to feel the stretch, but no further than necessary.

I think I must let grace play into this work on all levels; otherwise, I will simply default to my usual task-driven pattern, which was "mindless doing" just to get on to the next thing. The process of resetting my "default setting"—well, that is no small thing.

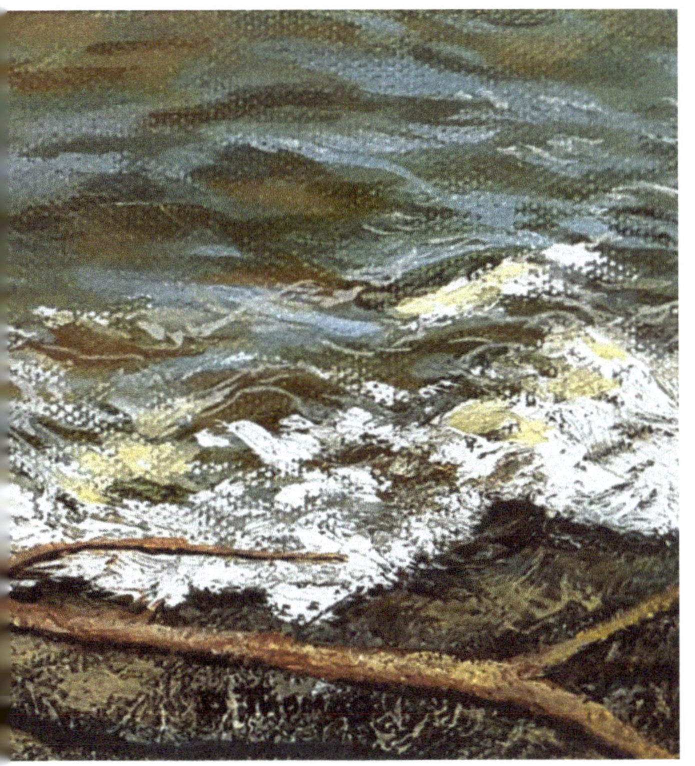

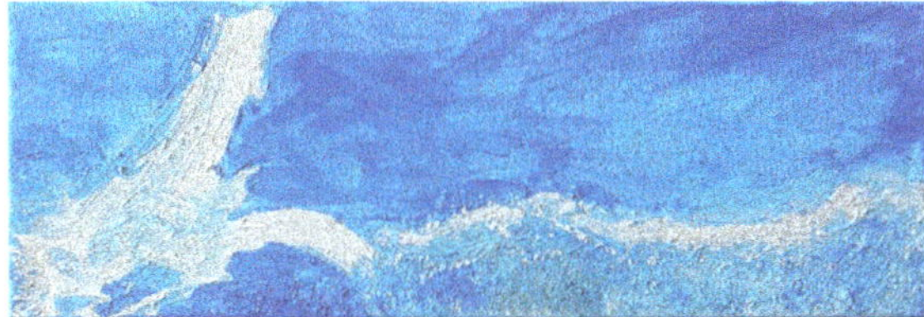

Blocking in color over some modeling paste in lower portion—instant texture!

MARCH 8–14, 2016

"Highways"

Highpoint Scenic Vista, Wrightsville, PA

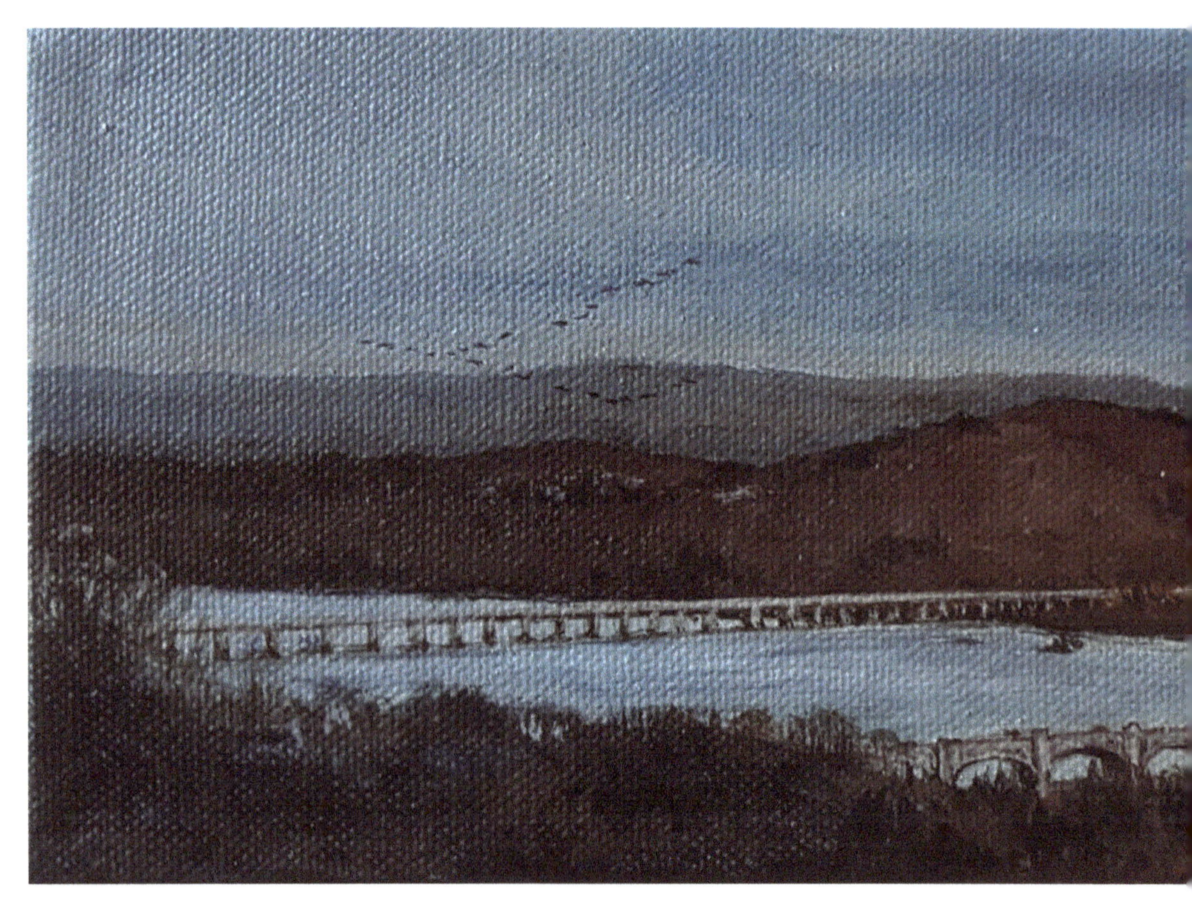

"For often the artist [God] even when not seen is known by his works."
(Athanasius 296–372 AD)

"The treasure secretly gathered in your heart will become evident
through your creative work." (Albrecht Durer, 15th century German
painter)

When this collection of work is done, it will be a "self-portrait" of sorts.

Since childhood I've been a collector of rocks, bird nests and insects, so why not
thoughts and images as well, treasures I've found along the way of life and along
the banks of a beautiful river.

I'm disappointed in the colors of this finished piece, but I have no time to go back.

Looking at images of the works in progress, I think the preliminary versions of
many are better than the finished ones. They are cleaner, looser and not so fussy.

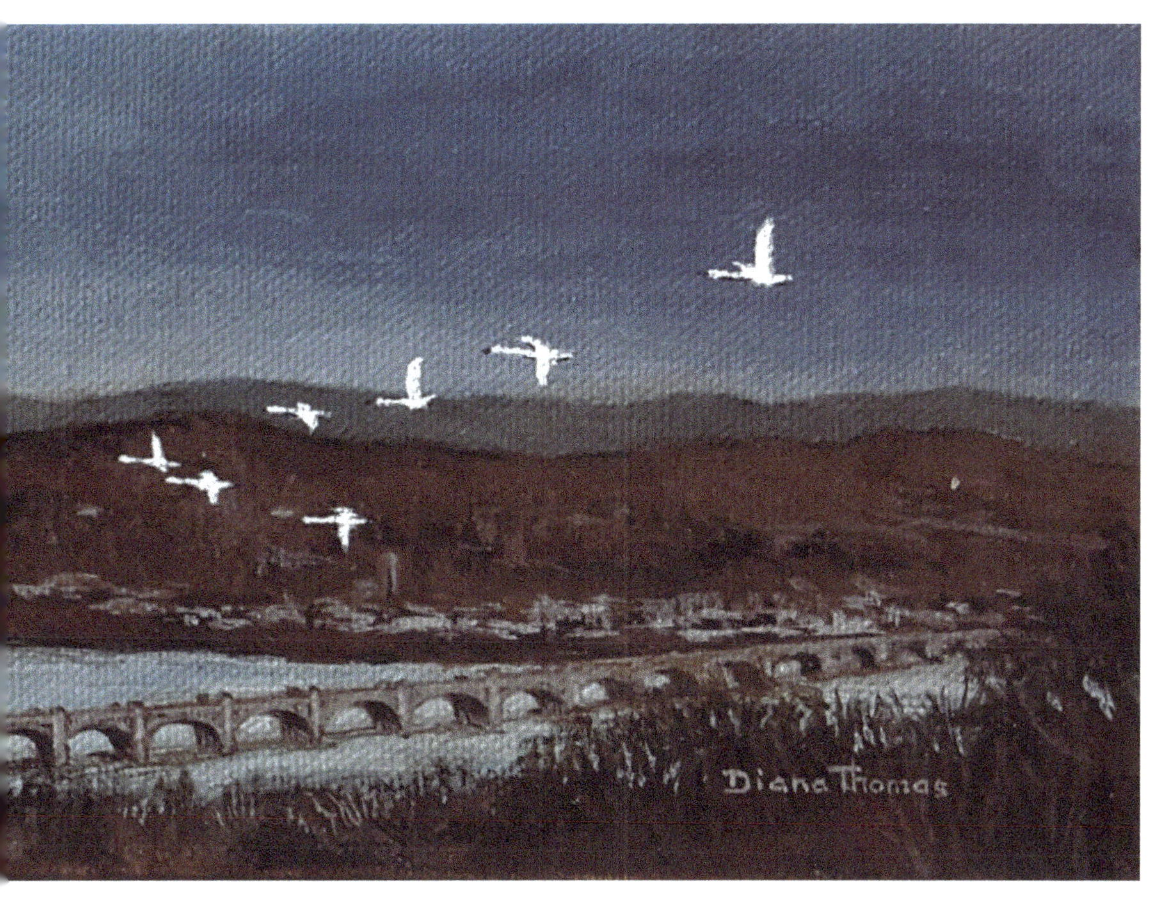

MARCH 15–21, 2016

"Mr. and Mrs."

Indian Steps, Otter Creek, York County, PA

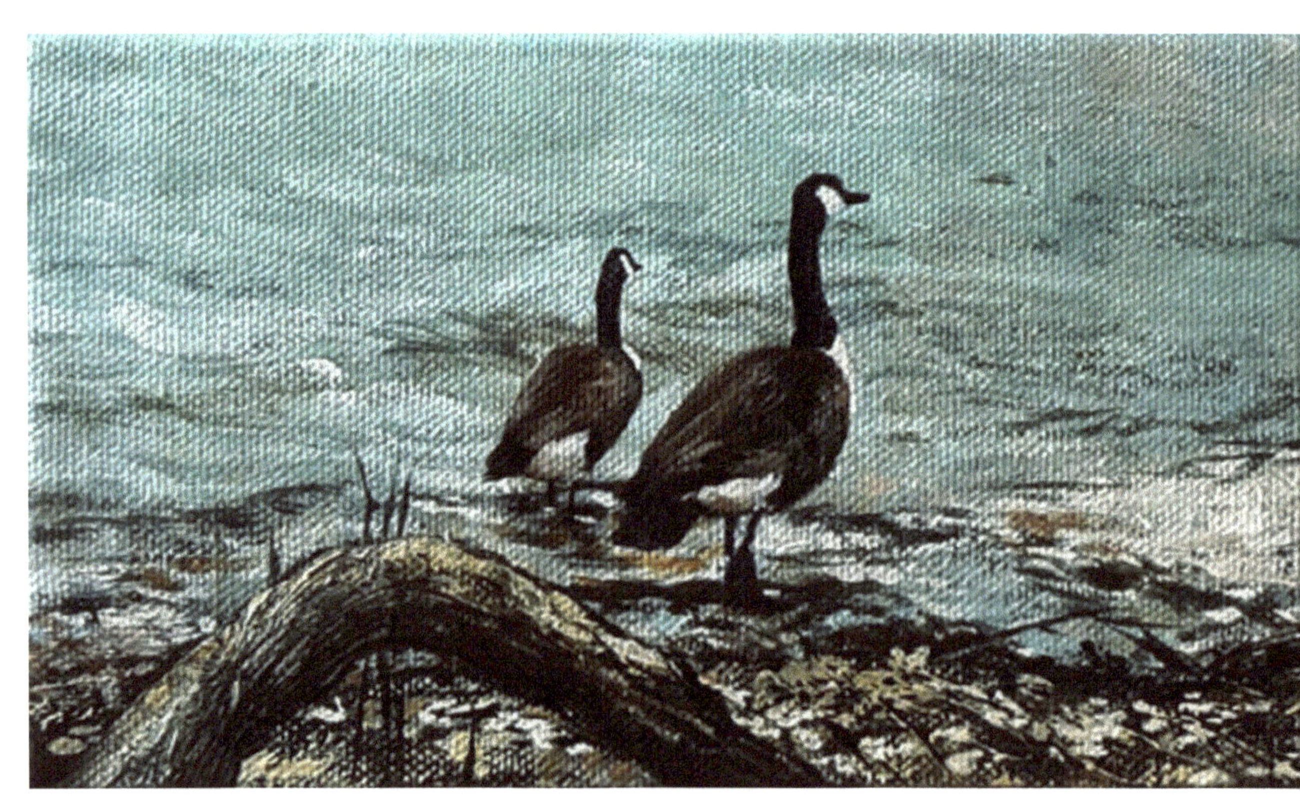

The first quarter of the "river project" is coming to a close, and with it, gone is the winter.

I'm moving from ultramarine, cerulean blue and Payne's grey with lots of white into the umbers, phthalo blues and greens—muddy, silver, shining true blue, brightest green, calm ivory and peach. I like the addition of the Canada geese. I had disturbed their rest on the bank trying to get this shot.

I have a color wheel that my dad painted in his art school days when I was little. Mom encouraged him to use his military benefits and go. Art became his lifelong career. My mom was a wise encourager.

Looking at it reminds me of the river's changing seasons, of life's changing seasons rotating and moving from one color into the next. Seasons move and change like the old song by The Byrds, "Turn! Turn! Turn!" which is based on a Bible verse written by King Solomon:

*"There is a time for everything, and a season for
every activity under the heavens."*

(Ecclesiastes 3:1)

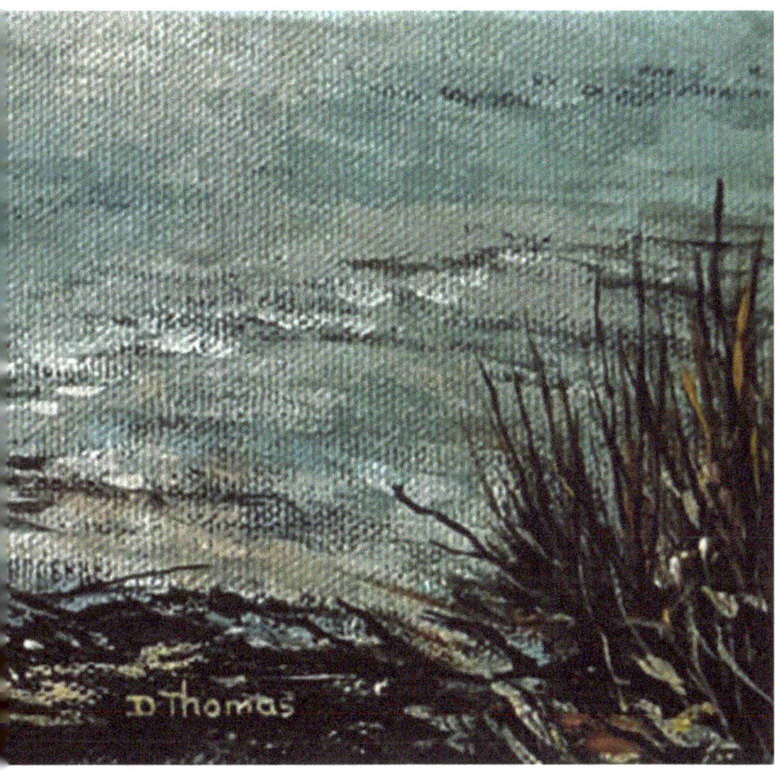

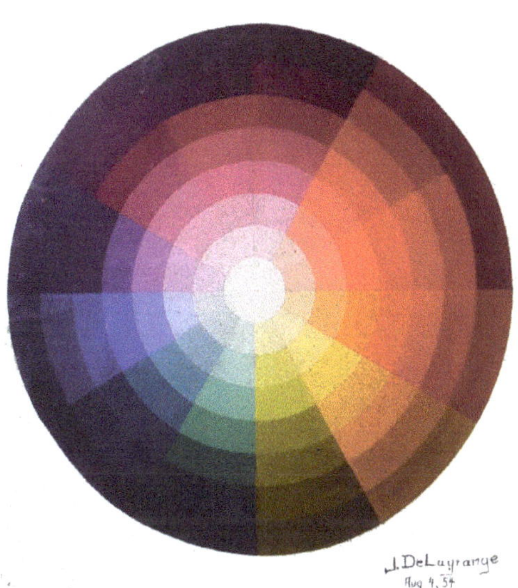

Dad's color wheel

MARCH 22–28, 2016

"Red Twigs"

Falmouth, PA

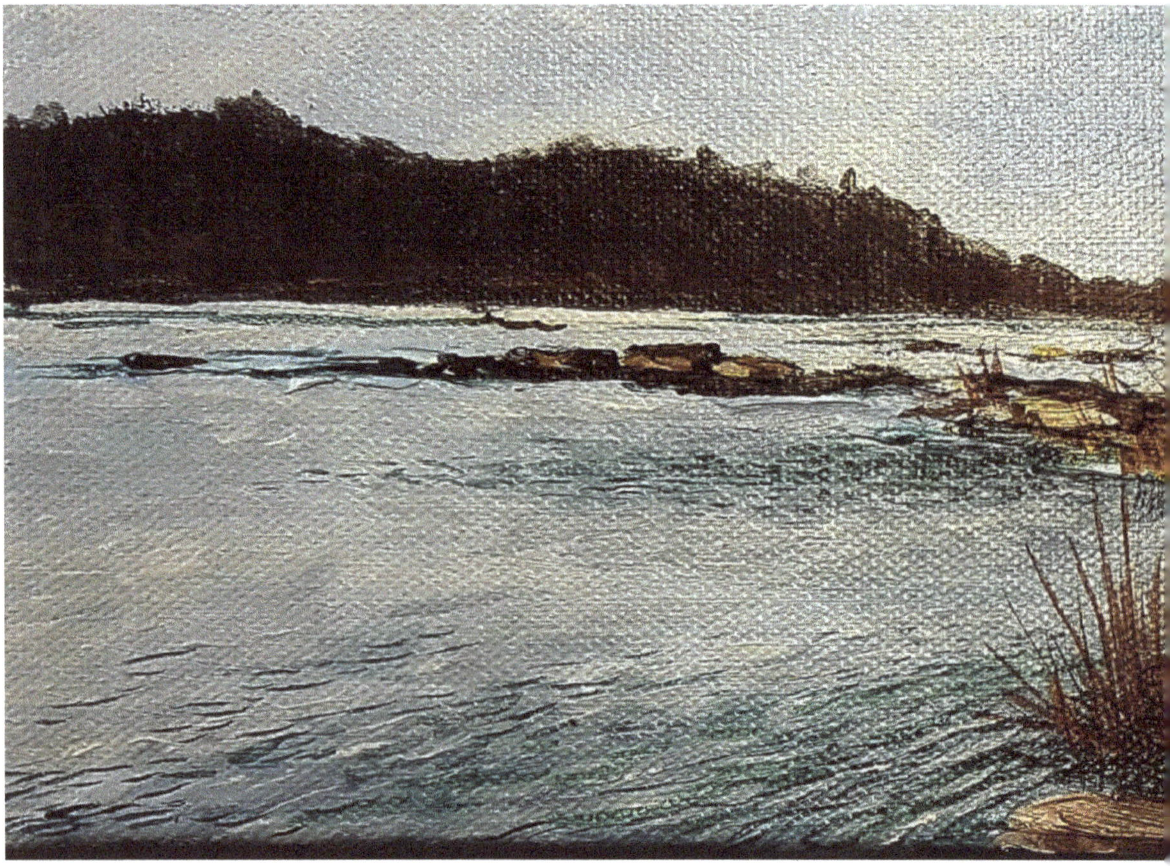

The past few days, it has been hard to make myself paint. There are so many things to do to get ready for the Easter season and the next Haiti trip in a few days. But this is part of my "lessons" for this challenge: how to do a better job of making time for some important business, including the artist part.

I think age helps some. I am just slower than before and must shorten my "to do" list. But the slowing down process is a strange adjustment. My brain still has the habit of creating very long (read, impossible) lists, and my body just laughs!

I think more seriously about one of my favorite verses, Psalm 46:10: "He says, 'Be still, and know that I am God….'" I picture a child being taught to sit still for a while and ponder something wonderful. Do people teach that to their children anymore?

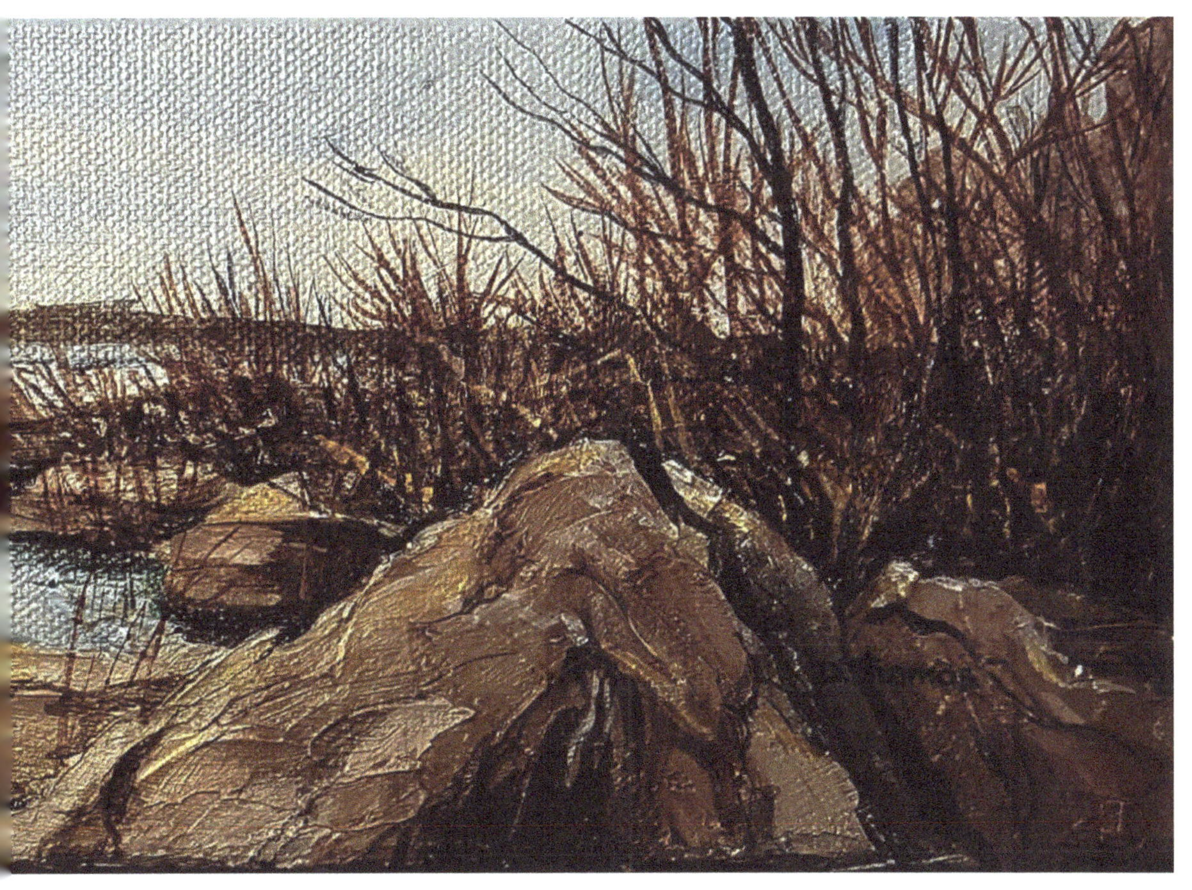

15

MARCH 29–APRIL 4, 2016

"Spring Morning"

Wrightsville, PA

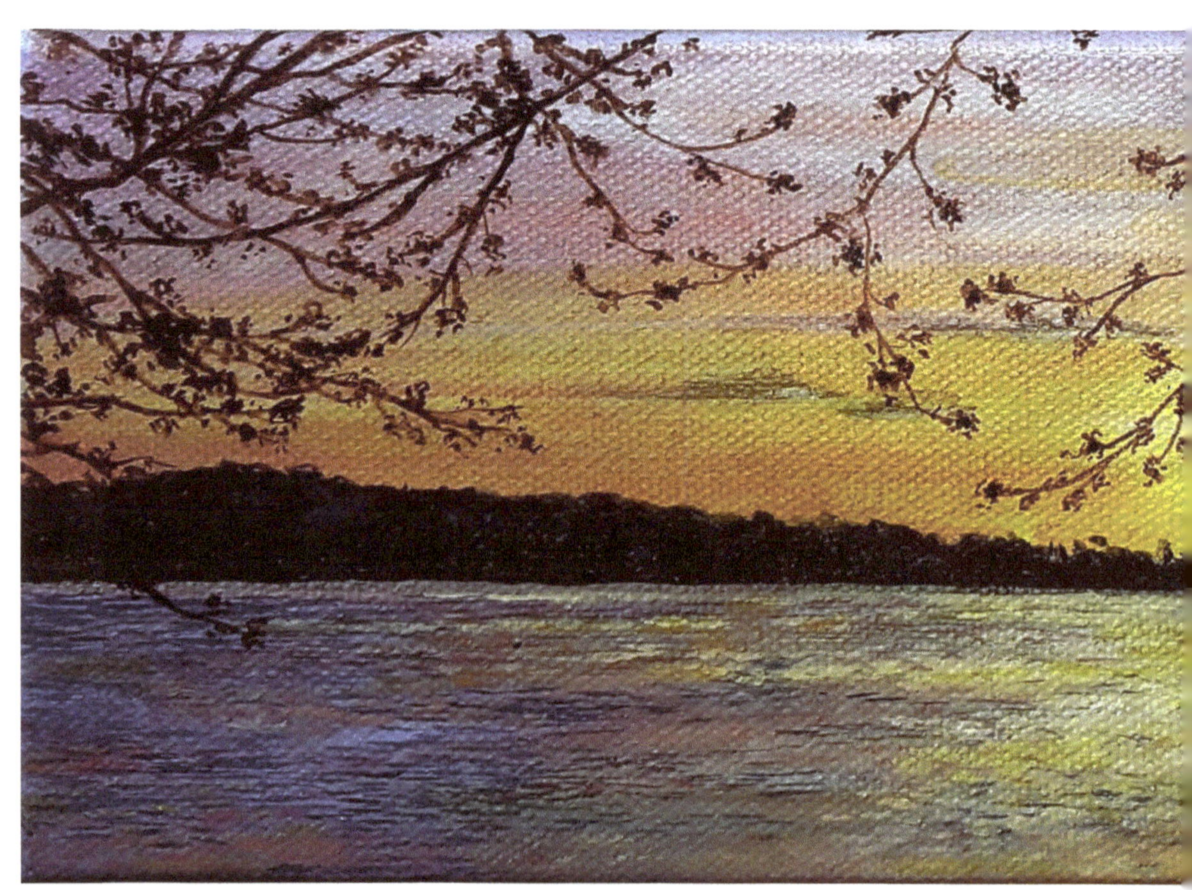

I went over to the West Shore to watch the sunrise. Bright, sunny, yellow sky; buds ready to pop open and send out leaves—I feel so hopeful. It's a new day, a fresh start, spring! The breeze on the water makes it appear that the water is flowing the opposite direction of the current. The main current goes along as it always does, though the surface is being pushed the other way. Life and our Creator have their way of going along where they plan to go, no matter what the surface winds bring.

This morning I read this verse while praying about leaving for Haiti, and it made me smile:

"The Lord will guide you continually, and satisfy your soul in drought, and strengthen your bones; you shall be like a watered garden, and like a spring of water, whose waters do not fail."

(Isaiah 58:11 NKJV)

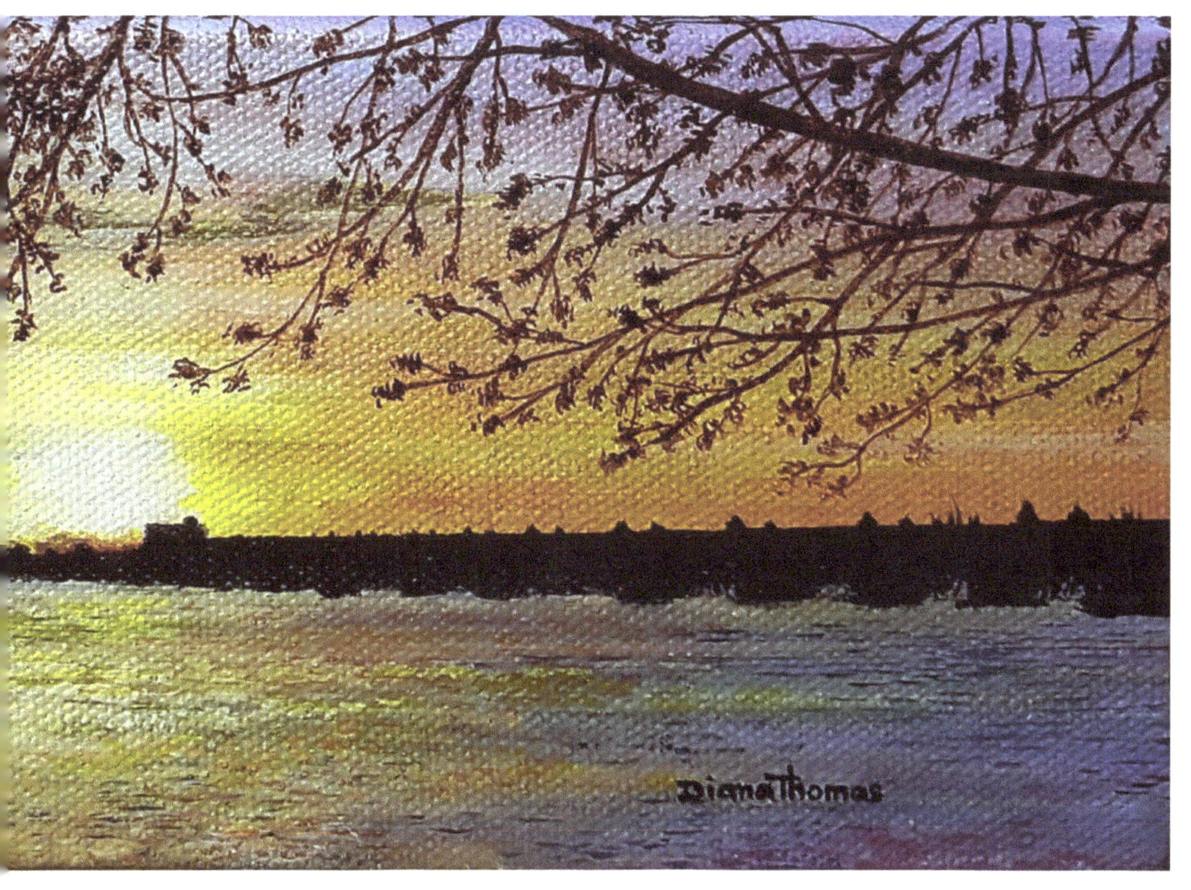

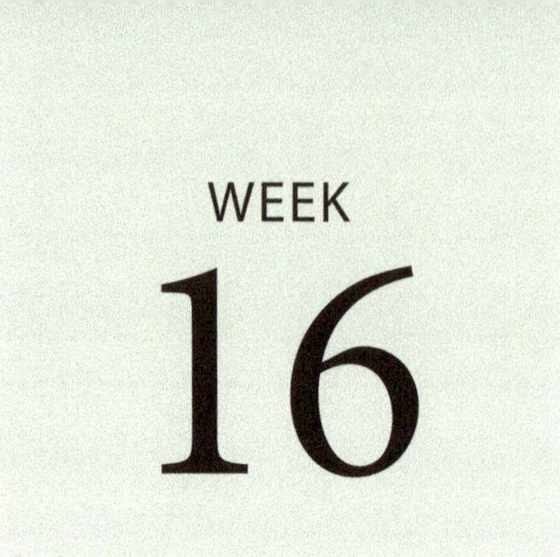

WEEK

16

APRIL 5–11, 2016

"Airborne"

Three Mile Island, Dauphin County, PA

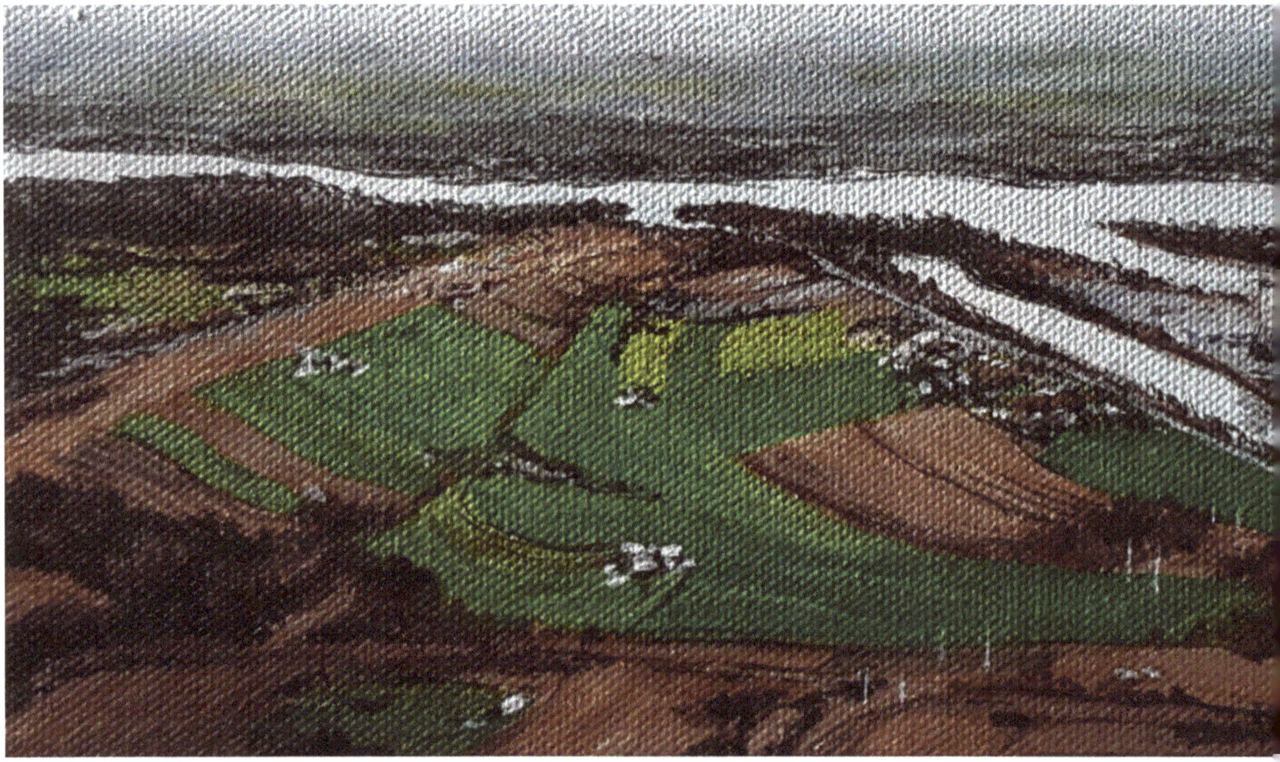

The only photo of the Susquehanna I got this week was when Ruth and I flew over Three Mile Island (TMI) on our way to Haiti.

I took my paints along and painted a scene of the rice fields I look at each morning. People are out just after first light, working their fields and walking along the canal singing, talking and scolding their children. Carrying buckets of water and other commodities on their heads, they look like little confetti dots of color against the green fields! Serene mountains in the background listening, looking strong, are colored by pink morning light.

The flow of life is a lot slower here—helping me practice living in "Haiti time" so I can carry it home with me. Haiti, teach me also to carry my load with grace and possibly bring some water to someone who is thirsty.

"I lift up my eyes to the mountains—where does my help come from?
My help comes from the Lord, the Maker of heaven and earth."

(Psalm 121:1–2)

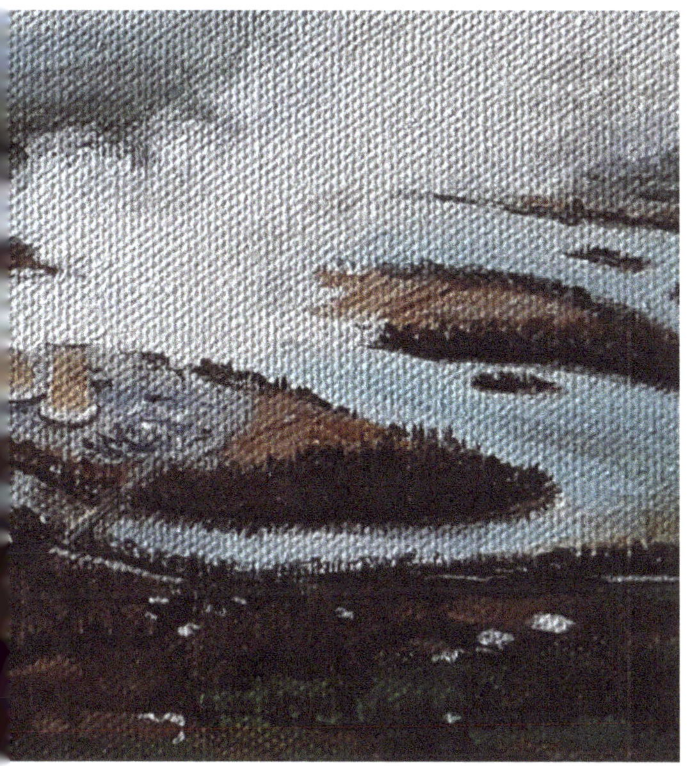

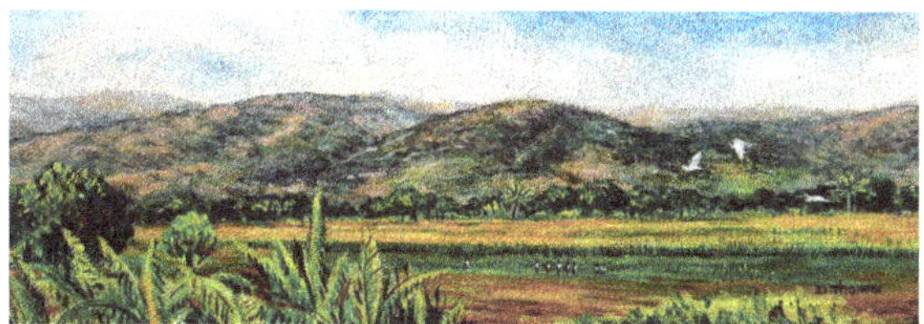

"Artibonite Morning," Borel, Haiti

APRIL 12–18, 2016

"Water Works"

Falmouth Boat Ramp

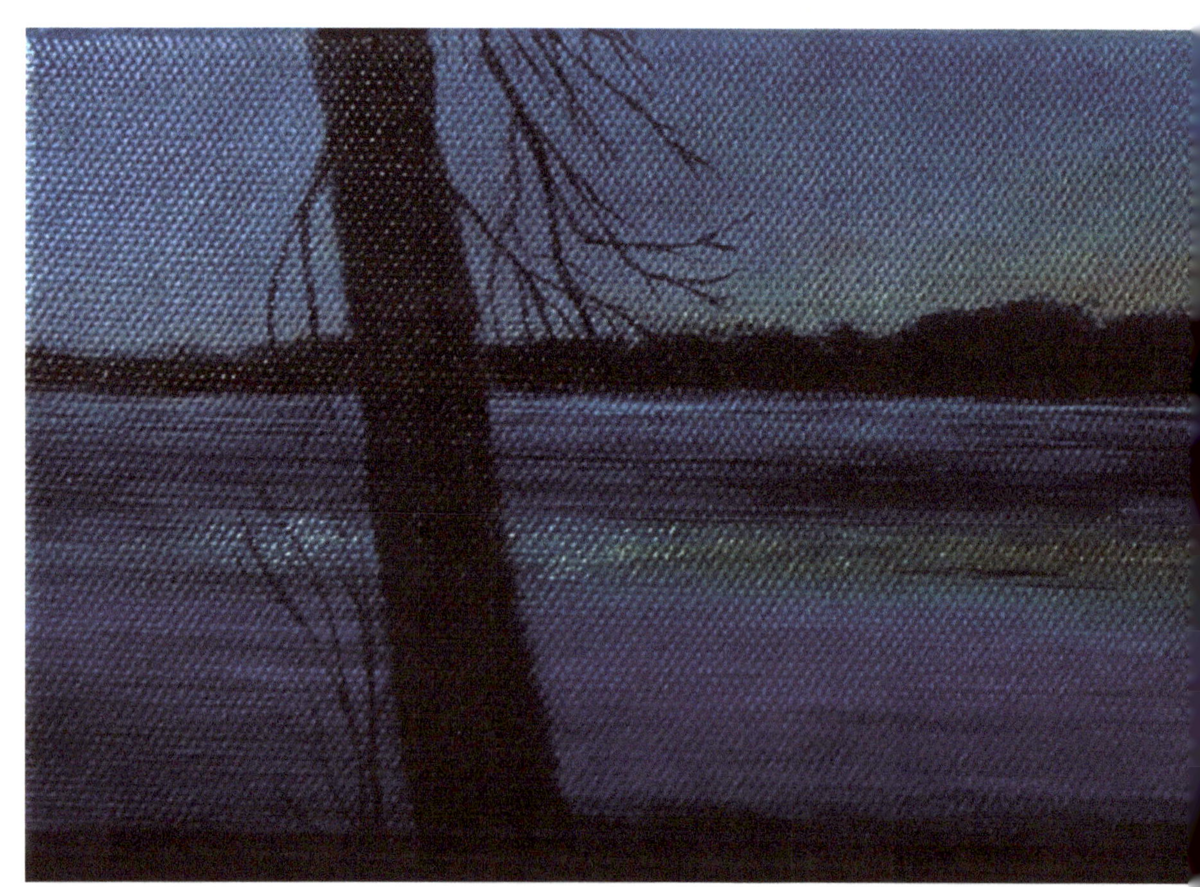

I returned to the U.S. on the 15th. A couple good nights of rest later, I'm getting back to "normal."

I needed to visit the river. I missed her like an old friend. Driving home from Perry County along Route 441, I could hear the lovely music of thousands of "spring peepers" (tree frogs), so I pulled into the boat ramp area at Falmouth right at dusk.

I sat in the car listening to that chorus, a springtime lullaby, gazing at the indigo river, breathing in the fragrance of water and vegetation, and watching the moon hang suspended in the clear and darkening sky. Soul food…such sweet refreshment….

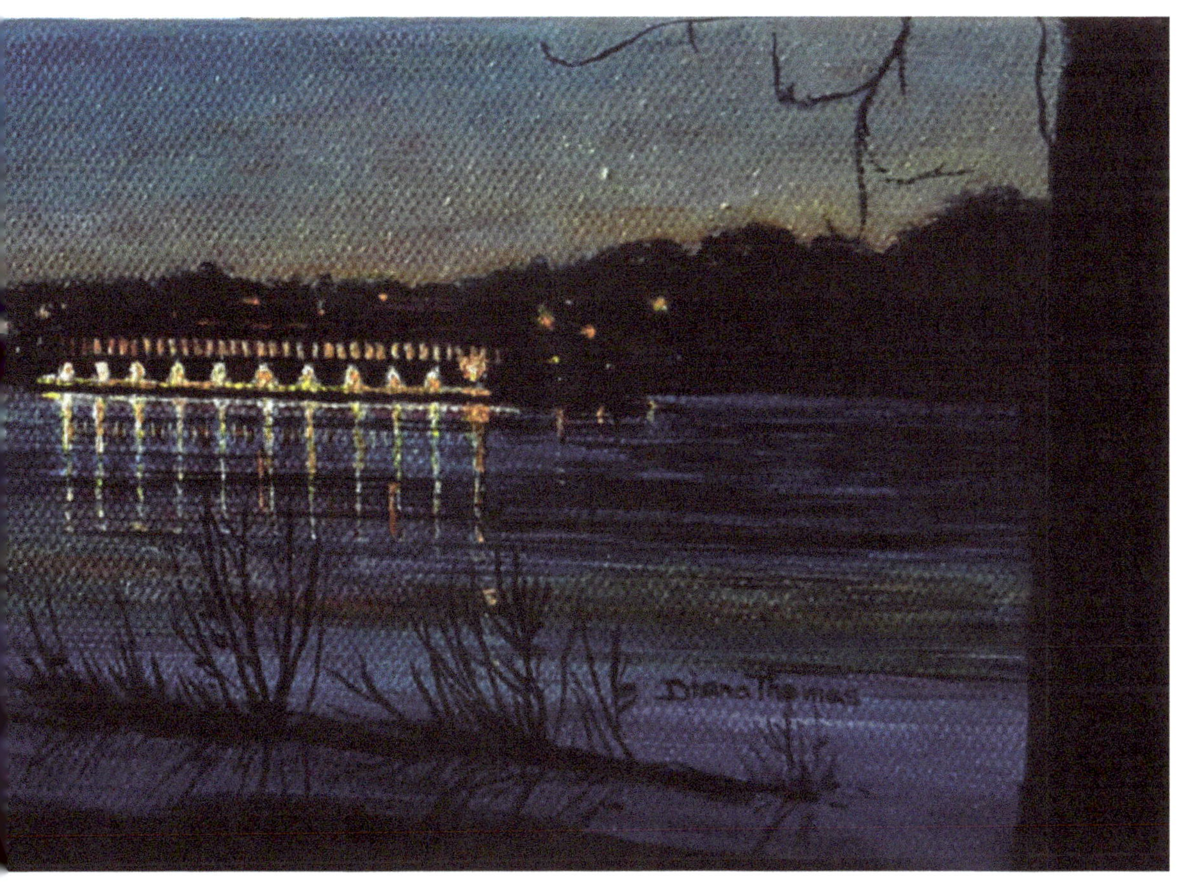

18

APRIL 19–25, 2016

"Fields of Gold"

Washington Boro, PA

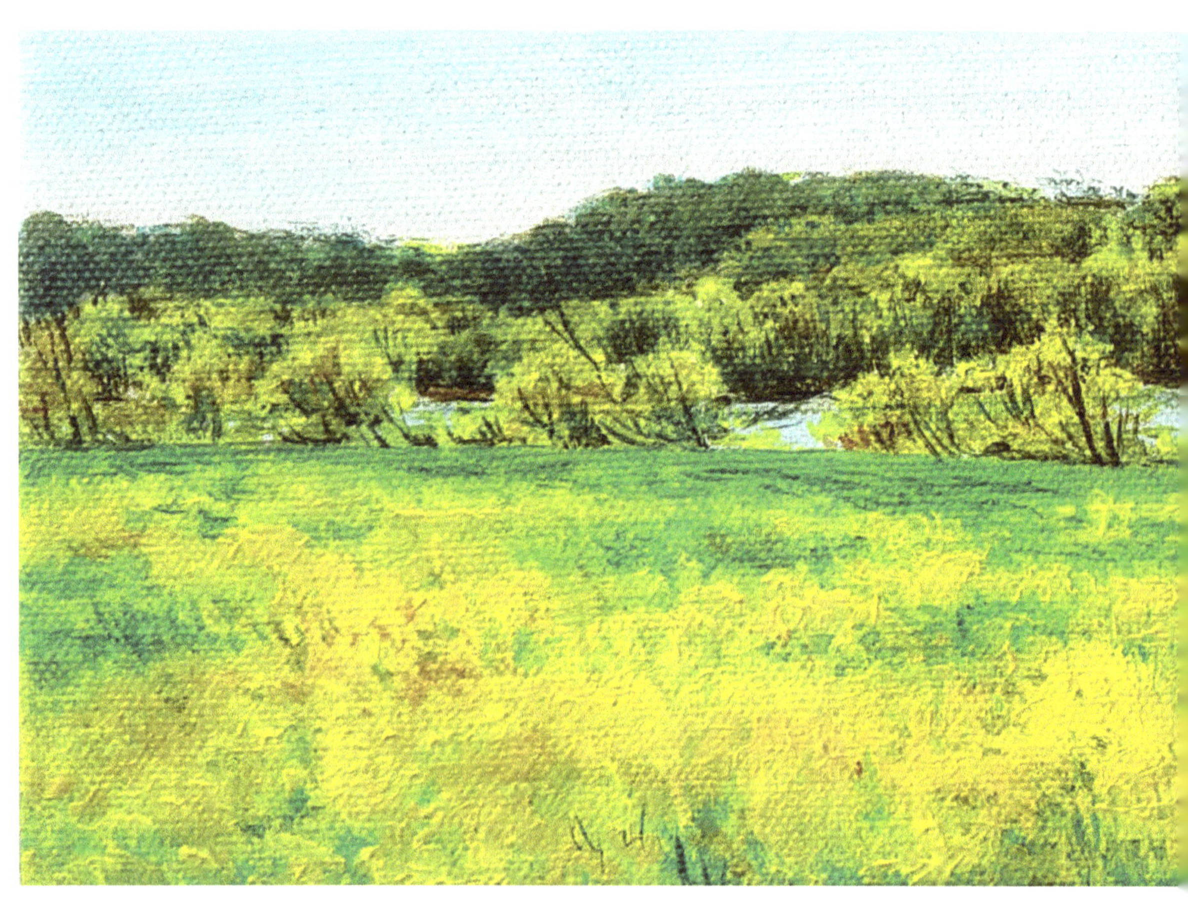

Weeks 14, 15 and 17 are still unpainted. This week I will take the paintings to Mount Bethel cemetery for a Fourth Friday show. It will be their debut! I am grateful for the invitation.

I pray that this body of work will say something greater than I can know at this point. Beautiful river, speak about your beauty; speak about life. Touch people somehow and bring healing as you so often do for me. Amen.

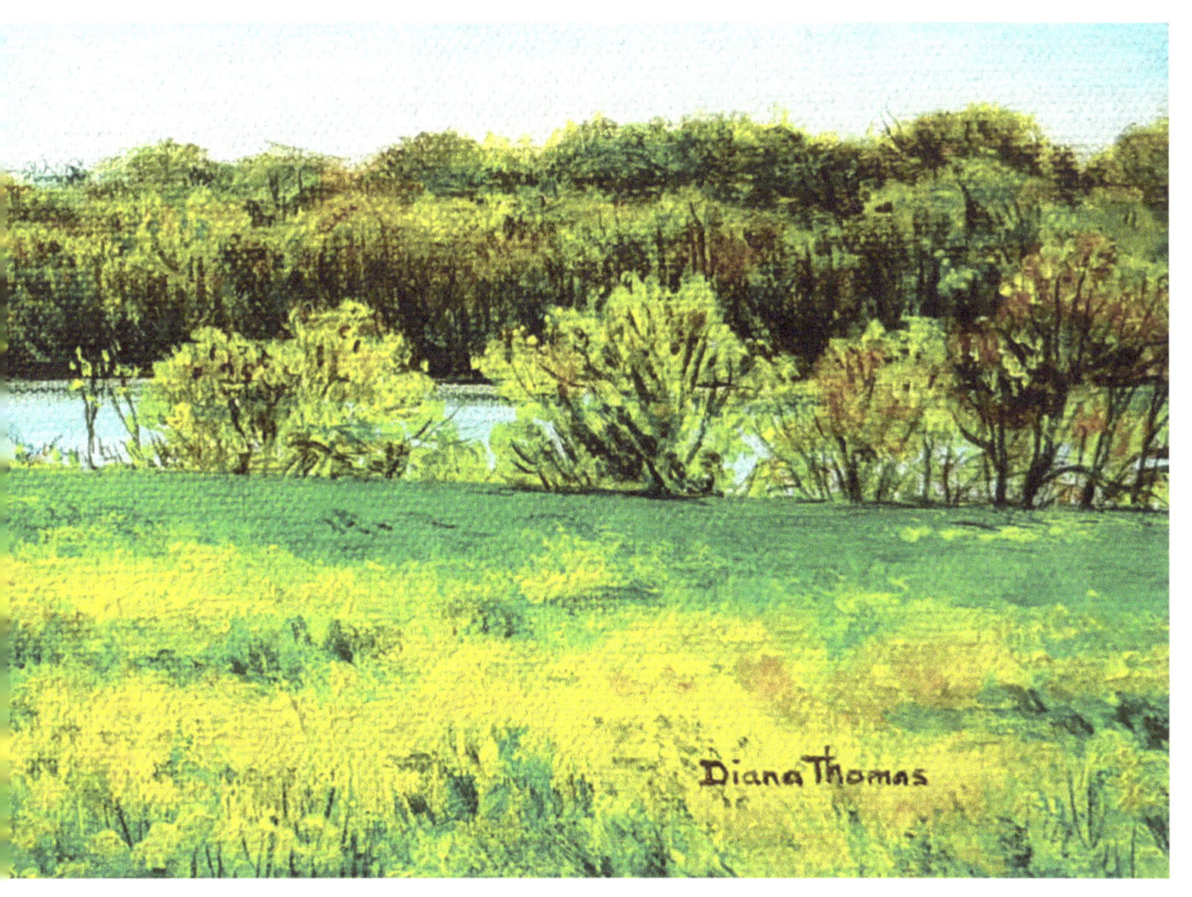

19

APRIL 26–MAY 2, 2016

First Public Appearance

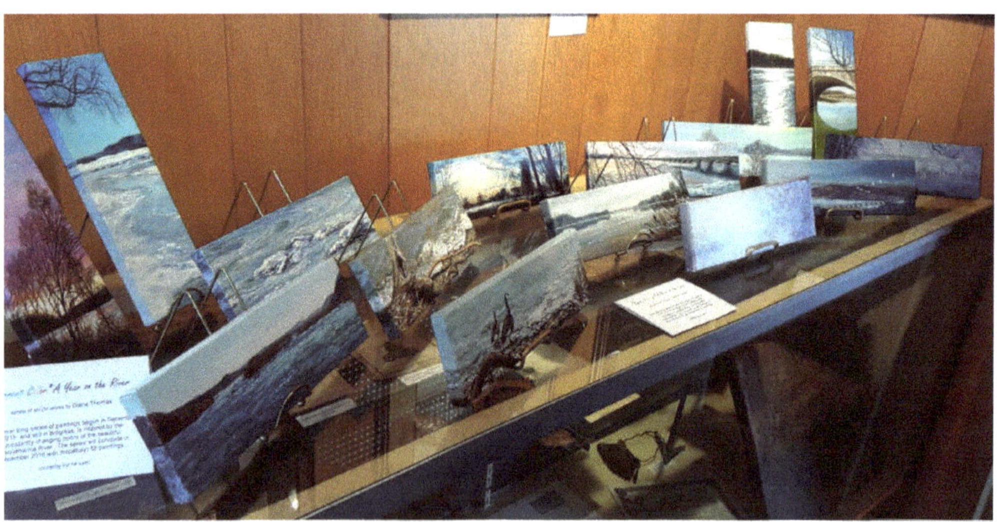

First showing at Mount Bethel

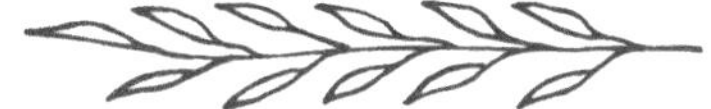

I like the name I chose for the
series: "Current Color: A Year on
the Susquehanna River."

I finally completed Weeks 14 and 15.
I have just finished painting the shot
of TMI from the air. I like it!

I'd like to keep a canvas or two in
progress at all times. That way I can
just take 30 minutes here and there,
and in between there would be time
to let some of the layers dry well,
before layering glazes. Sounds like a
good plan, but will I do it?

The comments I heard at the art show
at Mount Bethel were encouraging.
Many people who grew up on the river,
who call themselves "River Rats," told
me about their own experiences on the
river. That was really nice!

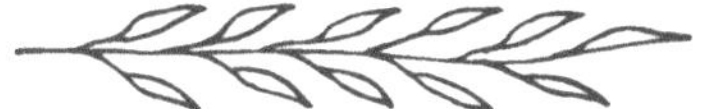

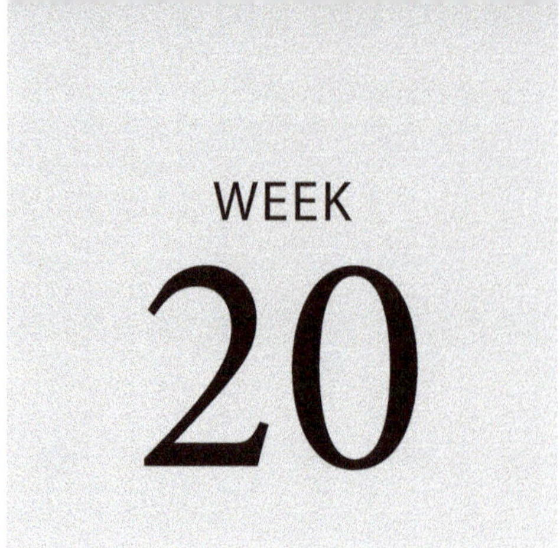

MAY 3–9, 2016

"Raining and Pouring"

E. Donegal Riverfront Park, Marietta, PA

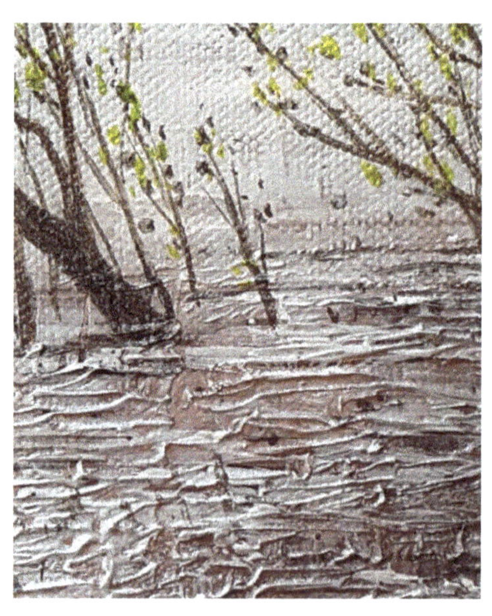

We caught a break in the rainy spell we've been having and drove to Lee's Landing in Port Deposit, Maryland, this afternoon.

I am getting ready to paint a shot of the river I took in the pouring rain. It is so fascinating to watch the little crowns of water splash up where each raindrop hits. Modeling paste will help with this one.

I'm humming the old song, "Raindrops Keep Fallin' on My Head." Like the song says, "the blues…won't defeat me" because soon "happiness steps up to greet me."[3]

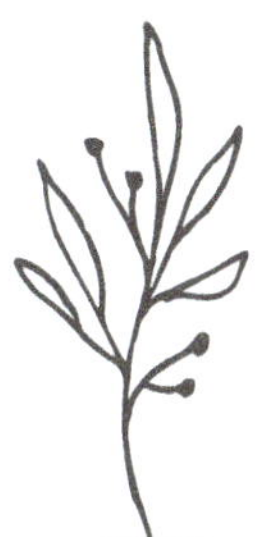

3 Burt Bacharach and Hal David, "Raindrops Keep Fallin' on My Head," Scepter, 1969.

MAY 10–16, 2016

"Gone Fishing"

Wrightsville, PA

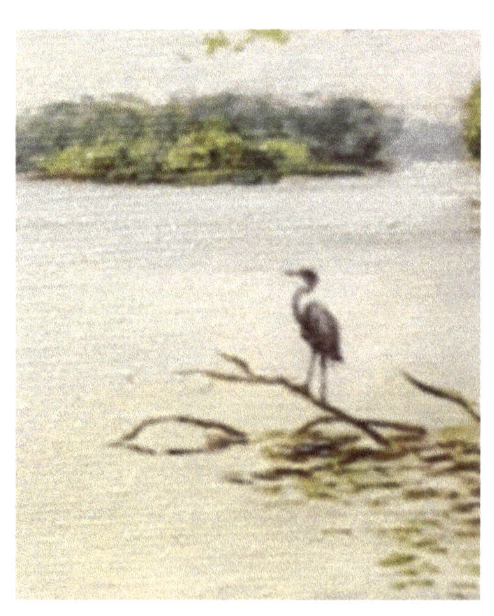

The river flows on and on—a constant reminder of the forever life that has been given to us as a gift!

Going often to the banks for photos is my regular practice in keeping a mindful pace in my "fast forward" life. I am working at living more in "Haiti time," which means not needing to look at a watch. It's freedom.

As I work, I want to make this journey a leisurely picnic on the riverbank, not a drive-through meal.

Breathe. Paint. Work. Flow along with the river's rhythm and be mindful in all things. Very few things really require rushing, when I think about it.

Painting is like praying. My mind is at peace.

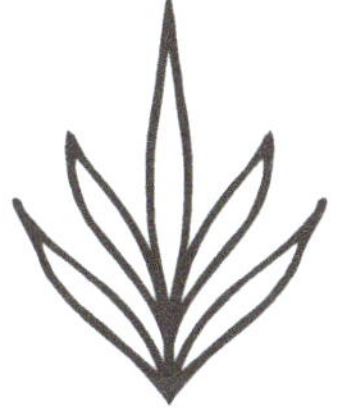

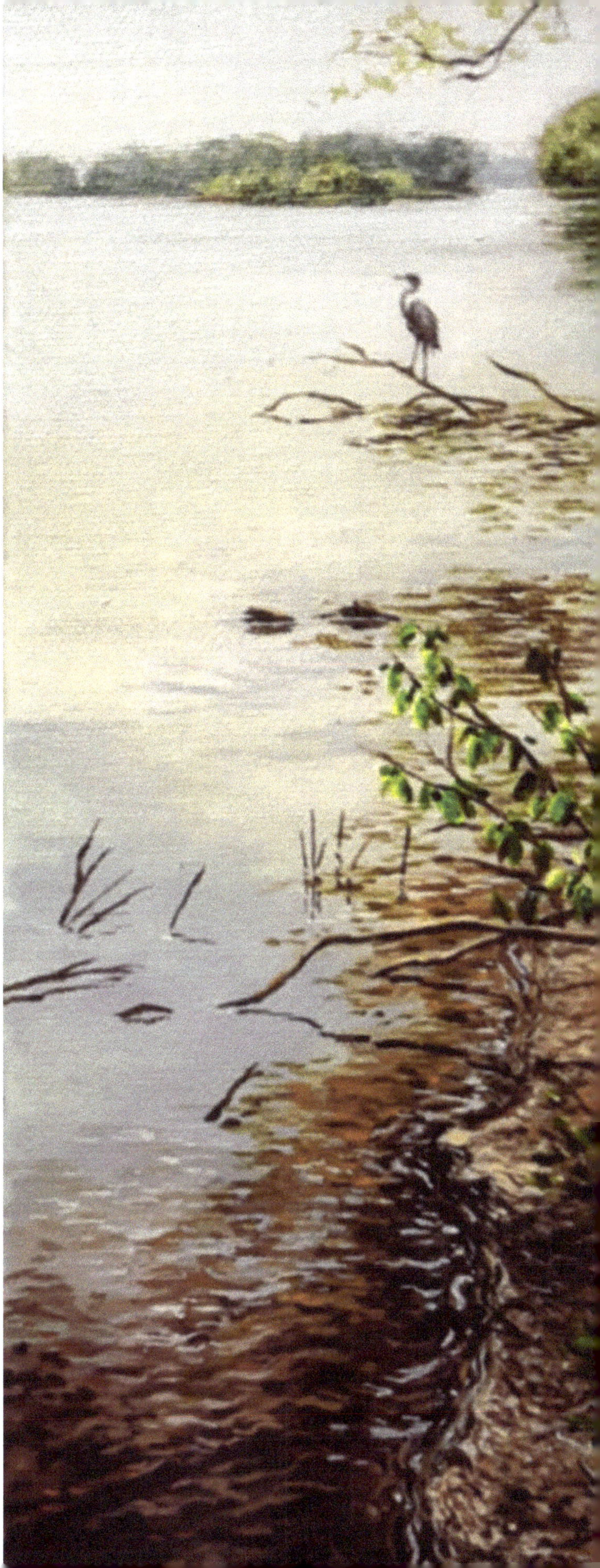

MAY 17–23, 2016

"Little River Rat"

Marietta, PA

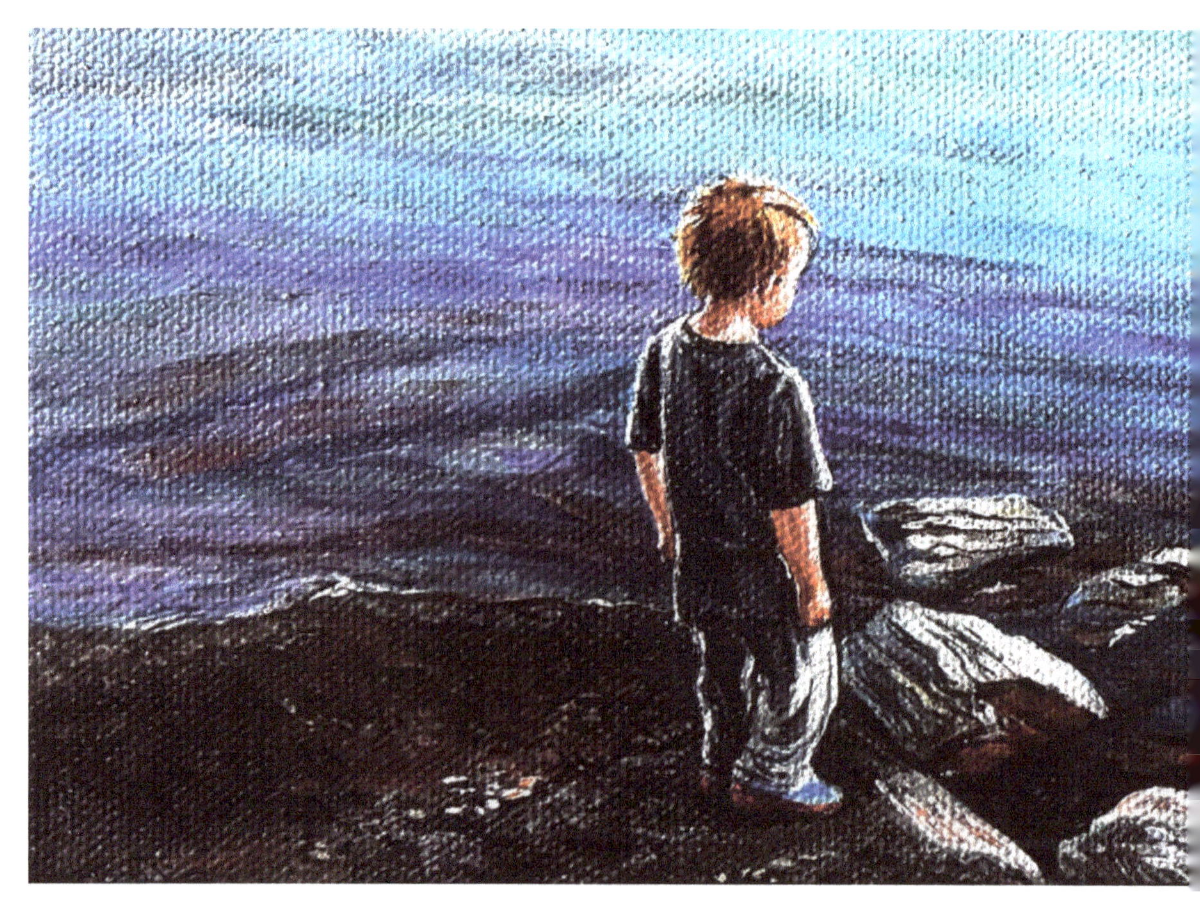

Okay, things are not going so good; I am still painting in fits and starts. I got uninspired by Week 19's lack of good photos, and Week 21's was sort of a "blah" one also. I repainted it (which I said I wouldn't do). This whole month has been extremely rainy, which makes me feel down.

We are getting ready to go to Michigan to visit Fred's folks, and I'm thinking of giving myself permission to leave a couple more weeks with no painting.

The river flows whether I paint it or not. Time moves on, and I can't get back what's passed. I don't want to be left with regrets.

"Go in your studio and paint!"

Okay. The paints and photos are packed!

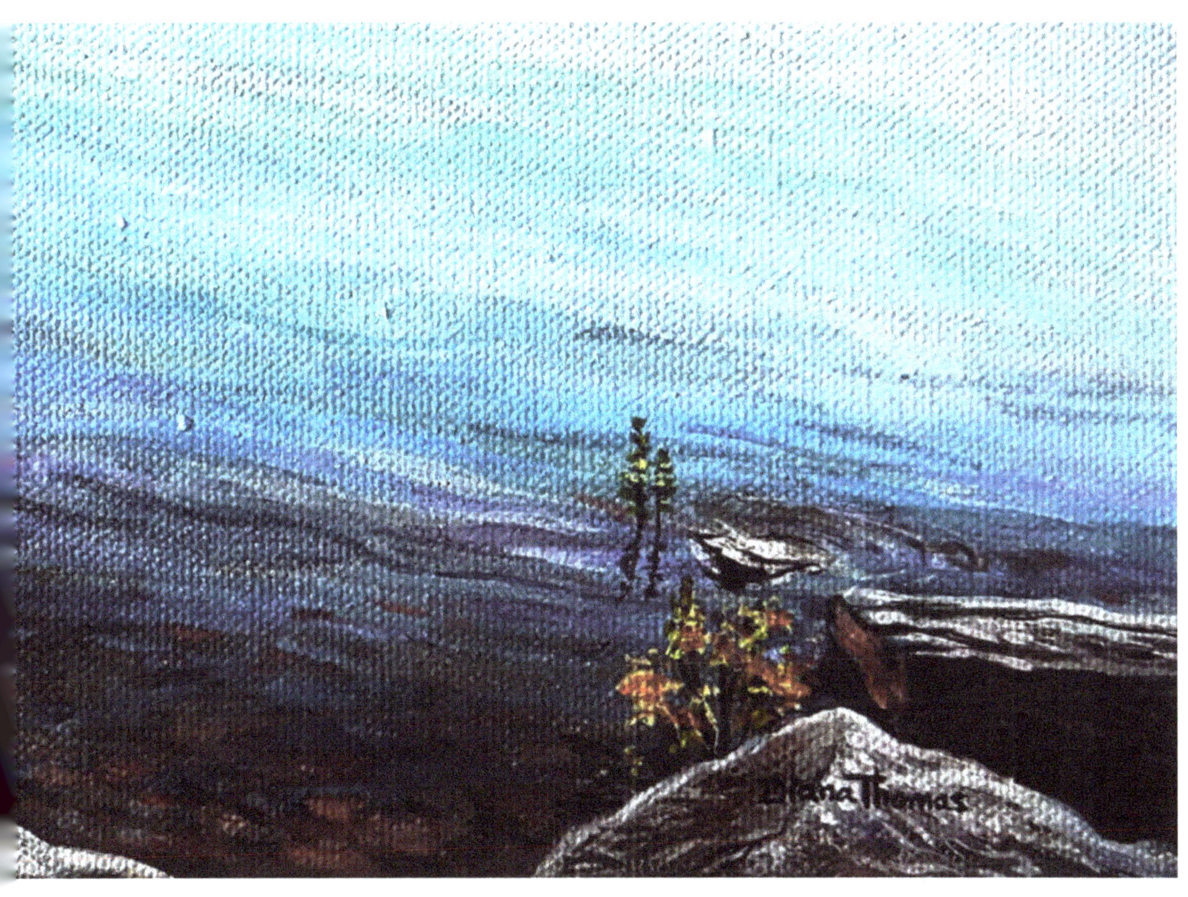

MAY 24–30, 2016

"Breezyview Overlook"

Columbia, PA

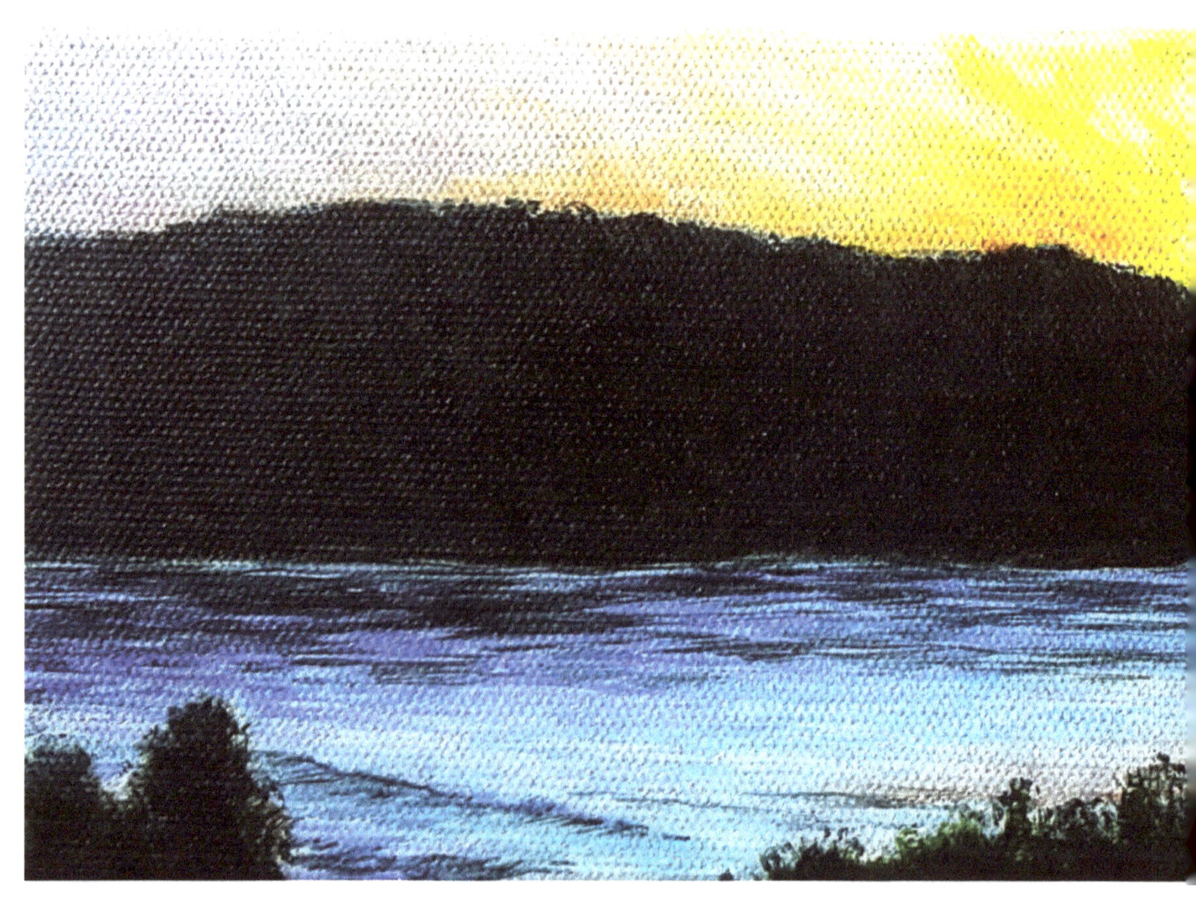

Stopped at Breezyview right about sunset on the way home from work. It will be my last chance to get a river photo before leaving for Michigan tomorrow.

There will be so many things to do when we get home. I wonder how I can think of the "*have* to-do's" the same way as the "*want* to-do's" so I can get rid of the negative energy that robs me of joyful living sometimes.

Oh, river, you flow under, over and around all the obstacles, moving some of them out of the way! Even a dam does not stop you, and you stay your course. Teach me how to have that same sense when I "have to ___________."

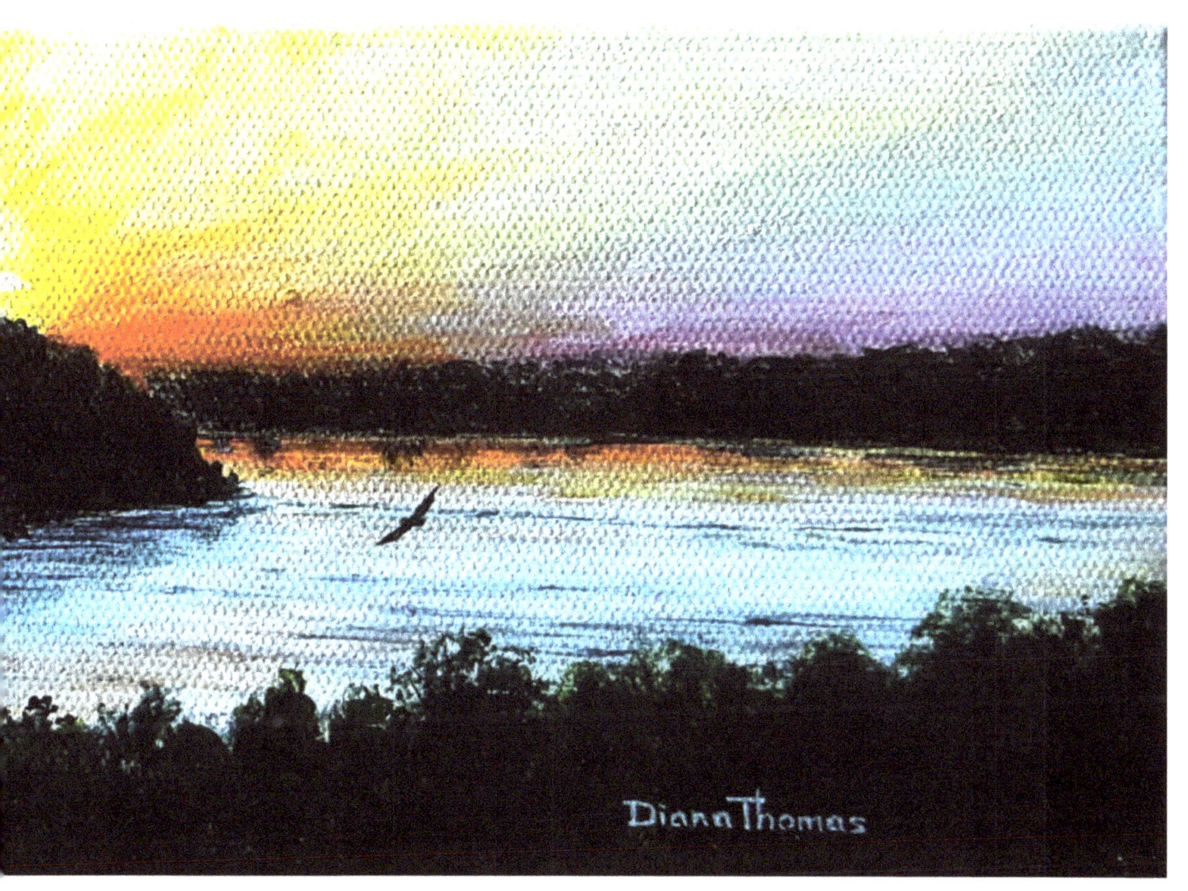

MAY 31–JUNE 6, 2016

No New Art

I returned from Michigan with two paintings in progress and am pretty happy with them (Weeks 22 and 23).

I am still not painting every day, although many days I am taking photos, editing them and putting them in the albums. It is almost halfway through the year! How can that be?

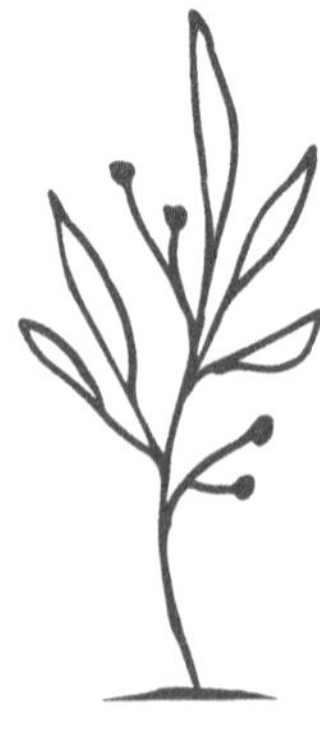

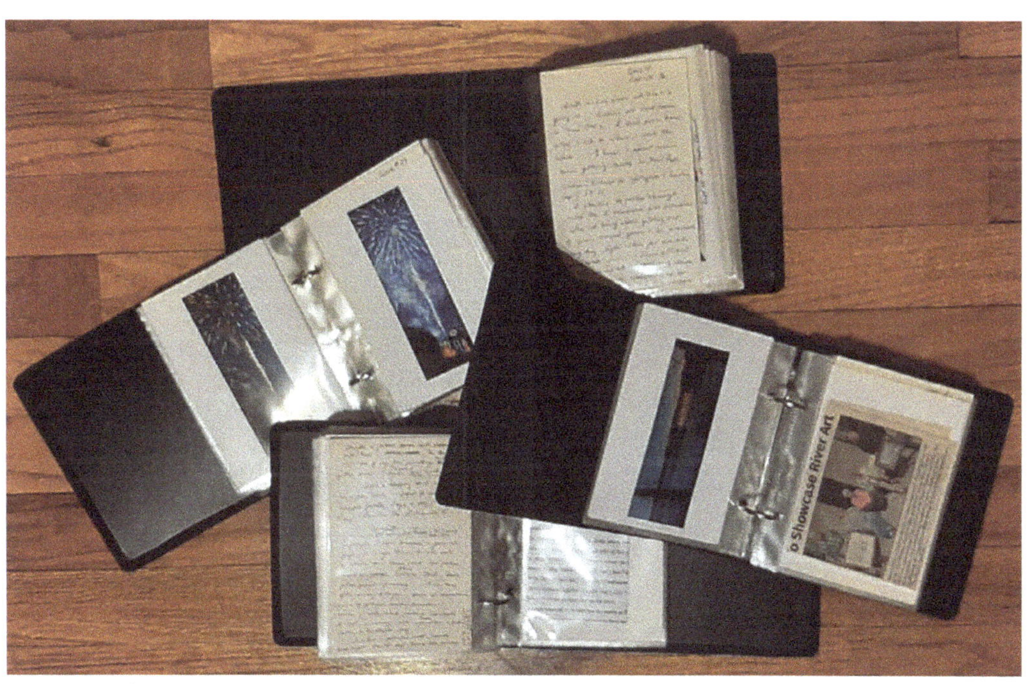

Albums for gathering photos and journal entries

JUNE 7–13, 2016

"Perfect Summer Day"

E. Donegal Riverfront Park, Marietta, PA

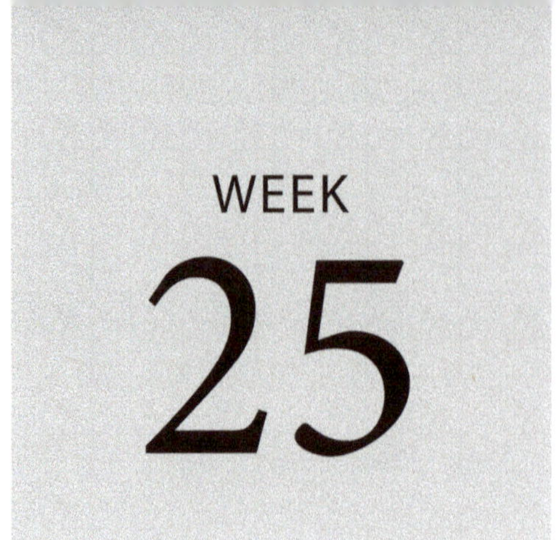

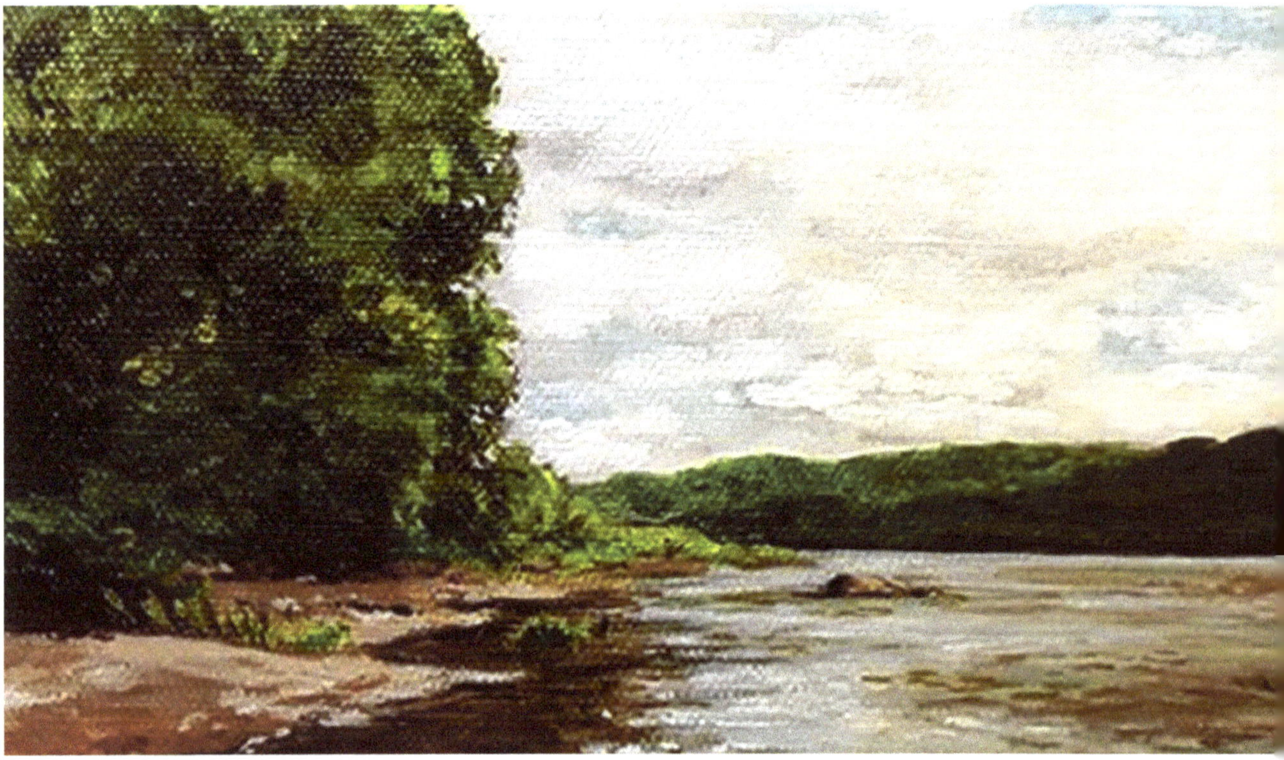

I walked the three-mile round trip to the Shocks Mill train trestle north of East Donegal Riverfront Park. I just needed to clear my head. The sound of the rapids here is sweet music. There are just too many "heavy" things on my mind right now—people I love struggling with hard things; friends and neighbors too—life is hard sometimes.

It is very windy today. Wheat is planted on both sides of the trail this year; their ripening heads sway like golden water. Puffy white clouds sail above. I hear a symphony by Redwing black bird, Indigo Bunting, Cardinal and Robin. I saw a Bald Eagle and watched the little Tree Swallows swooping and darting over the surface of the river like playful children.

"It Is Well with My Soul"

When peace, like a river, attendeth my way,

When sorrows like sea billows roll;

Whatever my lot, Thou hast taught me to say,

It is well, it is well with my soul.[4]

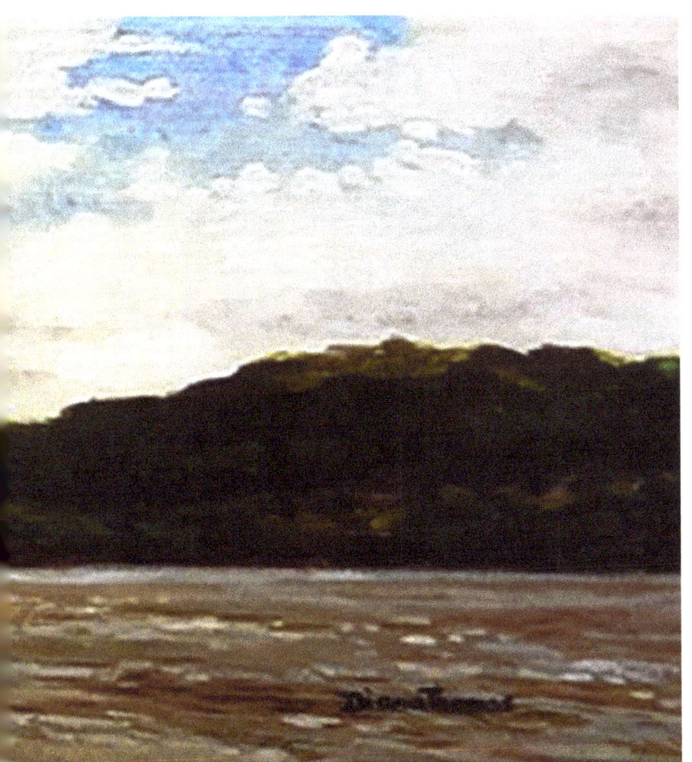

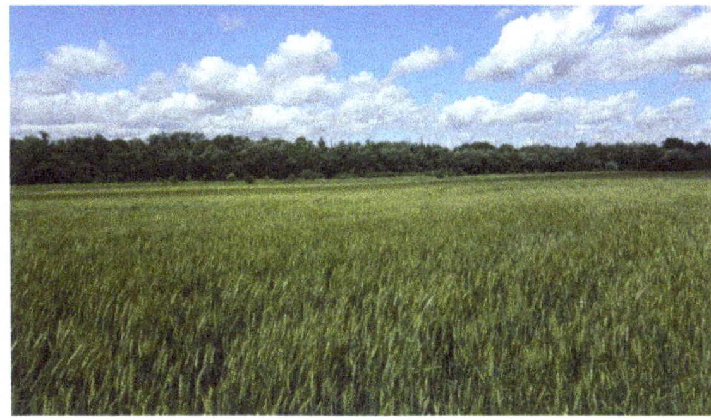

Summer wheat fields

---

4 Horatio G. Spafford, "It Is Well with My Soul," 1873. Public domain.

26

JUNE 14–20, 2016

"The Capitol"

Harrisburg, PA

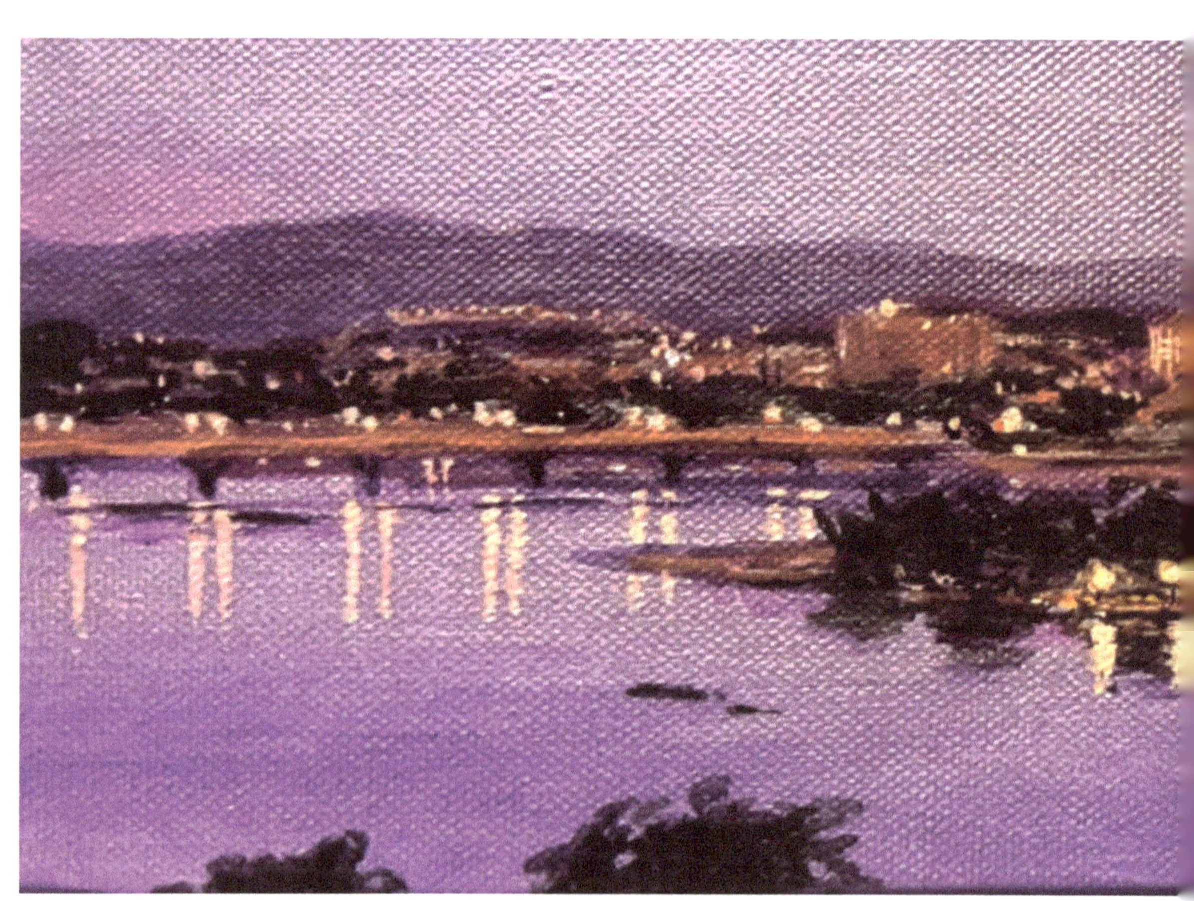

I am at the midway point already!

I've been blessed with such a peaceful life. Lord, show me how to use it to bring peace into a world with so much pain. I just heard on the news that there was another mass shooting in Orlando, Florida. Fifty or more people are dead at a nightclub. Senseless! God have mercy on this broken, sad world.

I am taking Dad out to see the new stone just put in at Mom's grave. Sigh. I will surely need some river time today. As I paint, there is a supply of refreshment whenever I need it. I am thankful.

I often think of these verses:

"He [God] will be the sure foundation for your times, a rich store of salvation and wisdom and knowledge; the fear of the Lord is the key to this treasure. ... There the Lord will be our Mighty One. It [Zion] will be like a place of broad rivers and streams...."

(Isaiah 33:6, 21)

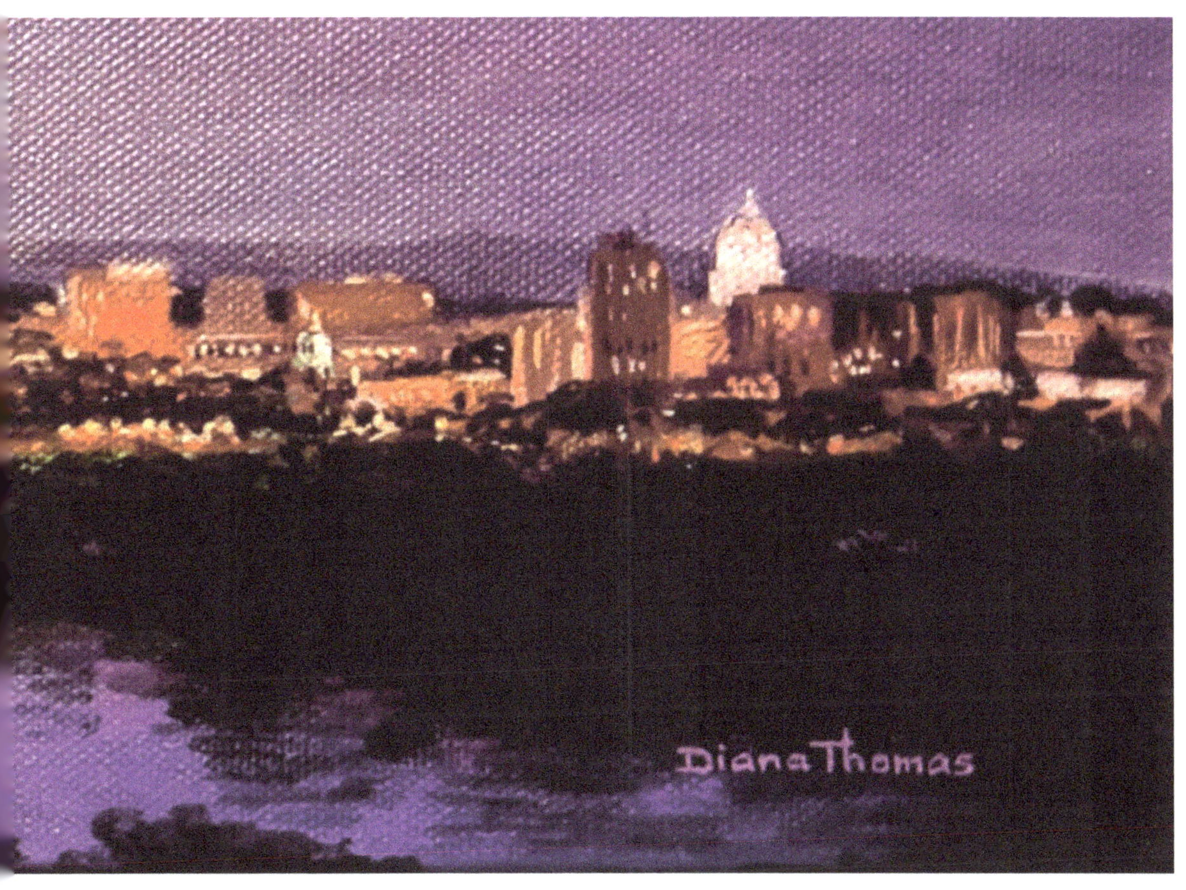

JUNE 21–27, 2016

"The Getaway"

Long Level, Wrightsville, PA

I haven't been to the river since last week's dinner date at a nice restaurant on the river at Wormleysburg. I got some great shots from Negley Park up on the hill at Lemoyne. It was a lovely evening with a beautiful full moon. Someone said it is called the "strawberry moon."

Anyway, I am feeling inspired, and I think I can get going again—refreshed! I'm up and down like a roller coaster, but the constant of the river and an enduring faith are steady and sure.

I almost titled this one "Redux" because I repainted the "dux"!

Here is the first try, which, as it turns out, I like better!

"Those who trust
in the LORD are like
Mount Zion, which
cannot be shaken
but endures forever.
As the mountains
surround Jerusalem,
so the LORD
surrounds his people
both now and forevermore."

(Psalm 125:1–2)

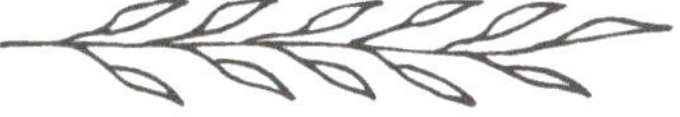

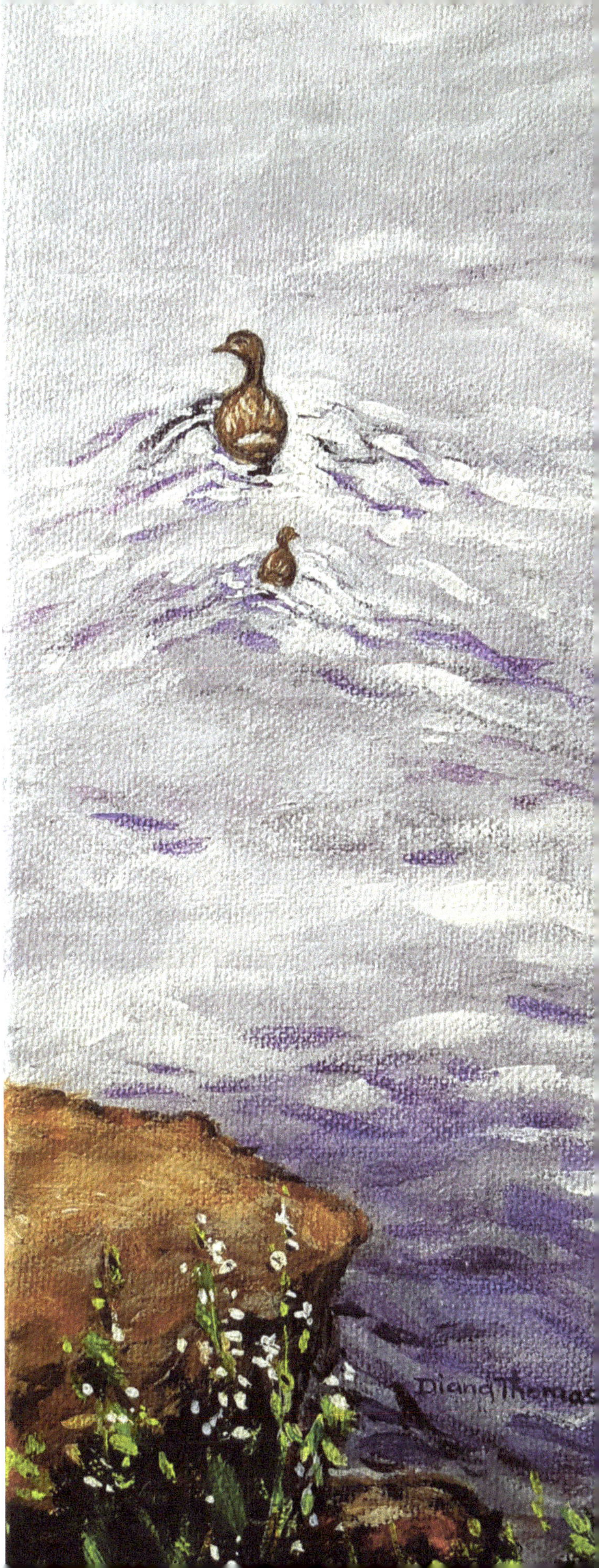

JUNE 28–JULY 4, 2016

"Boom" and "Boom 2"

Fireworks in the Rain

Wrightsville, PA

I went to Long Level for photos and was accosted by massive swarms of mayflies!

I finished the Harrisburg skyline scene, and it's what I pictured in my head. It's nice when that happens. I am working backwards to a couple of unfinished weeks.

I had fun when the grandkids took *me* to see the movie *Finding Dory* yesterday. I'm a big fan of the movie *Finding Nemo*.

I love Dory's unsinkable spirit in the face of her own limitations. She expects things to work out if she just keeps going and doing what she can.

So, I keep on practicing "walking by faith and not by sight" (2 Corinthians 5:7) as I go, carried on the "big current" through this life.

"Keep on painting, painting, painting…."

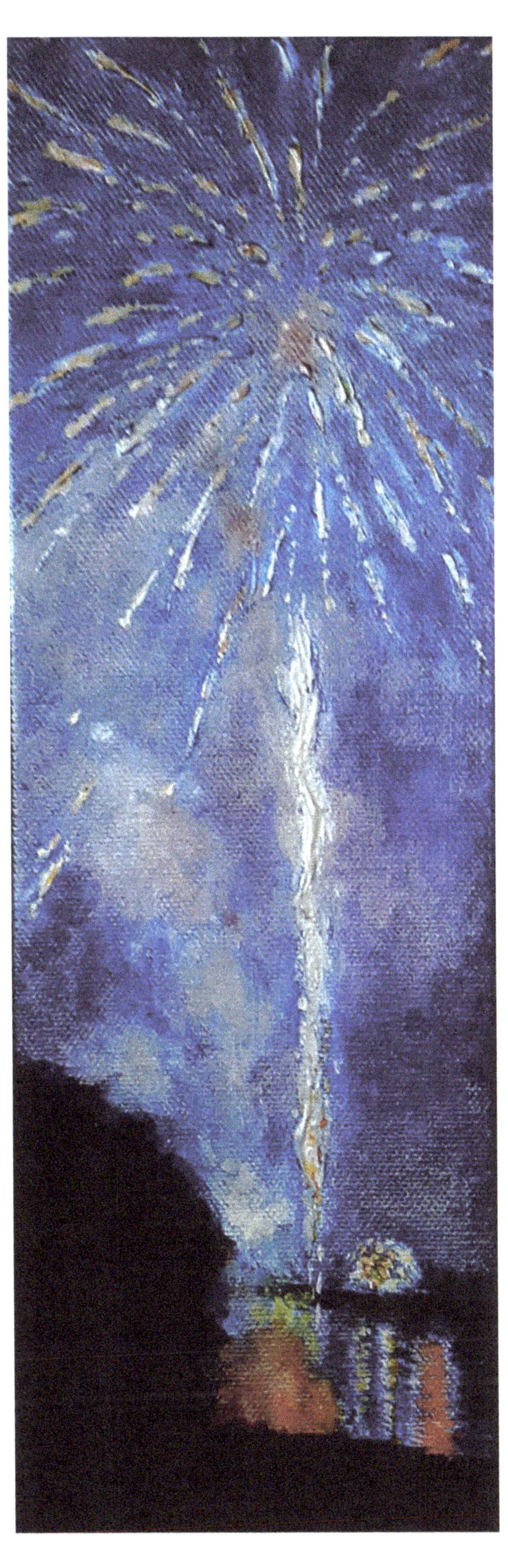
Diana Thomas

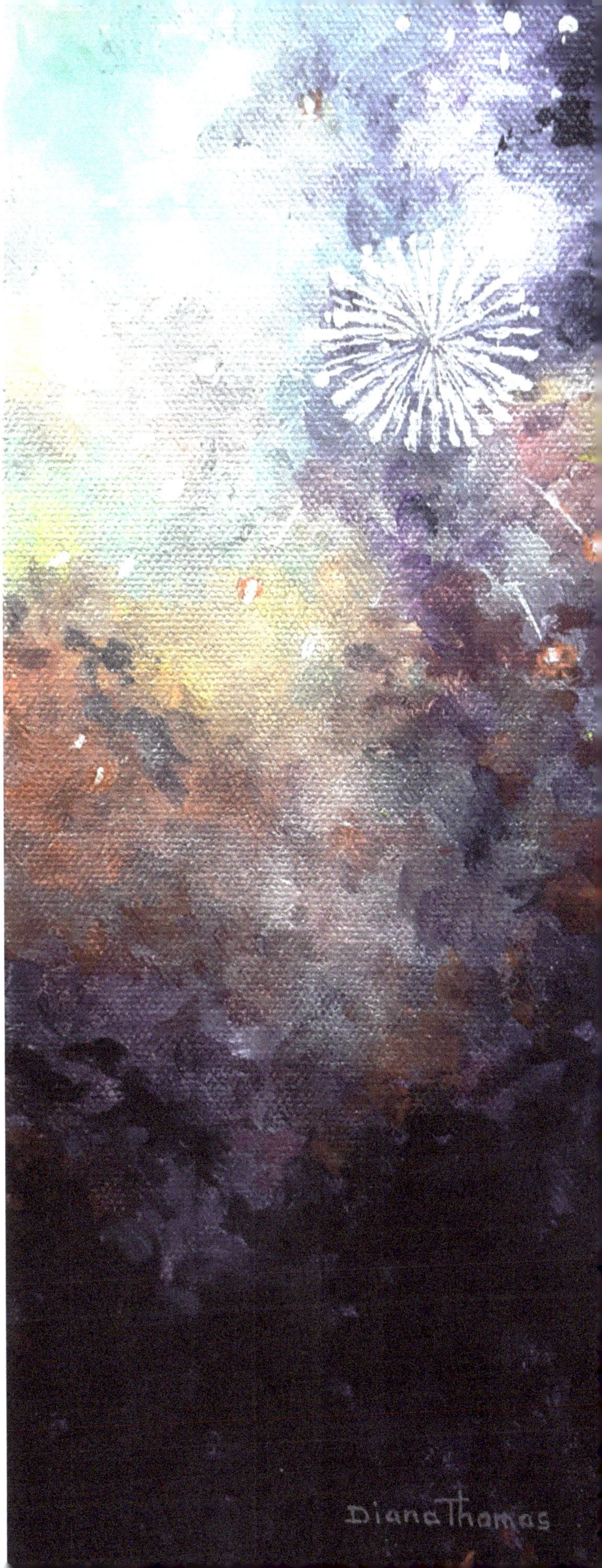

JULY 5–11, 2016

"Lightning Bugs"

Columbia, PA

It poured rain on the Fourth of July, but the fireworks went on as planned and my brave photographer friends joined me in trying to get some shots showing the fireworks' reflections on the river.

Today I actually want to paint (so I can avoid some other "'work'" that must be done first!).... Will I ever find the balance?

I promise to take me to the river for a break later today.

I'm looking forward to working more abstract on the firework shots.

I'm thinking of a poem that I wrote more than 15 years ago.

Summer Stars

Silver crescent moon

Hangs low in the sky

Towards the west and south.

Ten thousand golden stars

Rise from the wet grass

And swirl around my feet.

Higher, and higher,

Until they meet the silver stars

Who peek out of hiding

In their blue velvet bed.

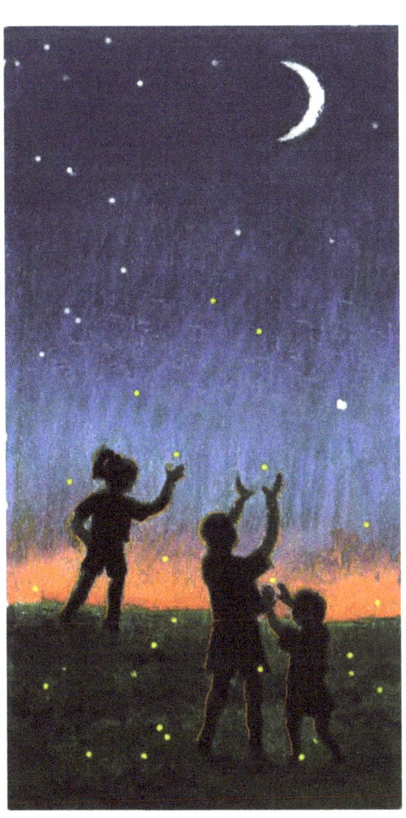

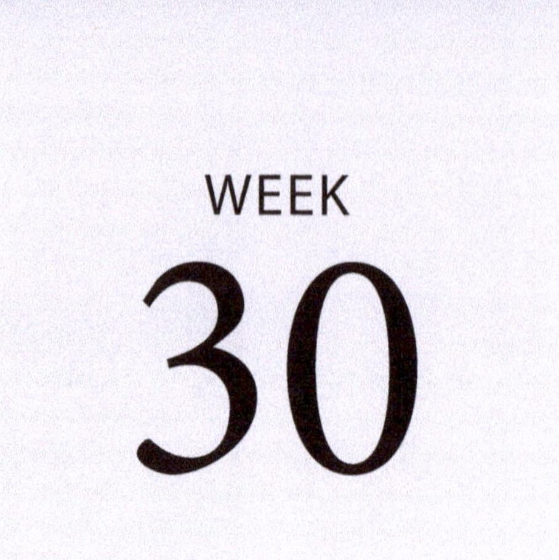

JULY 12–18, 2016

"Mayflies"

Enola Low Grade Trail, Manor Township, PA

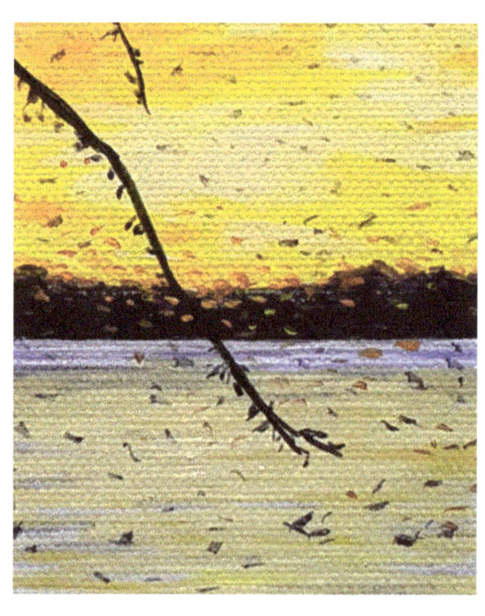

The mayfly hatching seems huge
this year. They deserve a painting
as well as my summer favorite,
lightning bugs.

We spent an evening at a favorite
restaurant in Havre de Grace.
Beautiful, beautiful, a peaceful spot
to rest and dine.

I hope to leave a footprint of beauty
and peace when I leave this place.

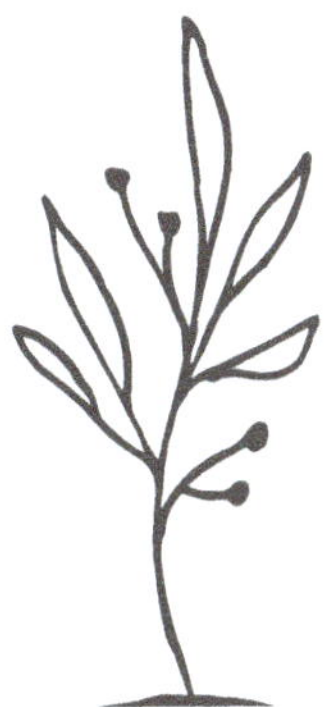

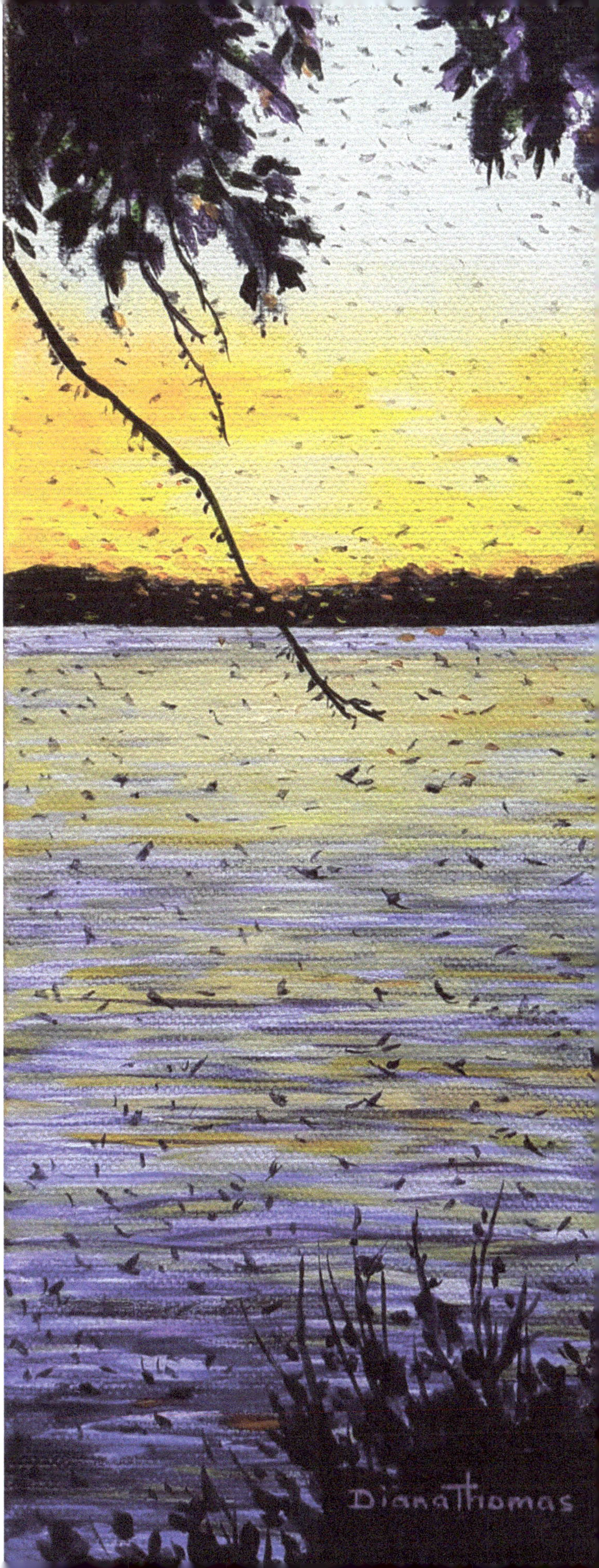

JULY 19–25, 2016

"Storm's Comin'"

Conejohela Flats, Washington Boro, PA

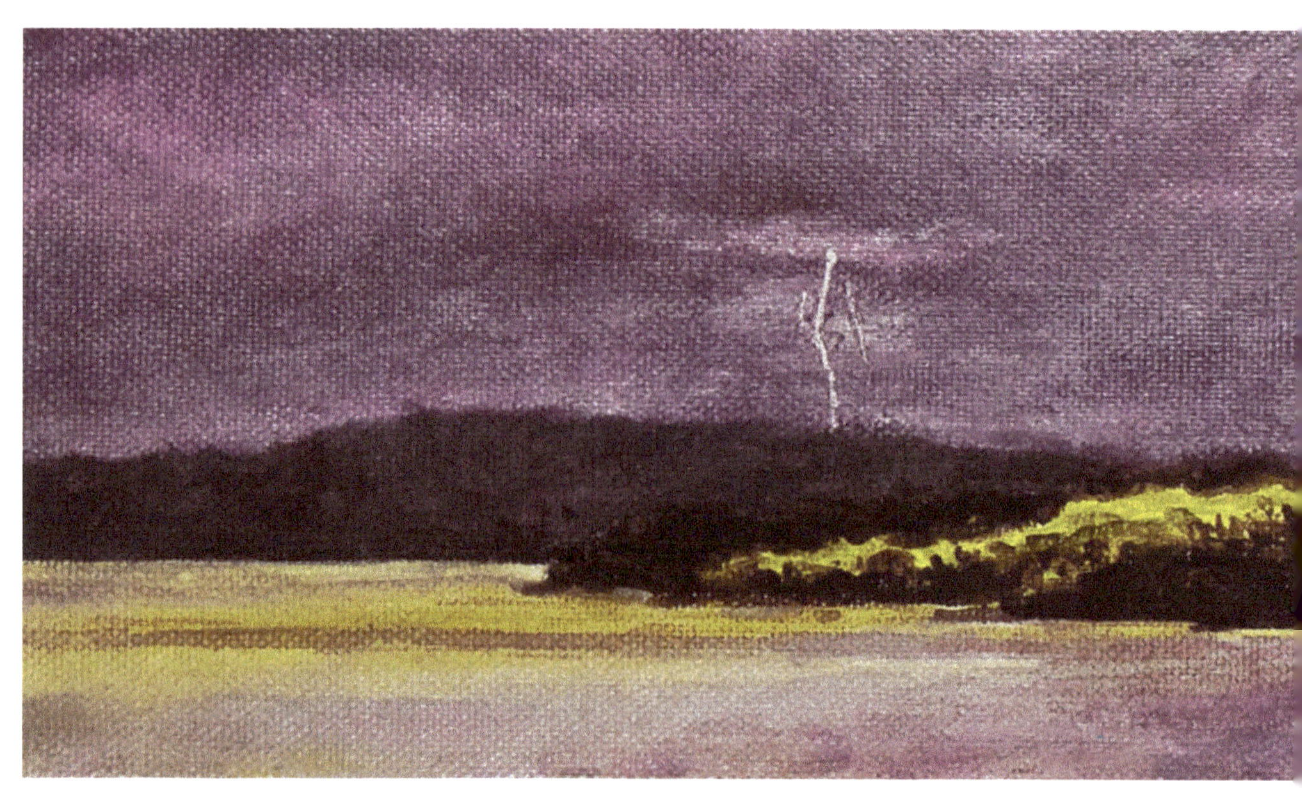

At six a.m. I drove to River Park (Columbia) with my coffee to look at the full moon setting over Wrightsville. The photos I got with my phone didn't do it justice. The river was so calm, like glass, and the rising sun flashed gold in the windows of the buildings in Wrightsville as if to make sure the moon didn't get all the glory at this time of day!

On another day, I stood at the Blue Rock boat ramp in the rain a long time, trying to get a shot of the lightning. I loved the colors of this one as soon as I did it!

"And there will be a tabernacle for shade
in the daytime from the heat, for a place of refuge,
and for a shelter from storm and rain."

(Isaiah 4:6 NKJV)

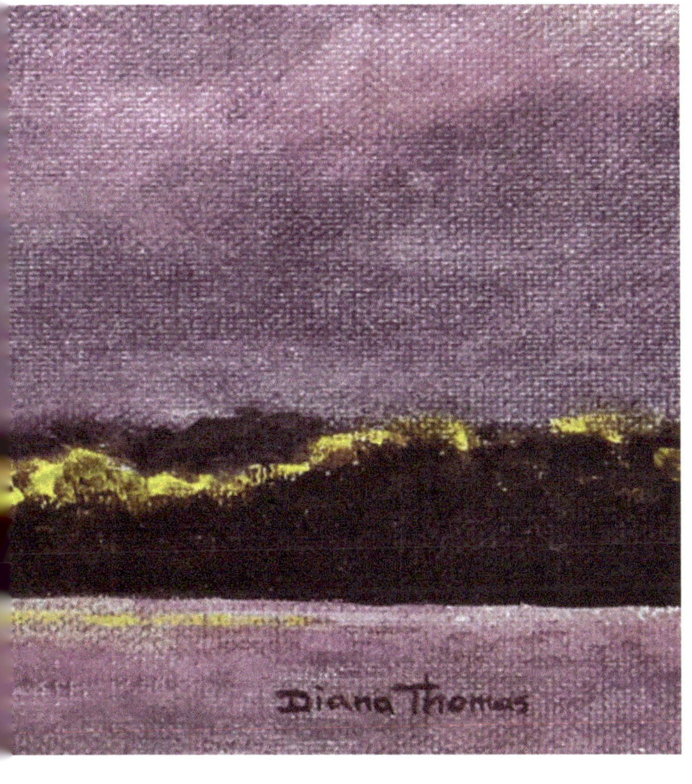
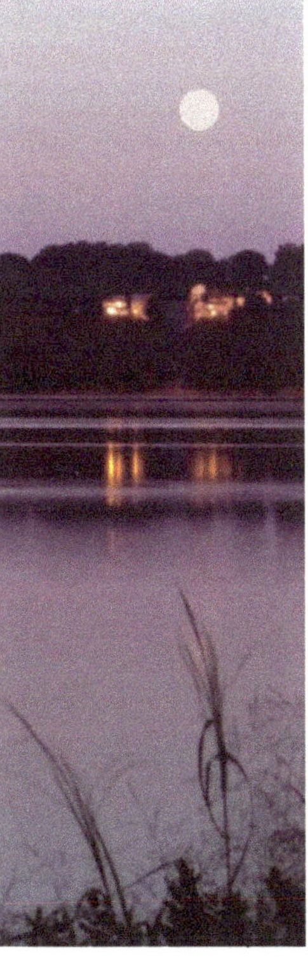

Full moon setting,
Wrightsville, PA

JULY 26–AUGUST 1, 2016

"Pink Loosestrife"

Wrightsville, PA

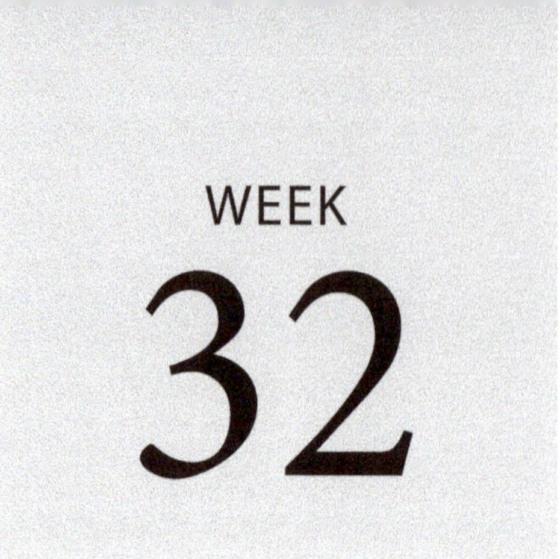

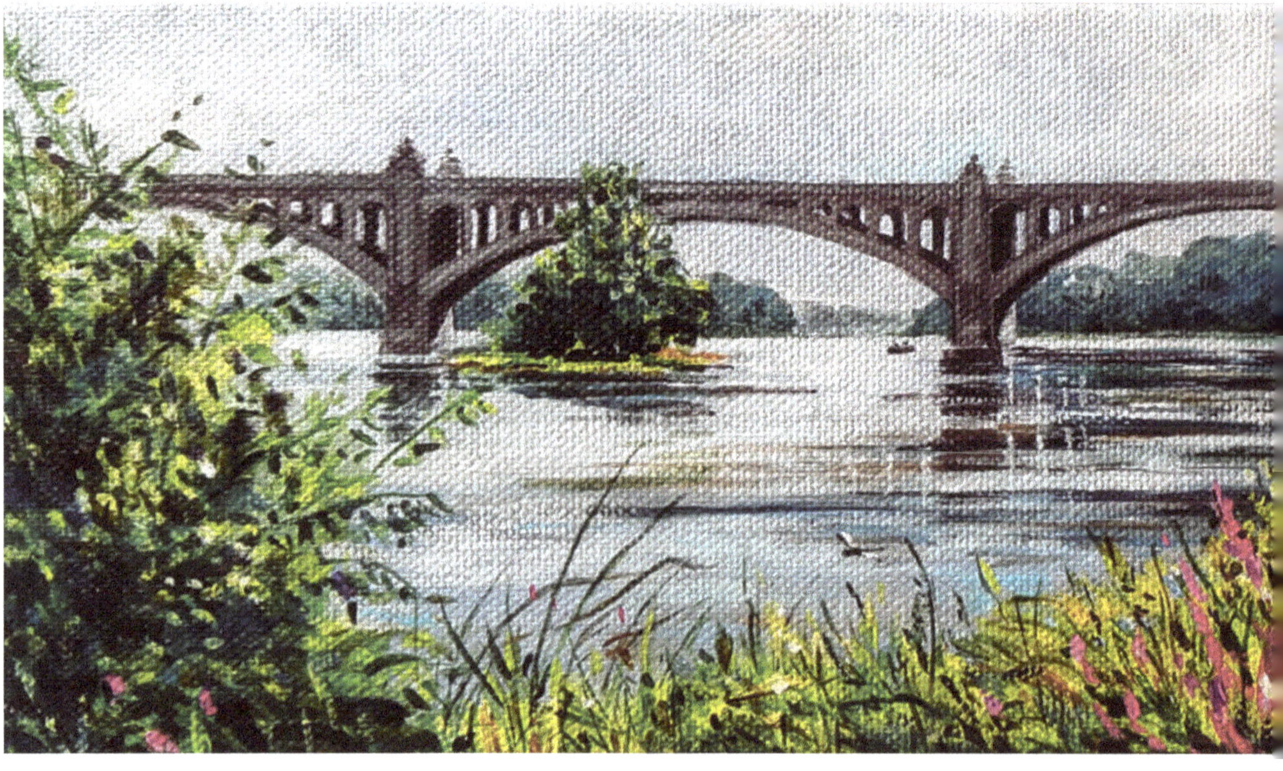

The dog days of summer are here, and the season drifts away like the puffy clouds overhead. I took our friends, who are here visiting from Missouri, to Columbia Riverfront Park for an evening stroll.

I hope my "photographer stand-in" friends can get some shots of the river when we are in Illinois next week. While Fred is busy taking care of his older sister's affairs, I will get to paint all day! Yes!

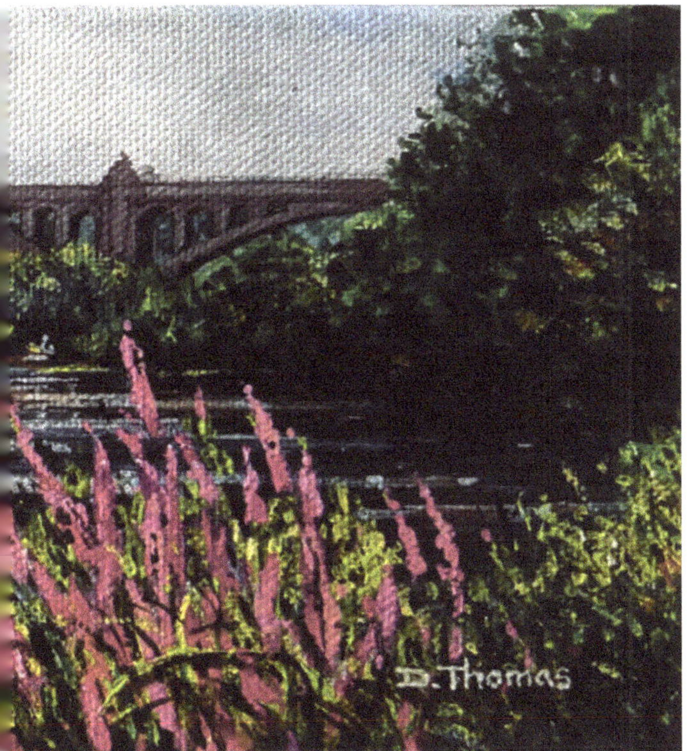

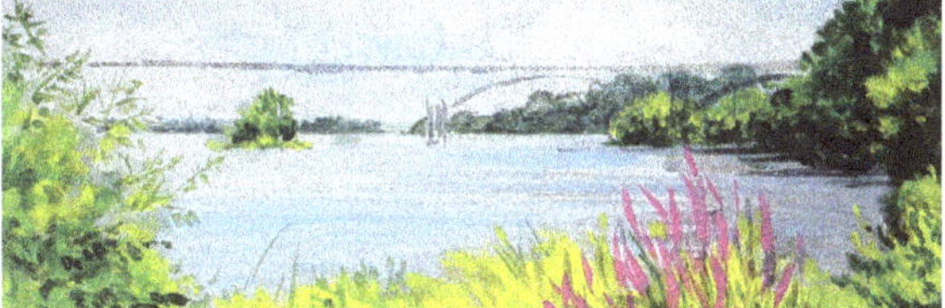

Work in progress

AUGUST 2–8, 2016

"Evening Commute"

Guest Photographer, Near Accomac

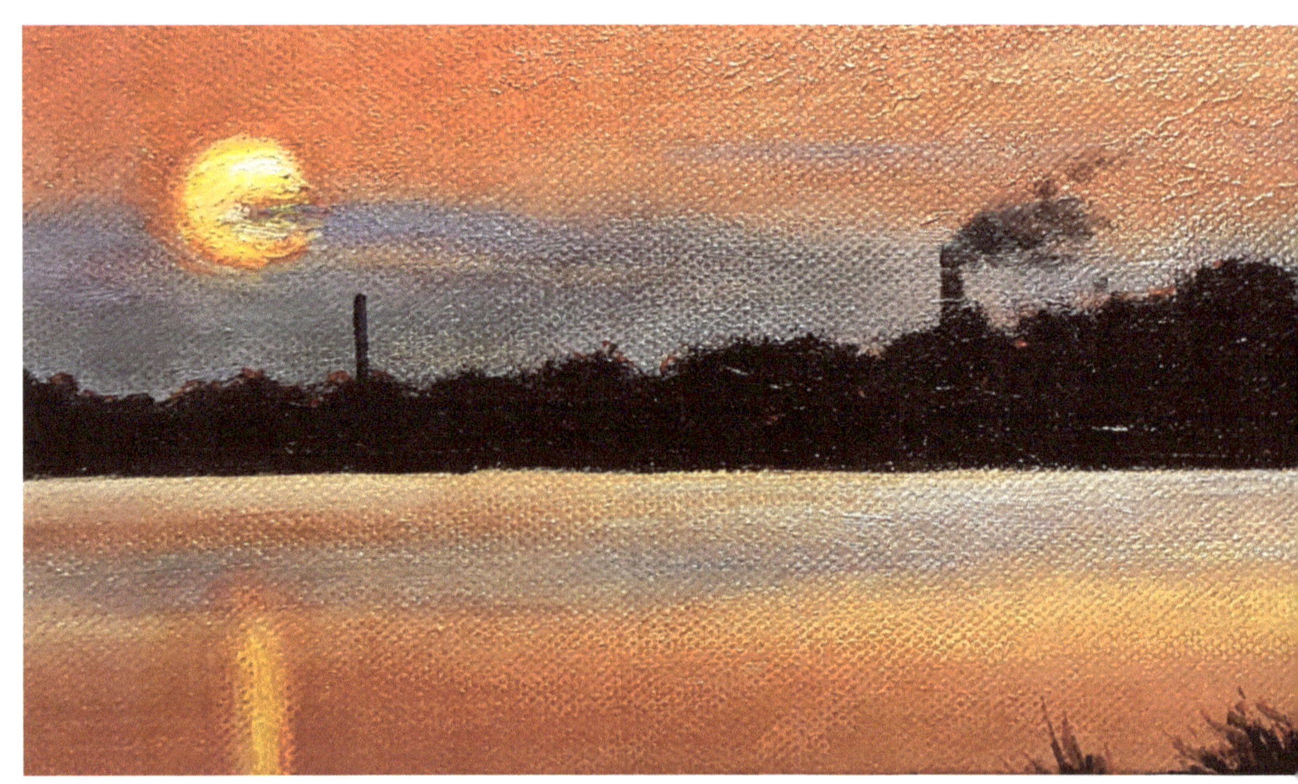

I loved the shot of a bronze and lavender sunset by my guest photographer. I can't wait to paint it.

We spent our 33rd anniversary on the "Big Muddy" Mississippi River enjoying dinner and a cruise. "Powerful and frightening" is how I would describe this river! Unlike the Susquehanna, which is the longest unnavigable river in North America, the Mississippi was bustling with work and pleasure boats of all kinds and sizes. What a lovely time.

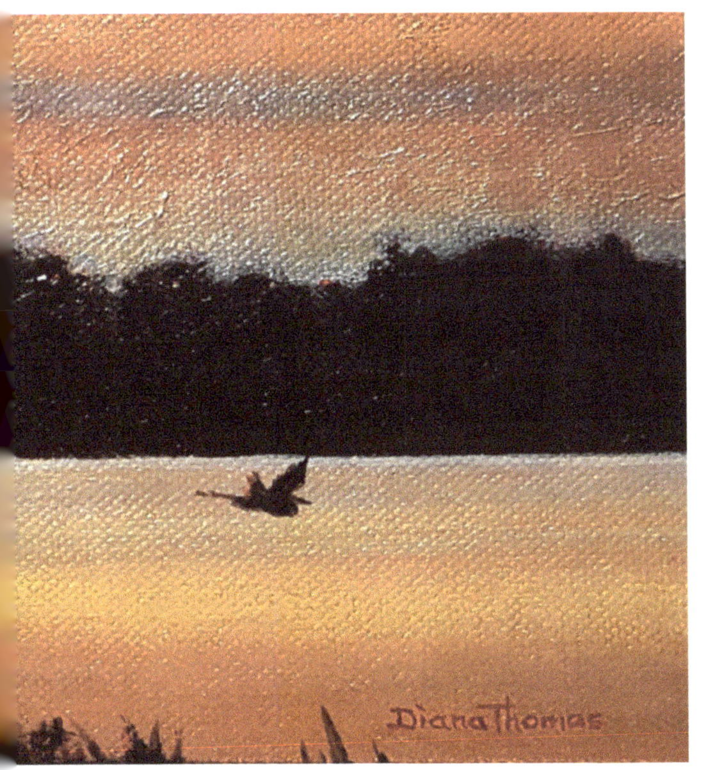

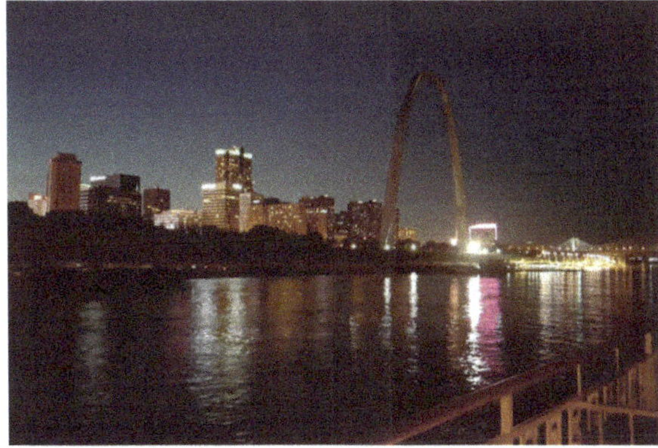

Mississippi River at St. Louis

AUGUST 9–15, 2016

"Port Deposit"

Looking toward Havre de Grace, MD

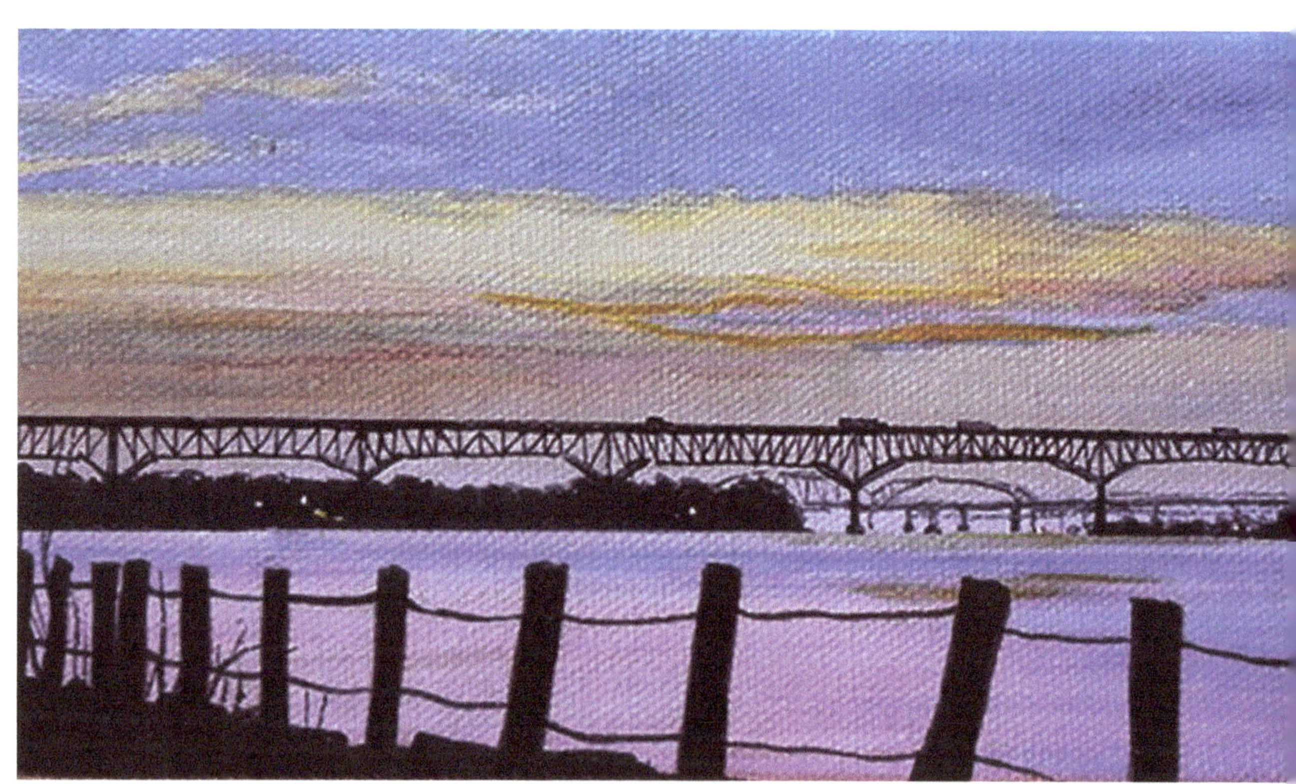

I got a few good photos from Lee's Landing in Port Deposit. I loved the streak of yellow in an otherwise purple scene and the layers of bridges, Route 95, Route 40 and the Amtrak train bridge, down at Havre de Grace where the Susquehanna empties into the Chesapeake Bay.

Lee's Landing is one of our favorite places to eat and relax during the summer. We go down to the Chesapeake Grille in Havre de Grace once in a while too. It's nice to stroll along the boardwalk afterwards and get an ice cream cone for dessert.

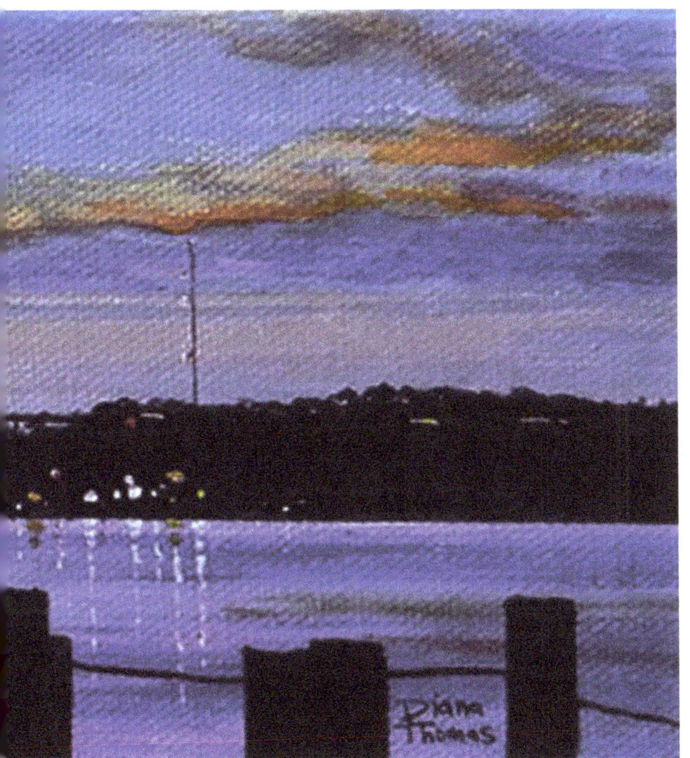

Tranquil, soft pastels to start this one

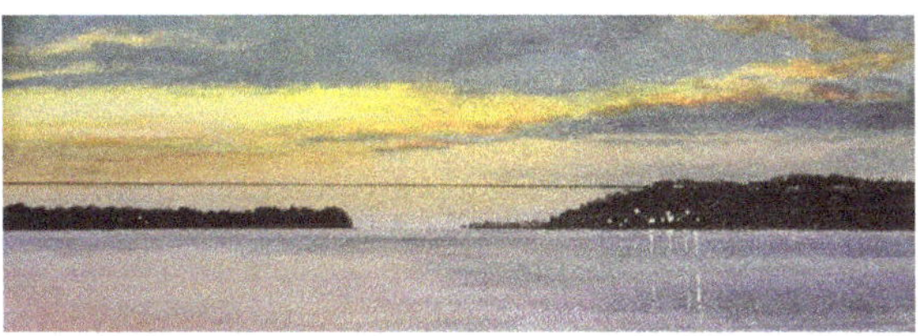

Adding the horizon line

AUGUST 16–22, 2016

"Reflections"

E. Donegal Riverfront Park, Marietta, PA

I started looking into contacting organizations that might want to borrow these paintings for promoting their work on behalf of the river. I figured that telling them I would have a year's worth of paintings will motivate me to make sure I finish.

As the river flows and days pass, I think about the special moments and people who are important to me. When we recently celebrated a grandson's second birthday, I thought about what things will flow from us down to the next generation.

A Prayer:

*May we send along
the experience
of being loved and
memories of laughter
and of understanding.
May we send along a de-
sire for meaningful work,
a faith in God
that endures, and a
reverence for life. May
we pass along a clean,
green environment for all
to enjoy. Amen.*

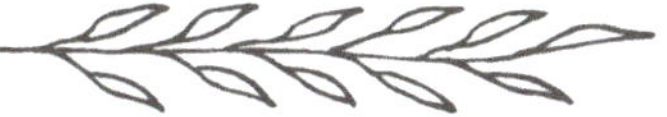

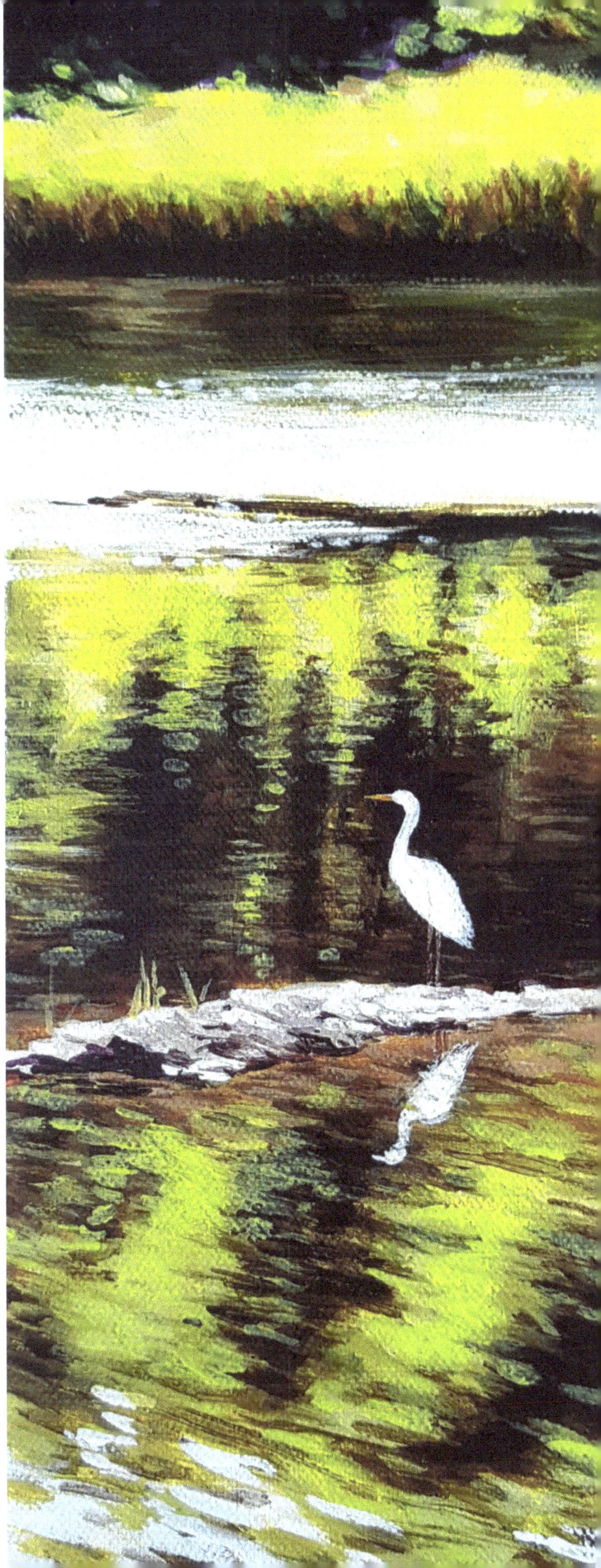

AUGUST 23–29, 2016

"Water under the Bridge"

Under the Route 30 Bridge, Columbia and Wrightsville, PA

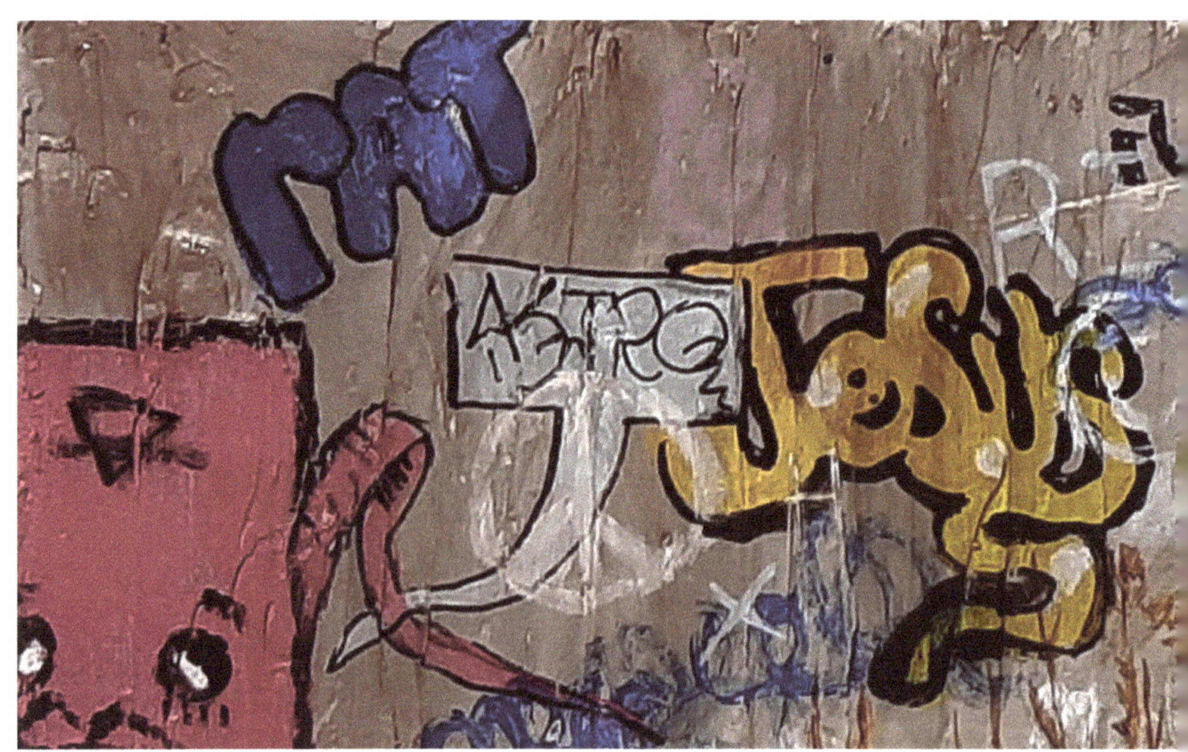

I got some photos under the Route 30 bridge on the York County side as well as some on the Lancaster side. This painting is a composite of the two, minus the stuff I didn't really want to replicate.

The sound of the trucks rumbling overhead is louder than thunder! But the creatures who make their home here don't care at all—dragonflies, ducks and a Kingfisher swooping in unaware of anything but their instinctual business.

What is our instinctual business? Is it a desire for a life of peace? I pray that is what my daughter Chrissy will eventually find. We had a nice afternoon together having lunch, shopping and singing in the car as I drove her to Harrisburg for another attempt at recovery. Oh, I pray she will find peace and leave behind thoughts that roar like thunder and the darkness that has been pulling her down and down like dark currents for so long.

I drove back home down Route 441 just so I could be near the comfort of the river, my old friend, always my constant beauty and peace.

"Do not remember the former things, nor consider the things of old [they are water under the bridge]. Behold, I will do a new thing, now it shall spring forth; shall you not know it? I will even make a road in the wilderness and rivers in the desert."
(Isaiah 43:18–19 NKJV)

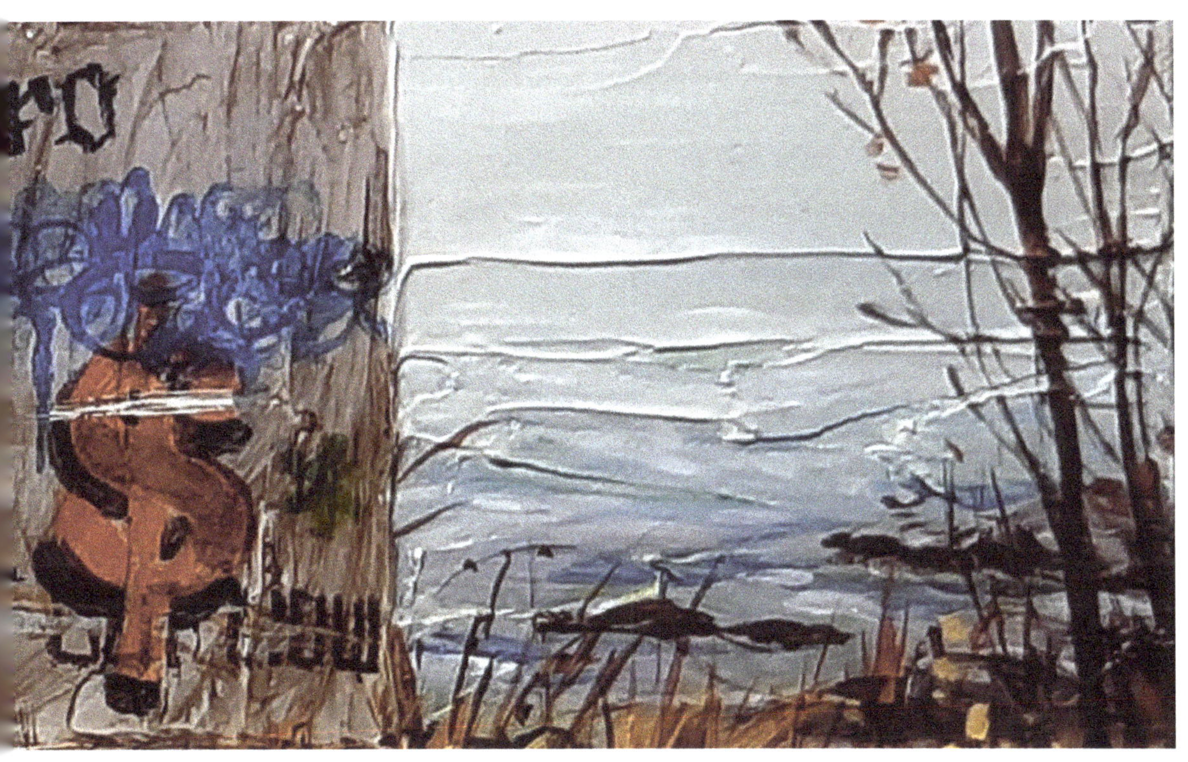

AUGUST 30–SEPTEMBER 5, 2016

"Camouflaged"

Safe Harbor, Conestoga, PA

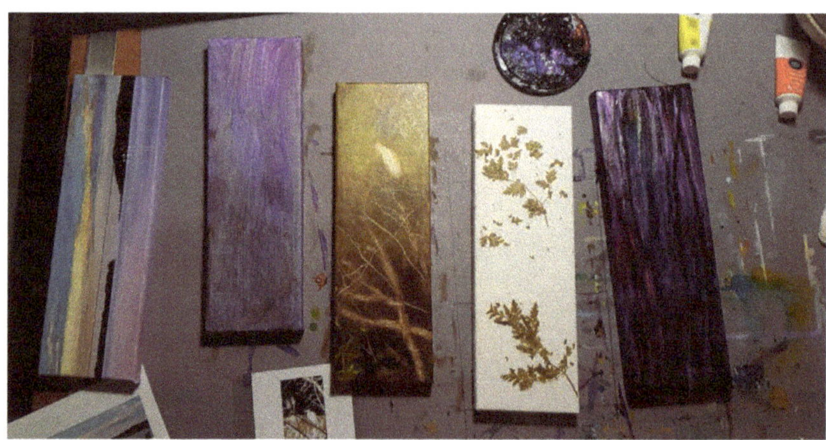

A little behind again

Okay, so I had a little talk with this stack of blank canvasses sitting on my table, staring me in the face, drumming their fingers impatiently.

"Look, you guys, just hang on. I'll be back from Haiti in a week. Believe me, it's hard to make you wait. If I could run away and elope with you to an island, I would. And I'd never come back to 'obligation land.'

"Really, I will be back, I promise. I can see in my head the images that will form on your white surfaces. I can feel the energy flowing from my hands through the brush as it strokes colors and shapes across your face. I see you coming alive and being shared with anyone who cares to gaze on you and let you call up forgotten memories of other times. I will be back soon because I need you."

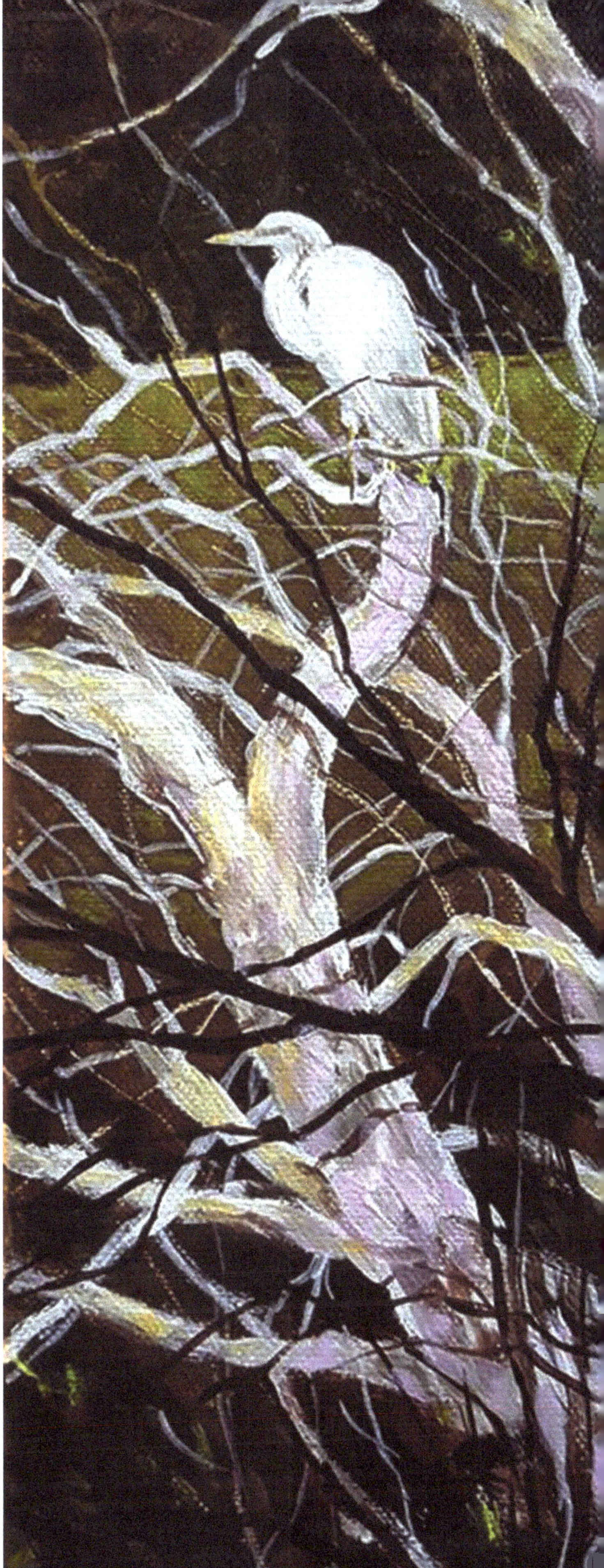

SEPTEMBER 6–12, 2016

"Clouds in the Water"

Washington Boro, PA

I was in Haiti from September 2nd to the 9th, so I only got a couple of shots of the river after getting home. I liked the reflections of clouds in this one, as if they came down to the river to drift there for a while.

In the airport in Port-au-Prince, I got a worrisome text stating that Chrissy had left the rehab.

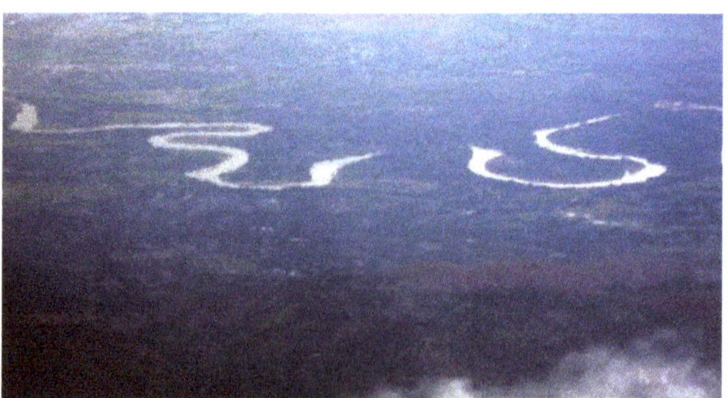

Artibonite River, Haiti

'Round and 'Round

The river flows,

And cold,

It washes o'er my feet.

It cannot wait,

Goes running on into the sea.

And upward drifts to skies of blue,

Becoming clouds all pink and white

That drop their rain,

Which washes down on me.

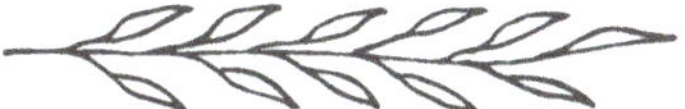

SEPTEMBER 13–19, 2016

"River of Tears"

For Chrissy

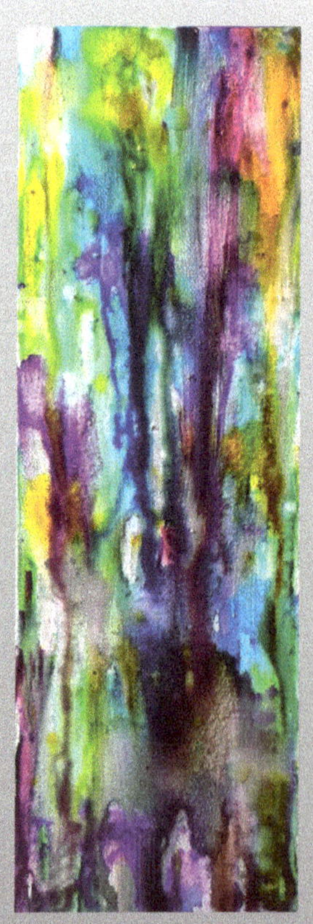 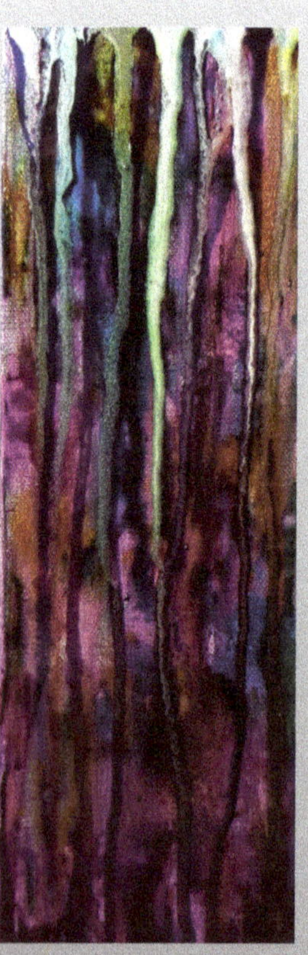

No, no, no, no…. Oh, Chrissy….

I want this to be just a very bad
dream, but it isn't.

Yes, we hoped for your freedom, but
not like this. Not like this.

My sisters came by car and plane to
be here and hold me up. And I am
so glad they have. But what will I do
when they go? What will I do, ever?

How deep was your despair? Too,
too deep.

A horrible, deadly riptide has swept
you away. No, no, no, no….

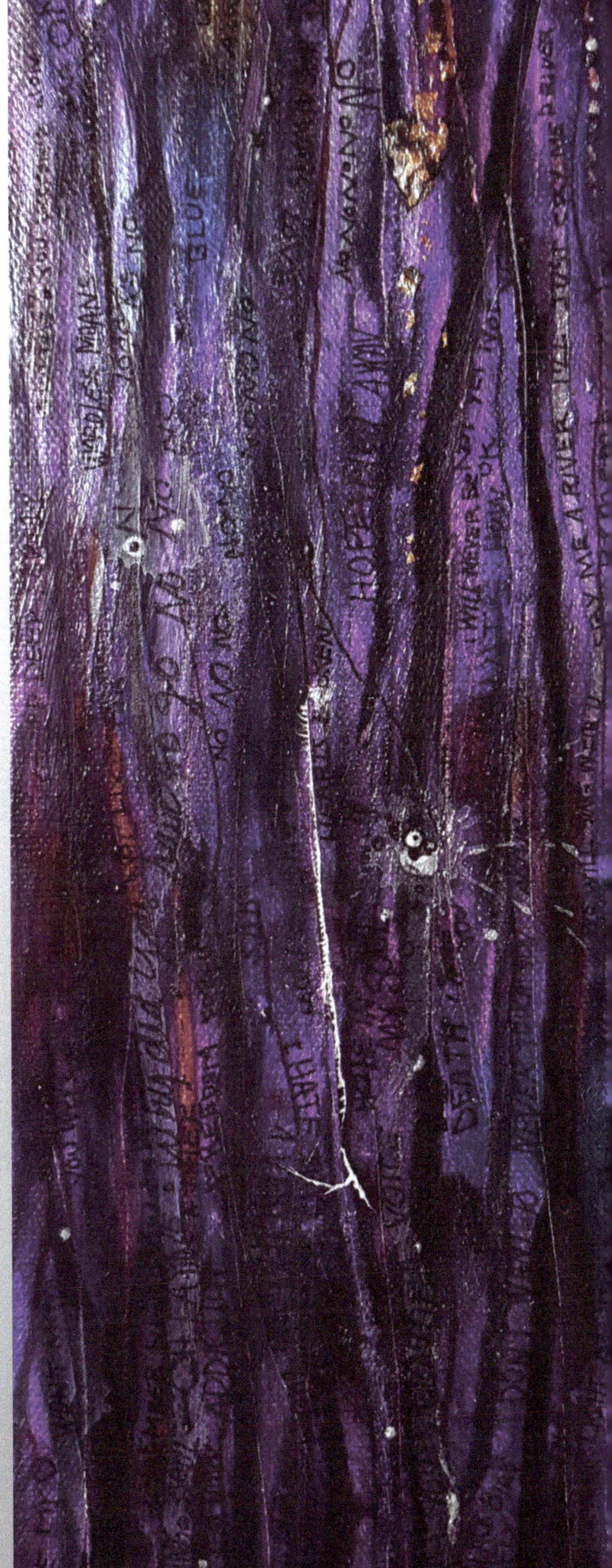

SEPTEMBER 20–26, 2016

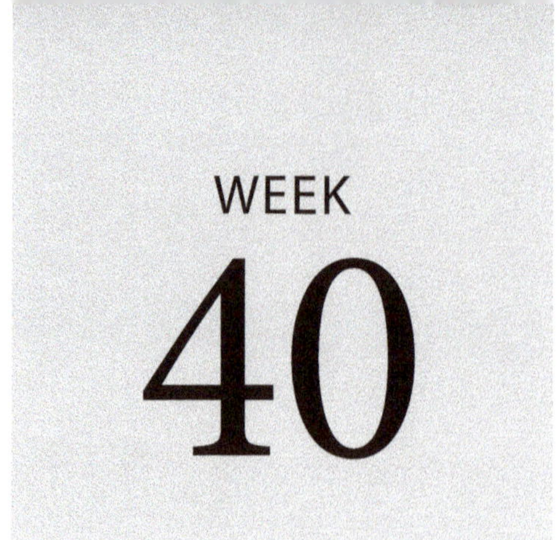

"Rolling Stones"[5]

E. Donegal Riverfront Park, Marietta, PA

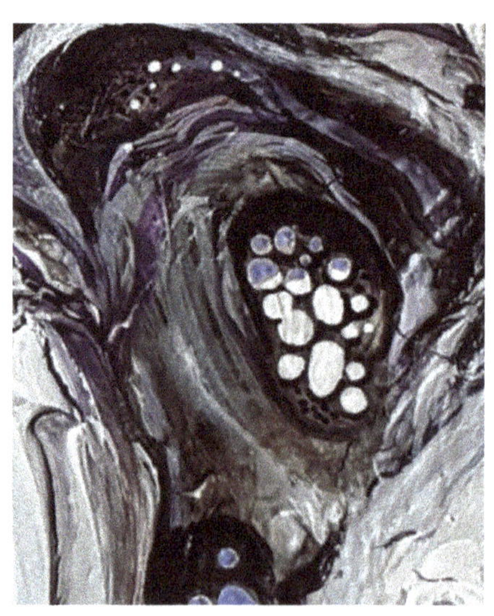

---

5 This painting was done weeks after the above date, but it seems appropriate here. In fact, for many weeks I only sat at the river and cried. I did continue to take photos every week in preparation for the time I might be able to paint again, but I did not paint the remaining weeks in chronological order. Eventually, I felt as if Chrissy had prompted me to continue the project. I often painted more than one each week to get caught up.

We are all still reeling. All my sisters
have gone home. I don't know what I
did or where I went this week. There
are no river photos. I got a little rest at
a women's retreat with friends.

At low water there are places where
the riverbed of solid rock is carved by
rocks and pebbles rolling 'round and
'round in a divot that is made deeper
and rounder by erosion as water swirls
the smaller rocks around. The little
rocks, though grinding agents, get
worn smooth in the process.

Life has a way of doing that same sort
of thing to our souls. The sharper
edges are rubbed smooth as we roll
along through life, and that is usually
a good thing.

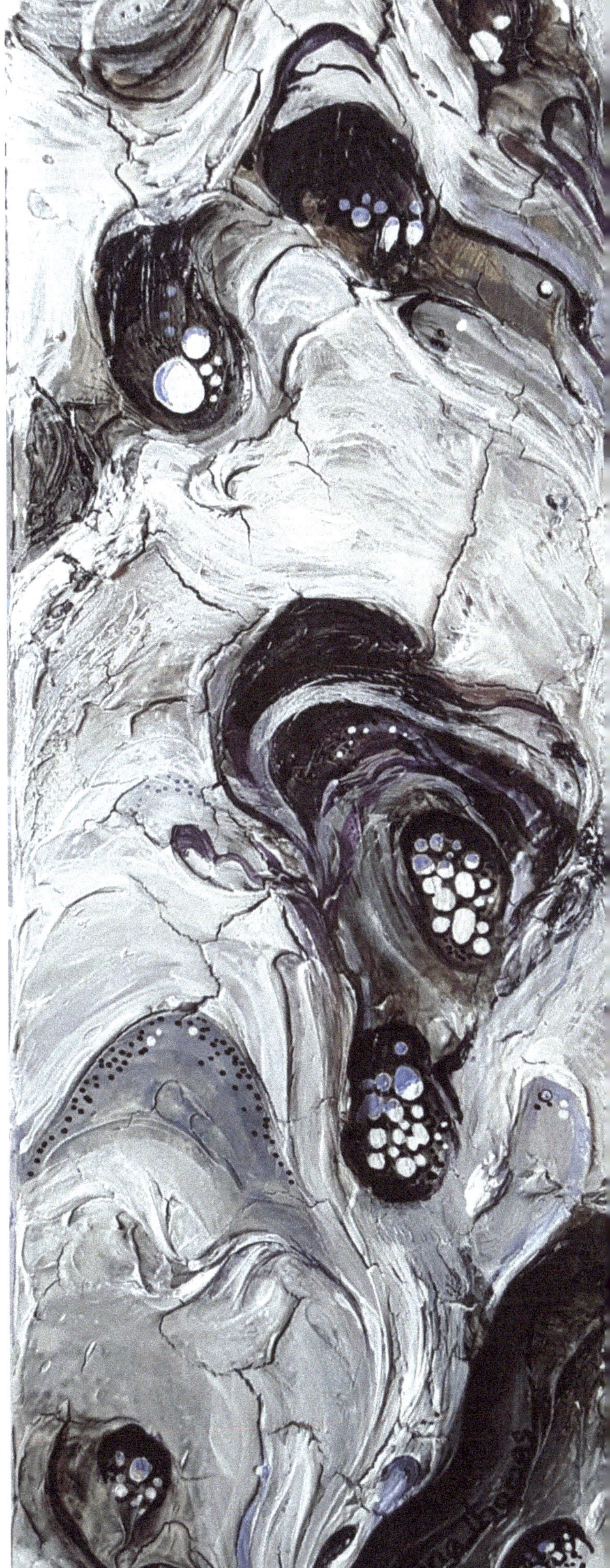

SEPTEMBER 27–OCTOBER 3, 2016

"Cloud Shadows"

View from Highpoint, Wrightsville, PA

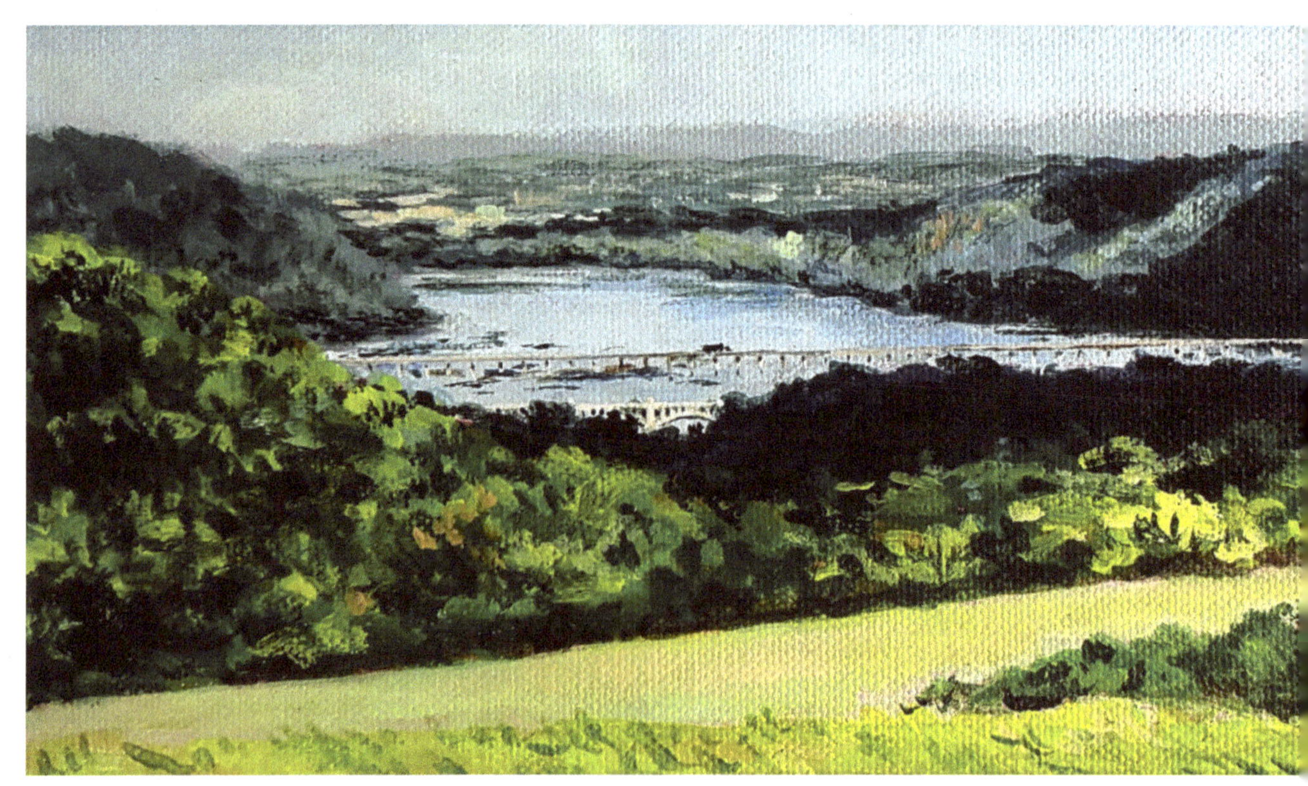

Everything is just a blur, so I walked up to the top of Highpoint to try and get a different perspective. It's such a lovely view. I enjoyed watching the shadows of clouds drifting over the landscape, creating nice contrasts of lights and darks.

It will be good to paint again soon. I feel the pull of this series wanting to have a conclusion.

I keep thinking about what I want to say at Chrissy's memorial service. I want to make sure that her beauty outshines all the pain she had at the end. The pain of losing her this way is the saddest thing I have ever known. Oh, it hurts too much to think.

"Yea, though I walk through the valley of the shadow of death, I will fear no evil; for You are with me...."

(Psalm 23:4 NKJV)

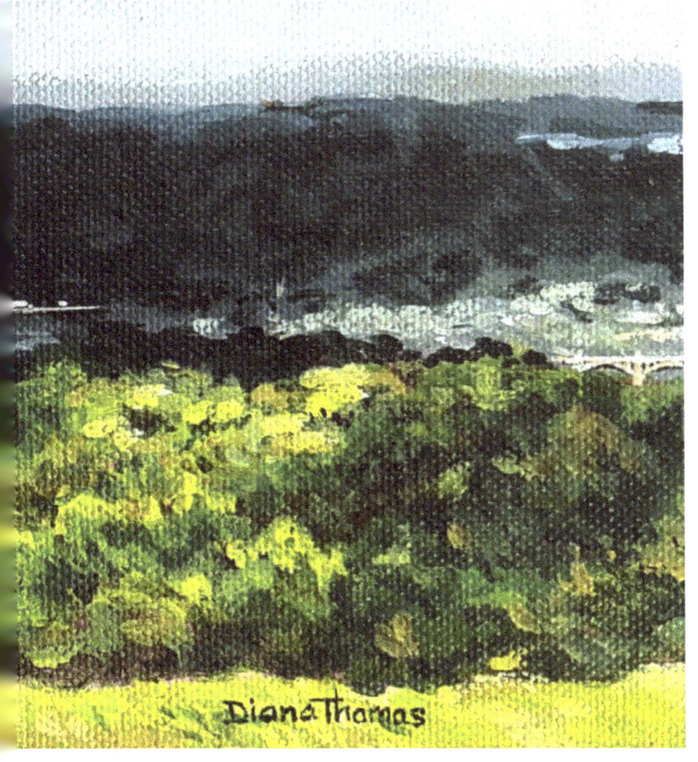

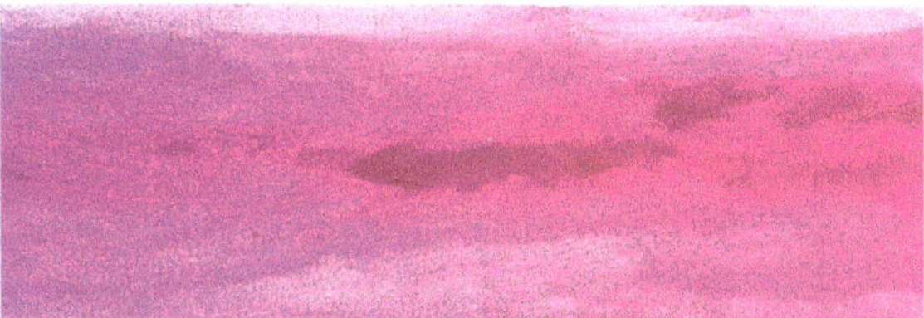

A surprising color to underpaint this one in order to tone down the greens

42

OCTOBER 4–10, 2016

"Calm"

Long Level, Wrightsville, PA

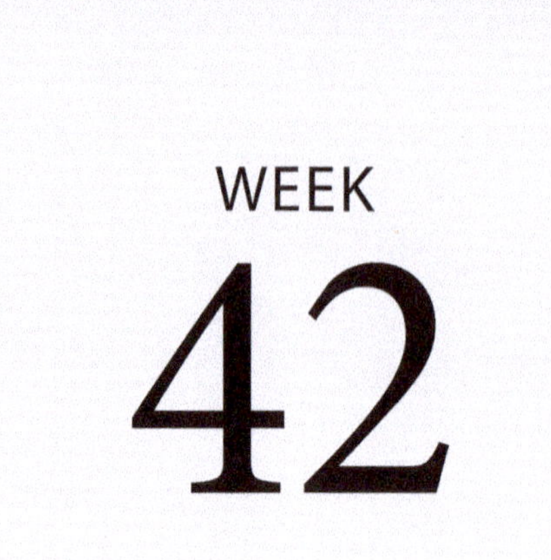

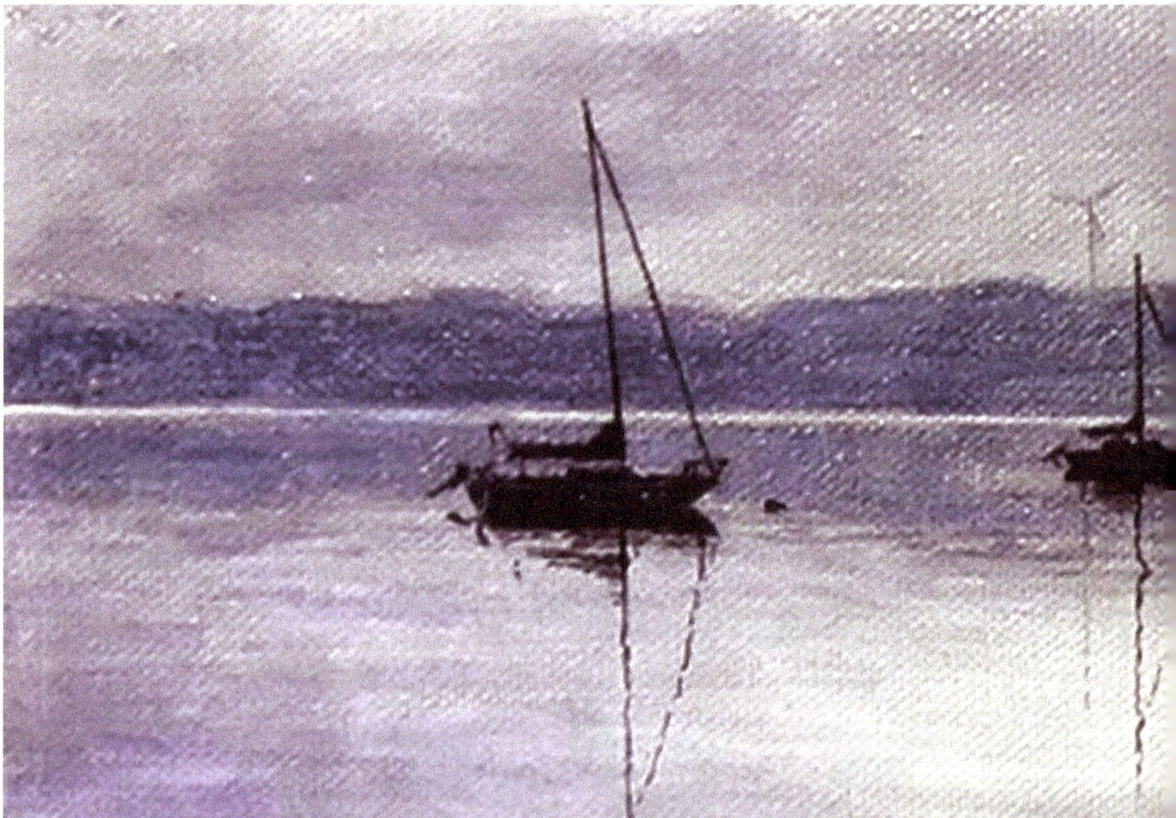

The art for this week is the opposite of what life is like. We are consumed with so many details for Chrissy's service. I am so thankful for friends and family who step in and do what is needed.

Dad found some old tapes of Chrissy singing when she was a little girl. I have been playing the CDs over and over that she made for us 12 to 15 years ago, and I know I haven't let her go yet, really. When I hear her voice and sing along, we are still together if I close my eyes. I love the parts of the recordings where she talks or laughs. And when she says, "I'll just do it the way I want," that is her to a T.

In this scene, the water was like glass and the reflections were as clear as in a mirror. I wonder what things I will see your reflection in as days go by, dear Chrissy.

"For now we see only a reflection as in a mirror; then we shall see face to face. Now I know in part; then I shall know fully, even as I am fully known."

(1 Corinthians 13:12)

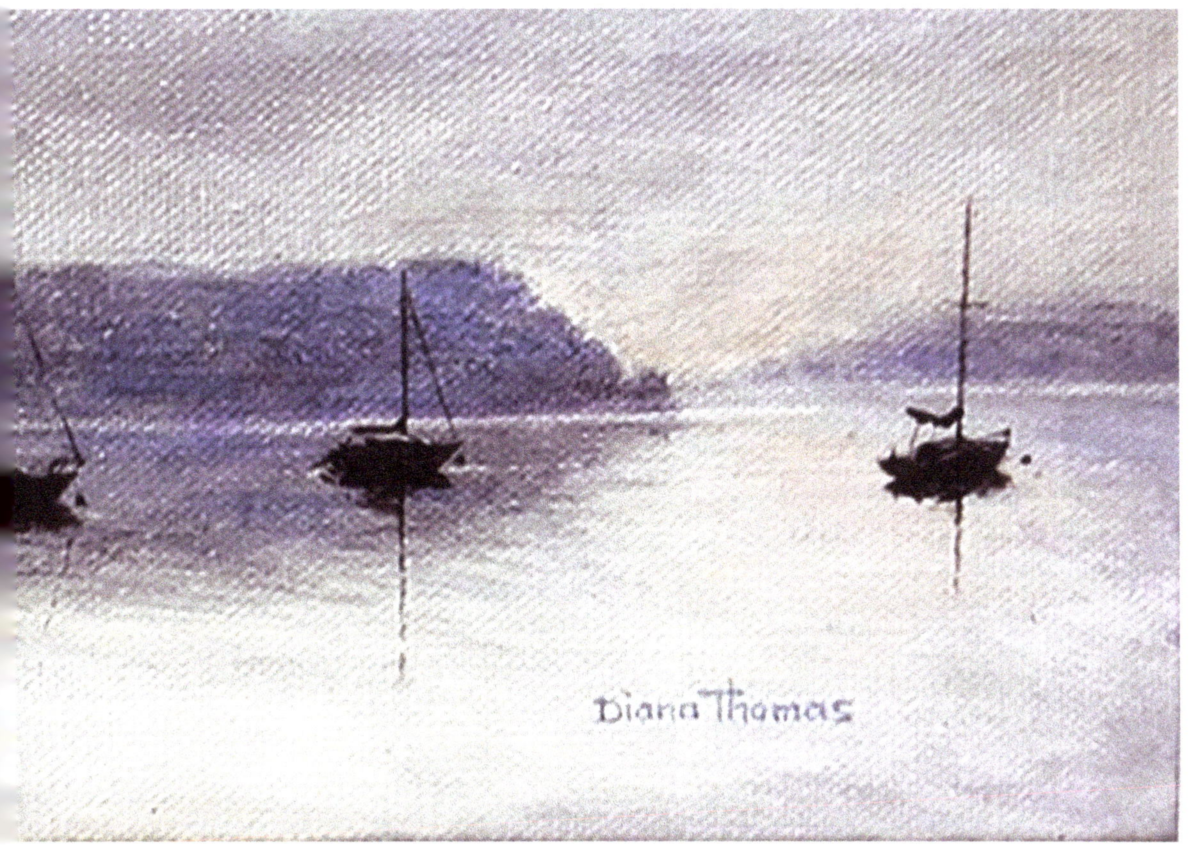

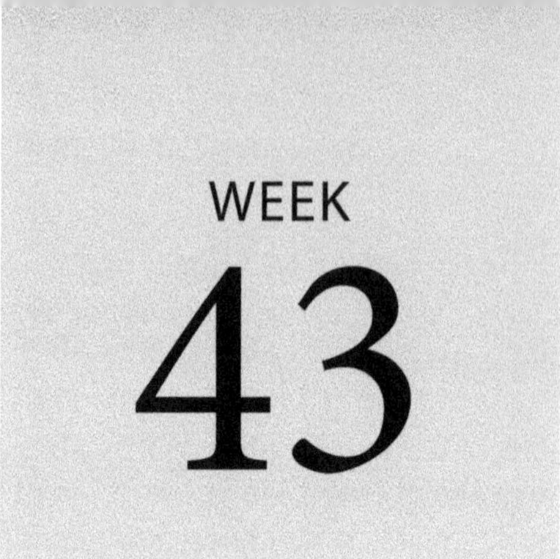

OCTOBER 11–17, 2016

"Even the Moon Cried"

Super Moon from Columbia Bridge, Columbia, PA

I am finally feeling a little better. I started to paint again today. I'm working on the one I'll call "River of Tears," trying to paint something from my heart and soul for Chrissy. I'm only ten weeks behind!

This evening, the 12th, I walked down to the old bridge. The "super moon" was so bright that I stood there looking at it for a very long time. I made a video of the gorgeous silver sparkles shimmering on the water.

A phone call….

This can't be true.

I can't take in the words….

Chrissy's mate, Cory, died this morning. His mom found him when she came home from work. God help her!

Oh, dear Lord, have mercy!

Our grandson is an orphan!

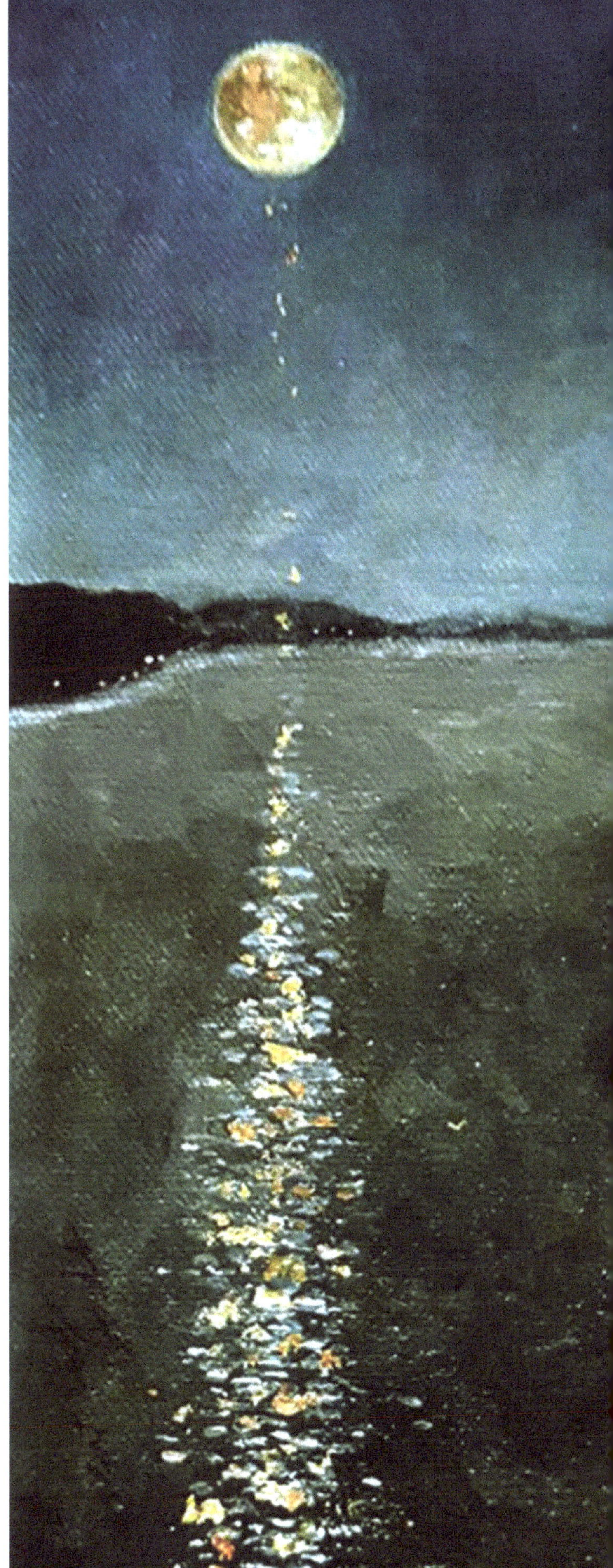

"The Spirit
prays for us
with groanings
too deep
to be understood
with words."

(Romans 8:26, my paraphrase)

OCTOBER 18–24, 2016

"Low Water"

Out on the Rocks and Looking South
from E. Donegal Riverfront Park, Marietta, PA

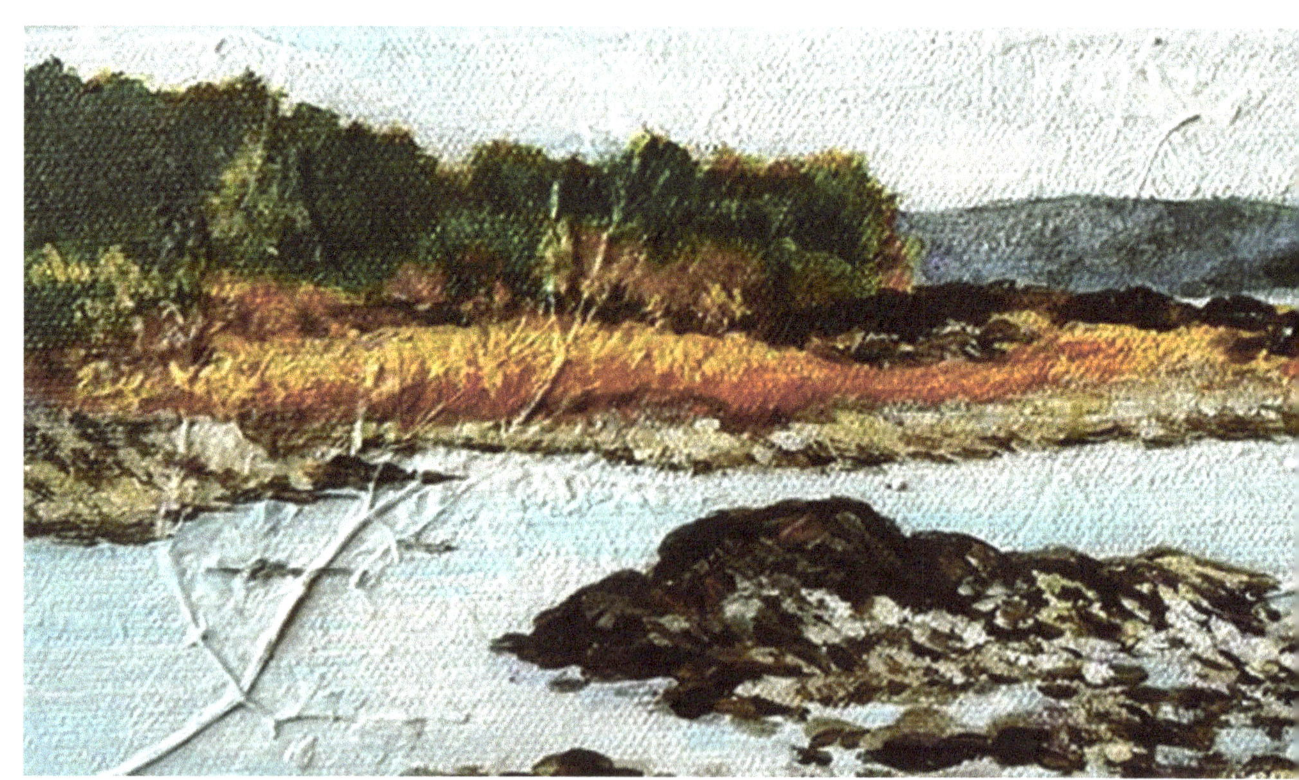

I'm spending a lot of days and hours just doing nothing. I can't process anything that requires thinking. (The system is running, but all the programs are shut down.) I guess that is good; it is just so unusual.

"Why did they have to go…to go…to go…?" echoes in my head.

I make myself go out for little walks. I went to East Donegal a couple of times and enjoyed walking way out on the rocks while the water was so low. Those photos will make for some interesting art. (See Week 40's art.)

I walked the whole length of the "Bridge Bust" market last Saturday. Sometimes I start my Christmas shopping there, but I didn't see anything I wanted. I did, however, meet a lady from Susquehanna National Heritage Area, which is located over at Long Level. They manage the new Columbia Crossing building at Riverfront Park. I told her about the "Current Color" series and she asked me to email her the info and some images. (She doesn't know that I pictured the works hanging in there even before I painted a single one!) This could be very interesting indeed. It felt good to smile for a while.

Life keeps on "rollin', rollin', rollin' like on a river."[6]

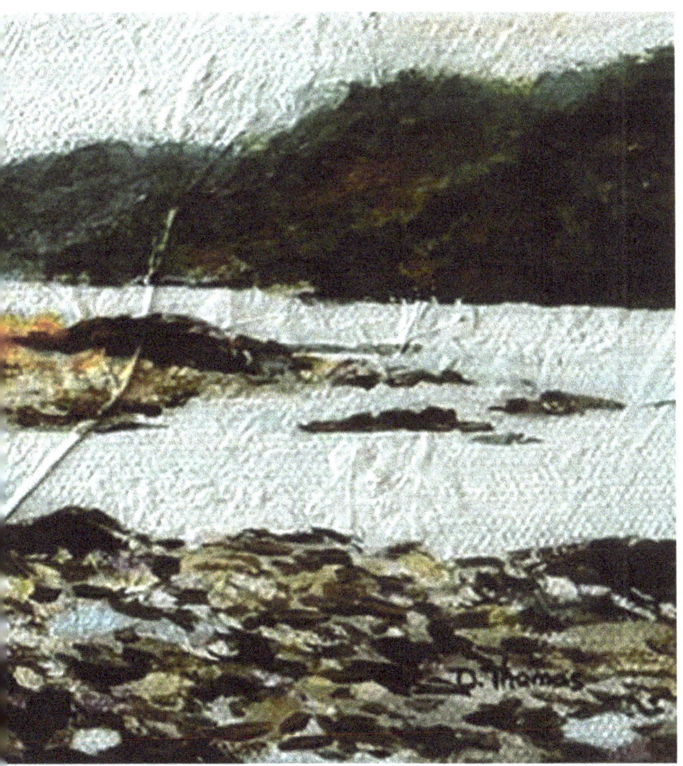

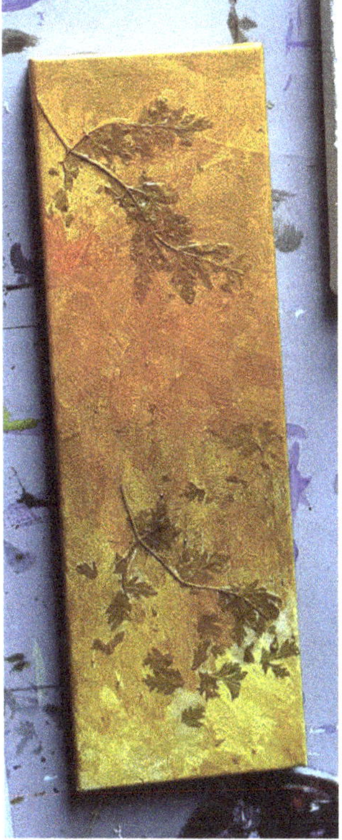

Leaves on the canvas for texture in this one

---

6 John Fogerty, "Proud Mary," *Bayou Country*, Creedence Clearwater Revival, 1969.

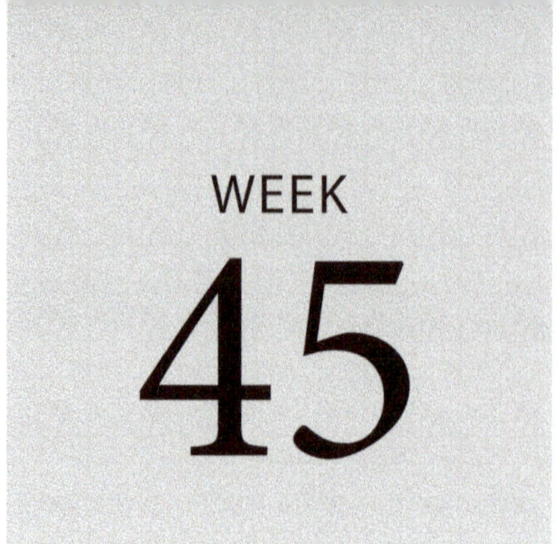

OCTOBER 25–31, 2016

"Golden Sycamore"

Millersburg, PA

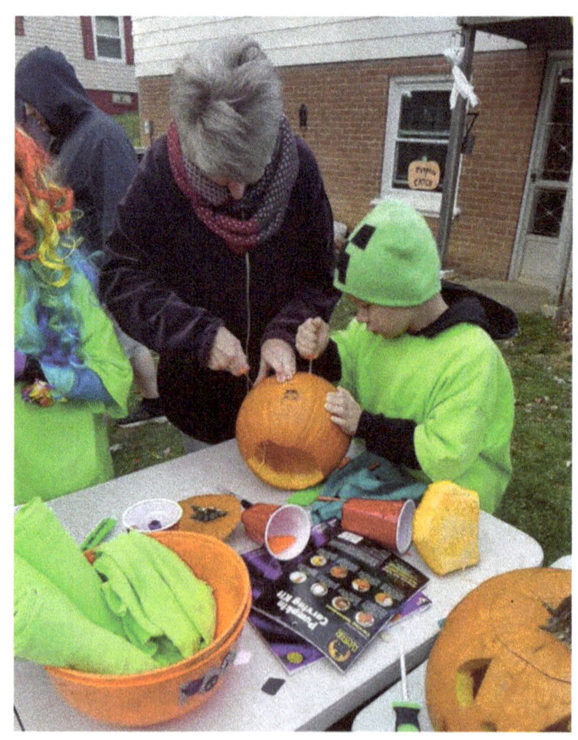

Unca Looj and Aunt Chris's punkin party
Pictured: Author and grandson Layne

I had some rest time with Fred at a pastor's prayer retreat at beautiful Doubling Gap Conference Center in Cumberland County. I'm just feeling like I'm in limbo.

My brother was here from Arizona, and we all had a good time at the annual "punkin carvin' party" at our son Louie's house. Sweet family traditions are part of the healing, even though living our "new normal" feels like a new shoe that doesn't fit too well. We'll just have to wear a band-aid for a while.

I'm plugging away on the "Current Color" pieces. I got some pretty shots in Millersburg one evening. We like to go up there to eat at The Wooden Nickel and walk around the Square.

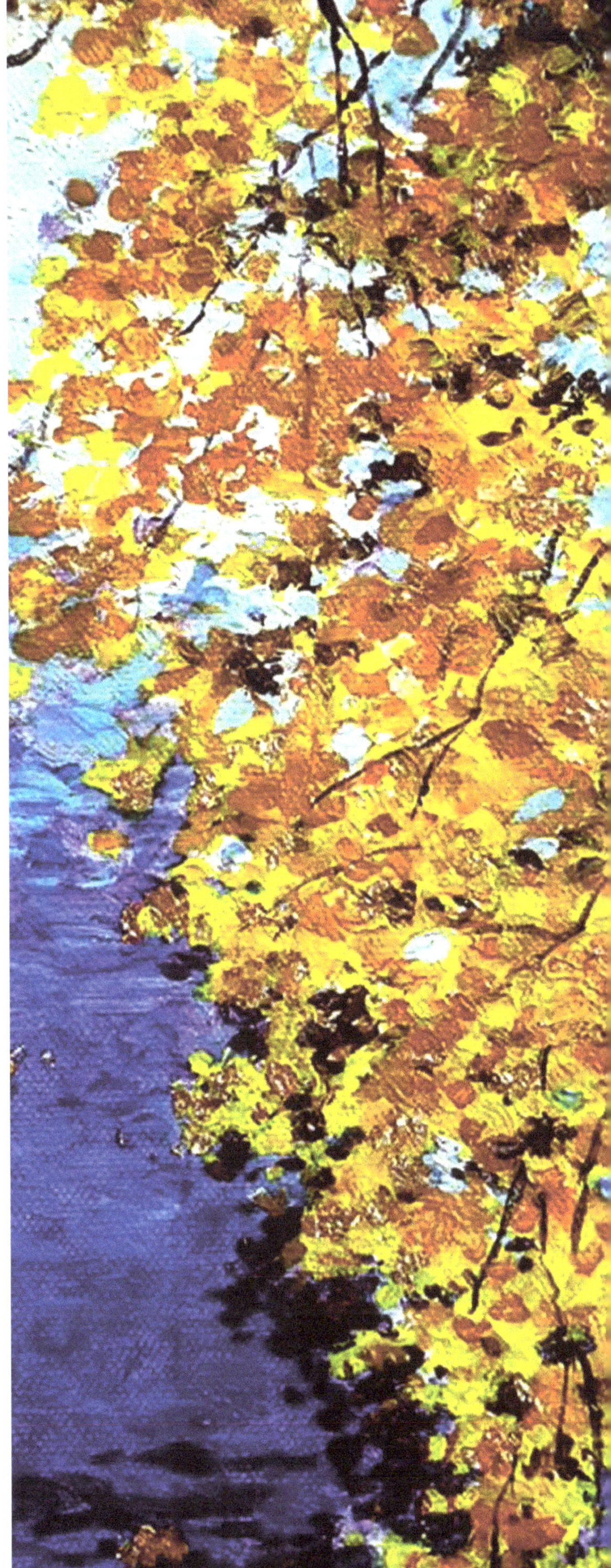

NOVEMBER 1–7, 2016

"The Kingfisher"

Conejohela Flats, Washington Boro, PA, by Guest Photographer

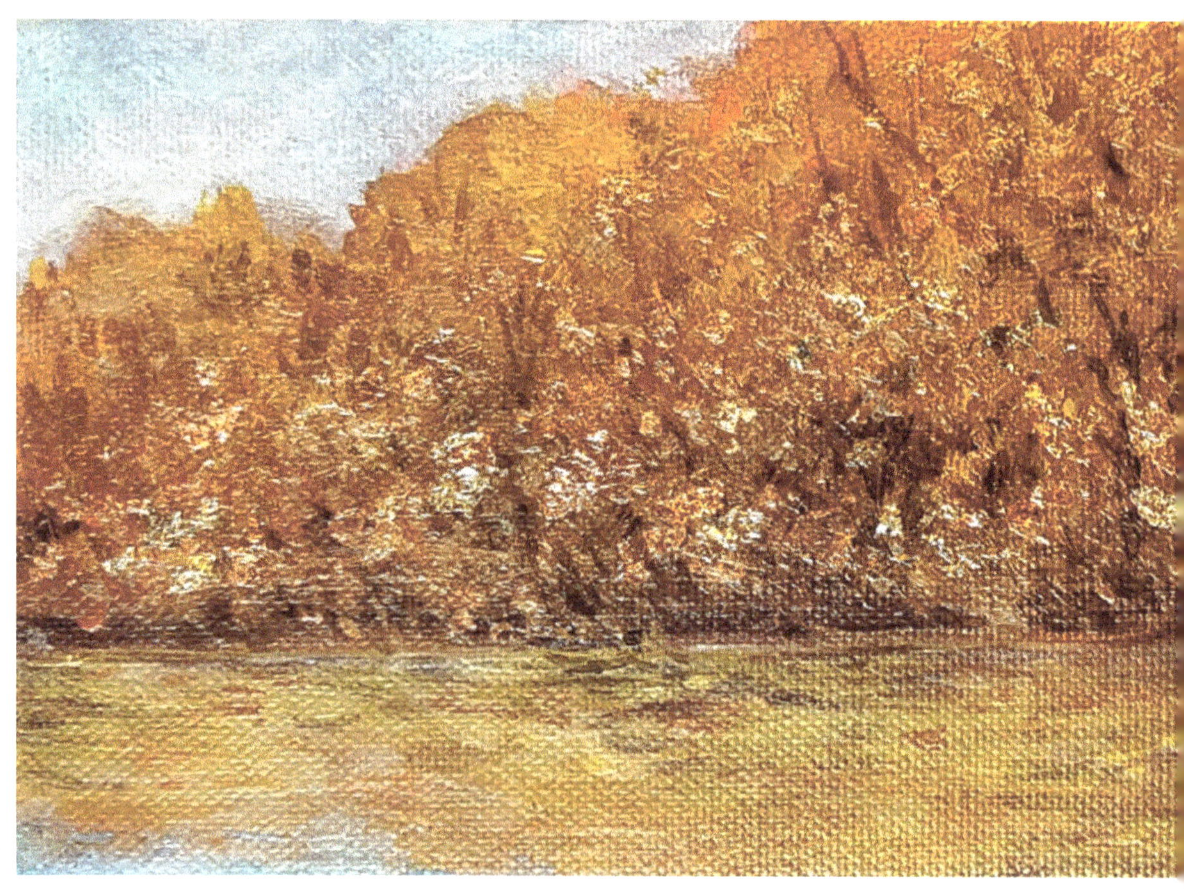

Mesi pou zanmi ki moun ede m'. (I'm thankful for friends who help me.) I have a guest photographer, Jeff, this week while I am in Haiti again.

My daughter prayed that I would get some rest and healing in my Haiti home. It is indeed very good to have a second loving family.

I believe that healing will come through the flow of life, disguised as "ordinary" moments, random beauty and sudden showers of kindness (received and given). I just lie back on the current and let it carry me, like a leaf on the surface. It brings back a memory from childhood of a canoe trip my dad took me and my sisters on. What a beautiful, lazy day. I am thankful for the store of lovely memories. I'm blessed!

I expect that the art may look a little different since I've started up painting again and trying to catch up. I purchased two new colors that I haven't used before. The artist is different, so the art will be too, I suppose. I am a new color.

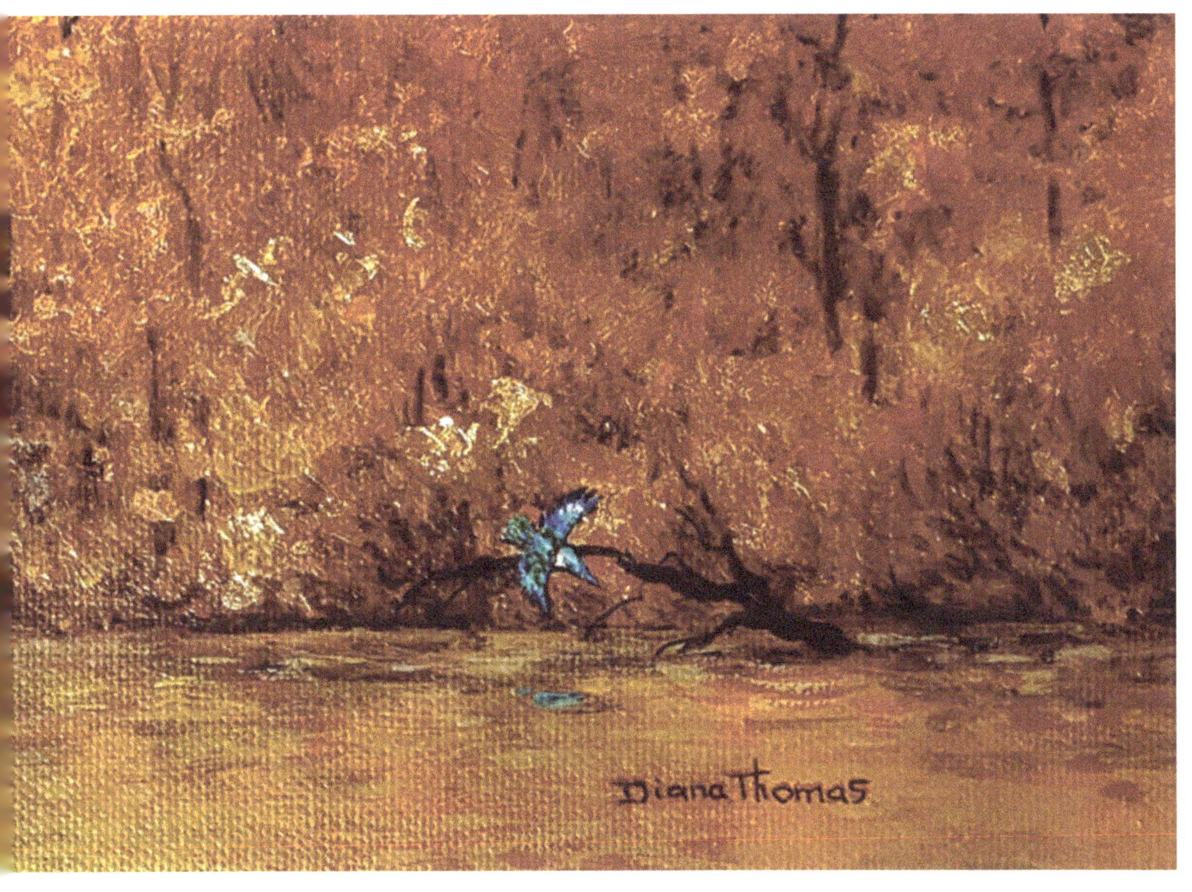

NOVEMBER 8–14, 2016

"Sumac"

Blue Rock Boat Ramp, Washington Boro, PA

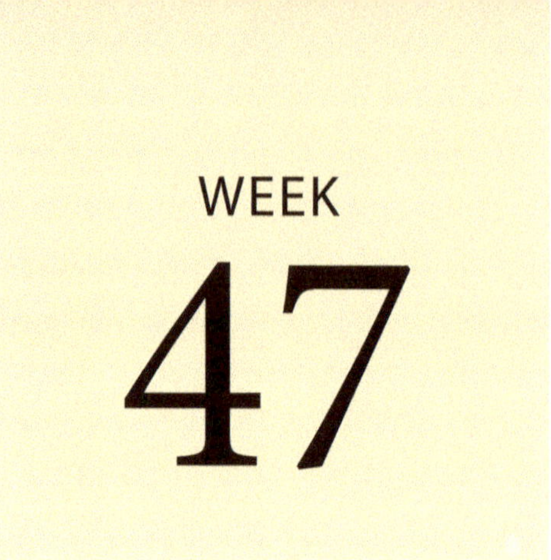

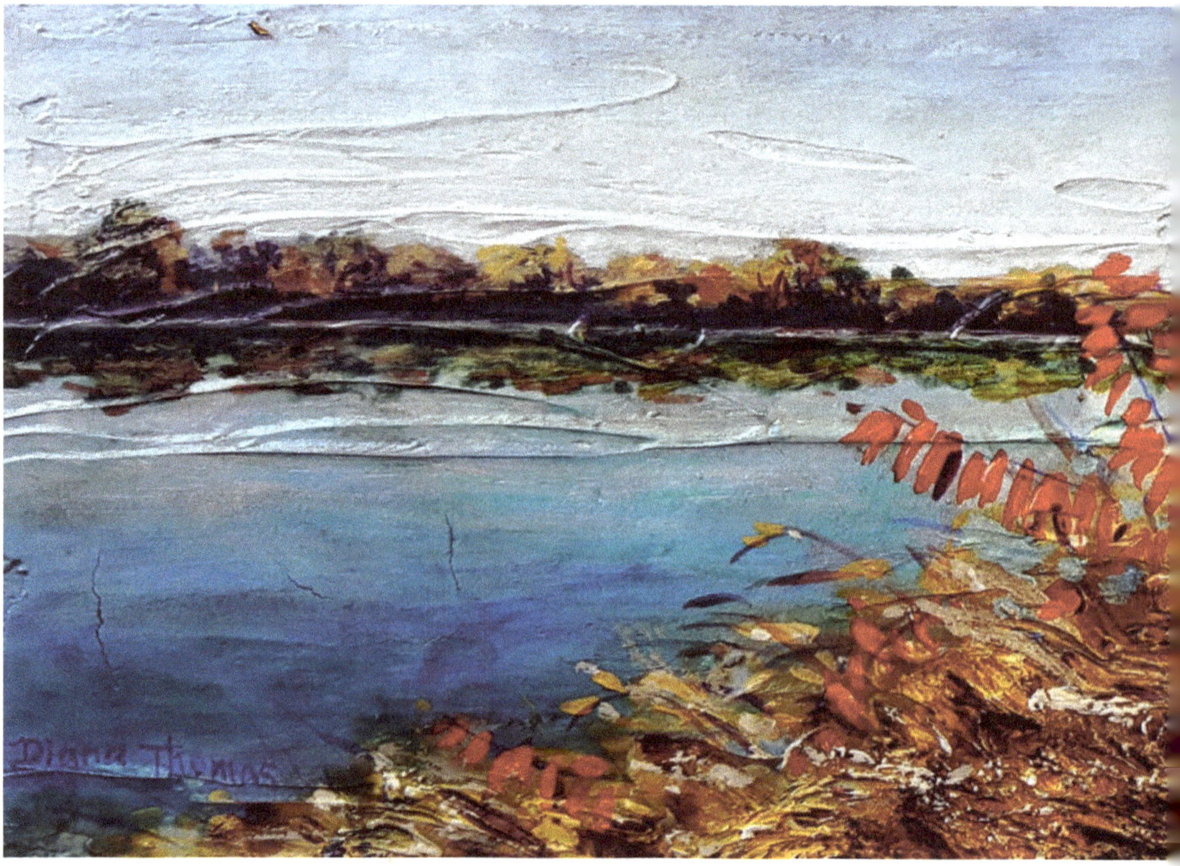

I am loving the autumn colors. I can't believe a year of photos will soon be finished. There are quite a few paintings waiting to emerge, but all in good time. I am just working random weeks' photos till all are done. As I look over the year's photos, there are many more than one per week that I still want to do. I think I will not be finished for a while, or the river will not be finished with me for a while. Thankfully.

While down at the "flats," I came across the grave marker of someone's faithful pet dog, Sabastian. Life and death must go hand in hand; nothing in this life is forever.

It will soon be time to meet with my graphics friends and see what they think about the undertaking of getting all these paintings photographed and color corrected for print making! That will be a huge endeavor, but it will be good insurance against loss or damage.

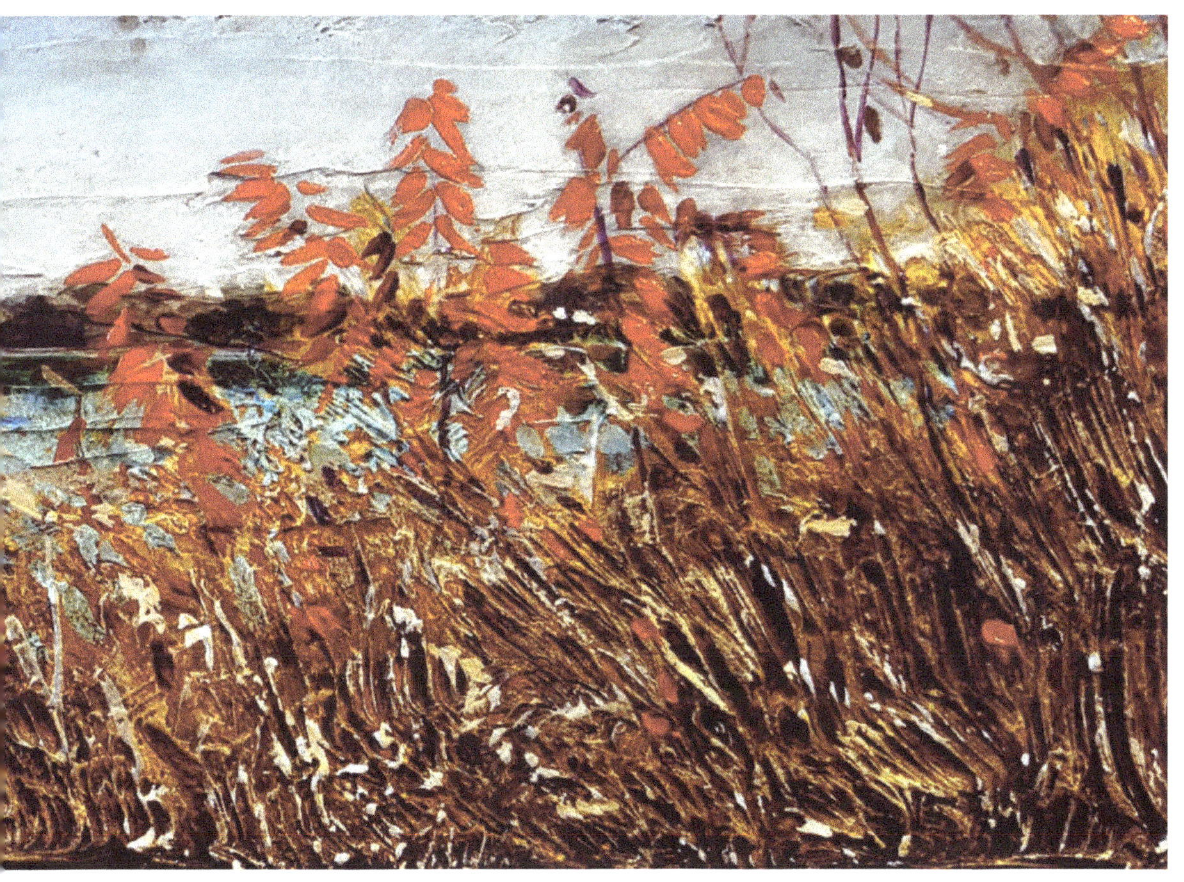

48

NOVEMBER 15–21, 2016

"Big River"

Photo by Guest Photographer, Harrisburg, PA

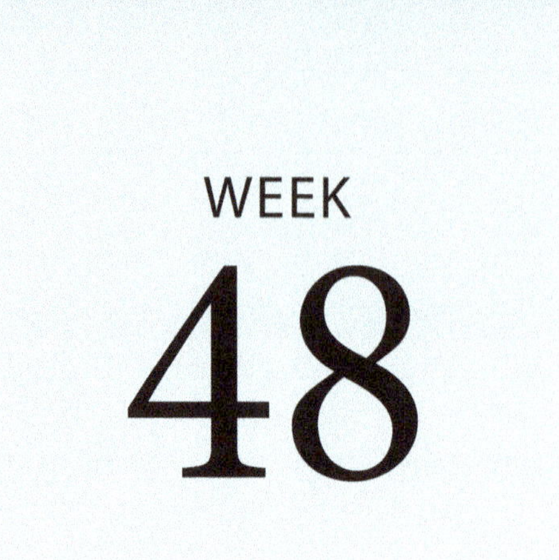

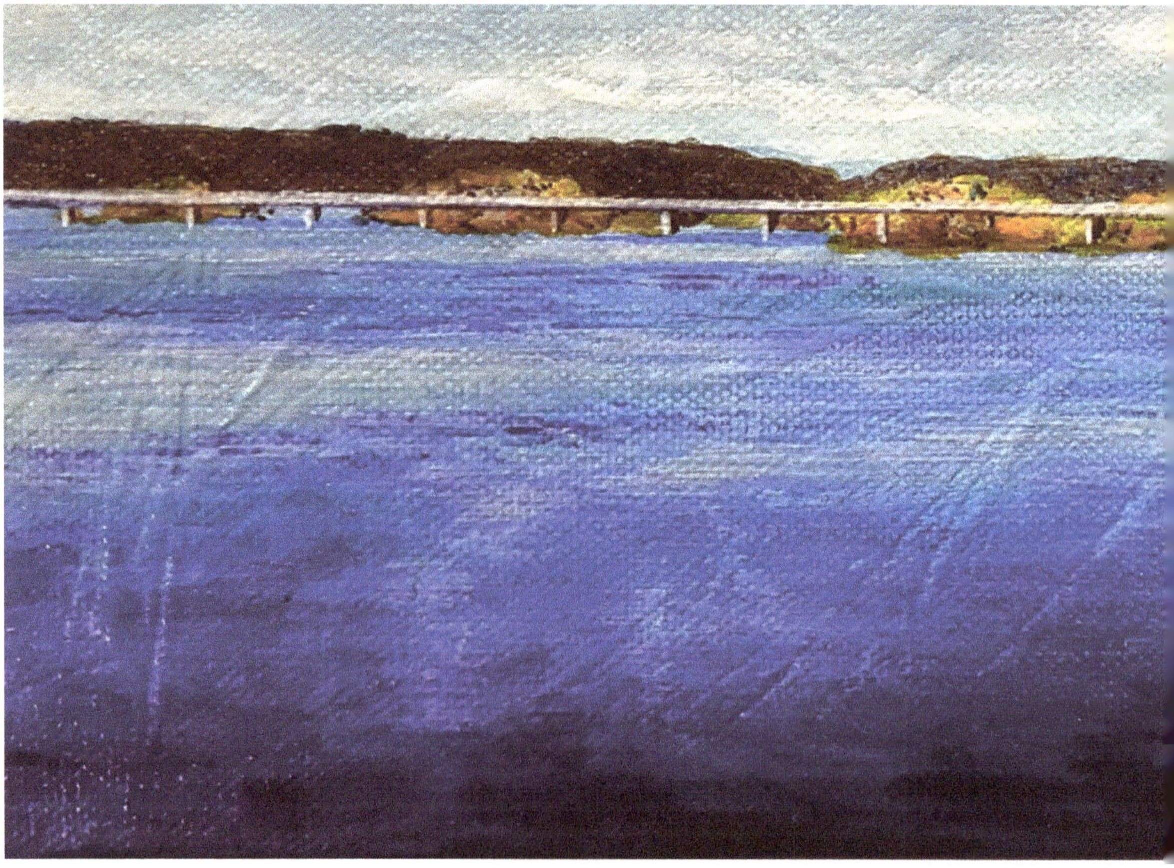

Guest photographer Lori is on call in Harrisburg, Pennsylvania, today. Thanks, friend!

I have had some terribly low lows this week. One day at a time, as they say in recovery. I am not used to having to be carried so much by the Lord. Looking back, I know that this arrangement is probably true much more often over the years than I've cared to admit. These days I'm simply like a helpless infant, thumb in mouth, tears in eyes, still shaking from hard sobbing.

The river has a set course to follow. It always flows in the same direction, toward the Chesapeake and then the ocean. I've given up all my best intentions for now and am thankful for my river resting place.

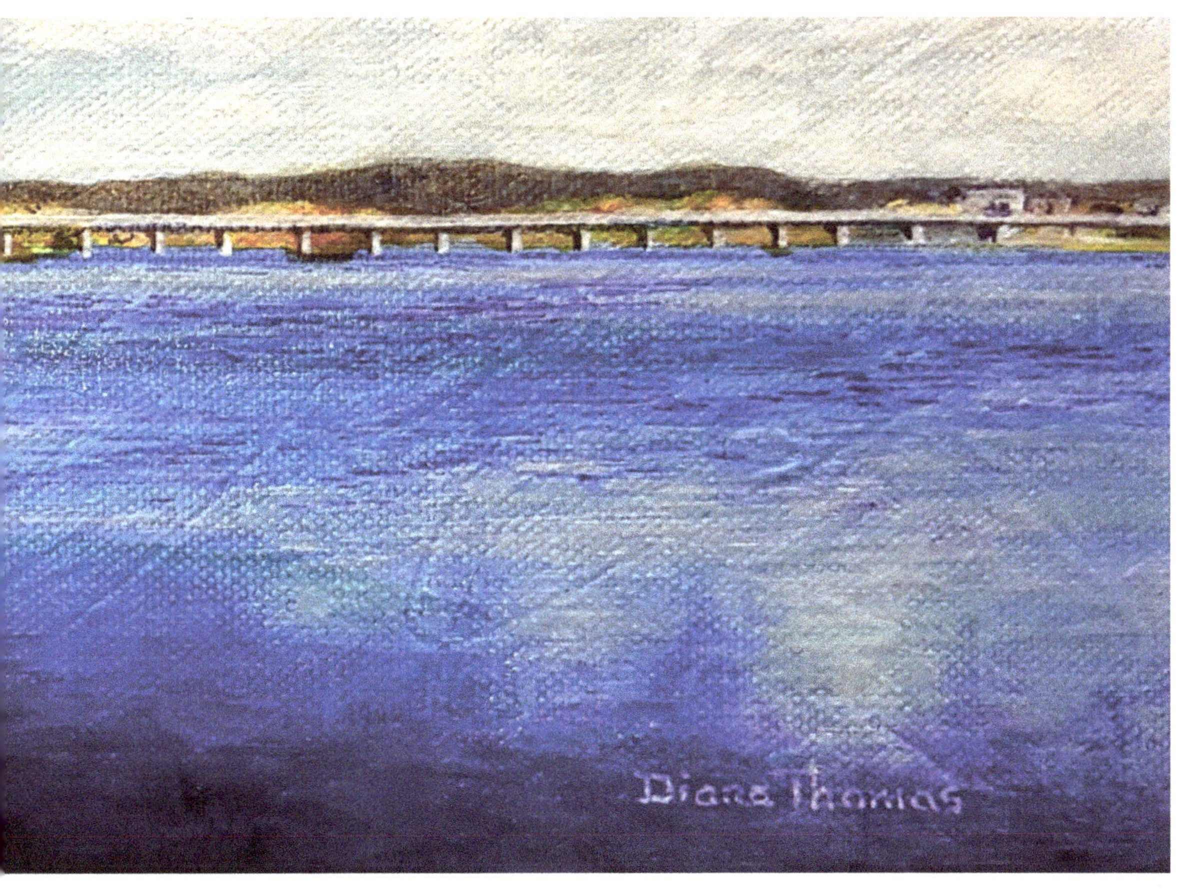

NOVEMBER 22–28, 2016

No Art for This Week

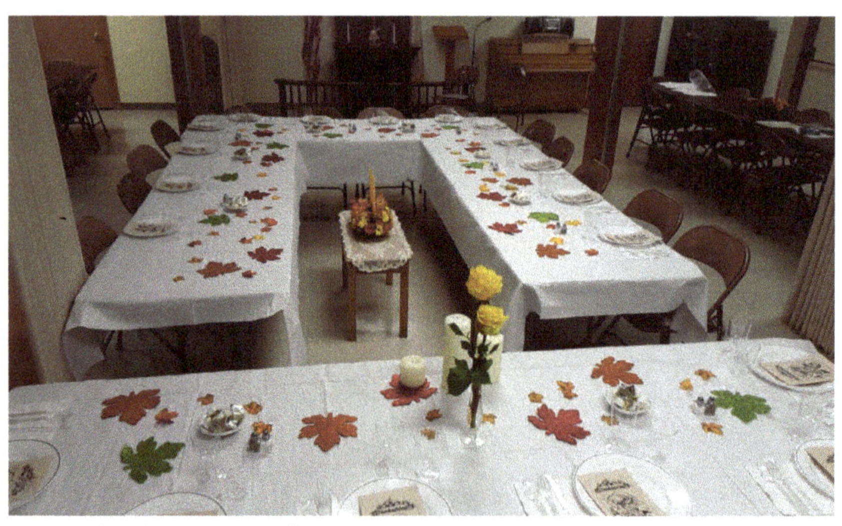

Our Thanksgiving table

Just moving along…. Though the river looks still and calm on the surface, there is a powerful current moving below.

Time spent with family doing ordinary things, letting the tears come whenever they feel like it. They soon subside. I enjoyed time with Dad at Root's Farm Market, buying flowers and produce for Thanksgiving. I used to do that with Mom, but this year will be the first anniversary of her passing.

In the kitchen the other night while making the stuffing for our big meal, Fred and I fell apart and just stood there a while, holding each other and crying. I hear that "weeping may endure for a night, but joy comes in the morning" (Psalm 30:5b NKJV).

I got an invitation from Susquehanna National Heritage Area last week asking me to show "Current Color" next fall at Columbia Crossing! Yes, I'm so thankful!

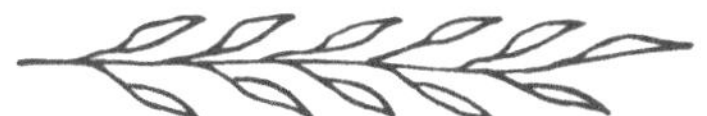

NOVEMBER 29–DECEMBER 5, 2016

"Misty Morning"

Looking toward Accomac from Marietta, PA

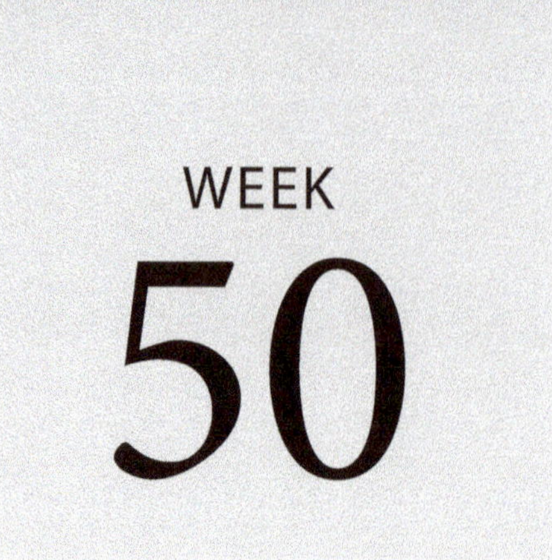

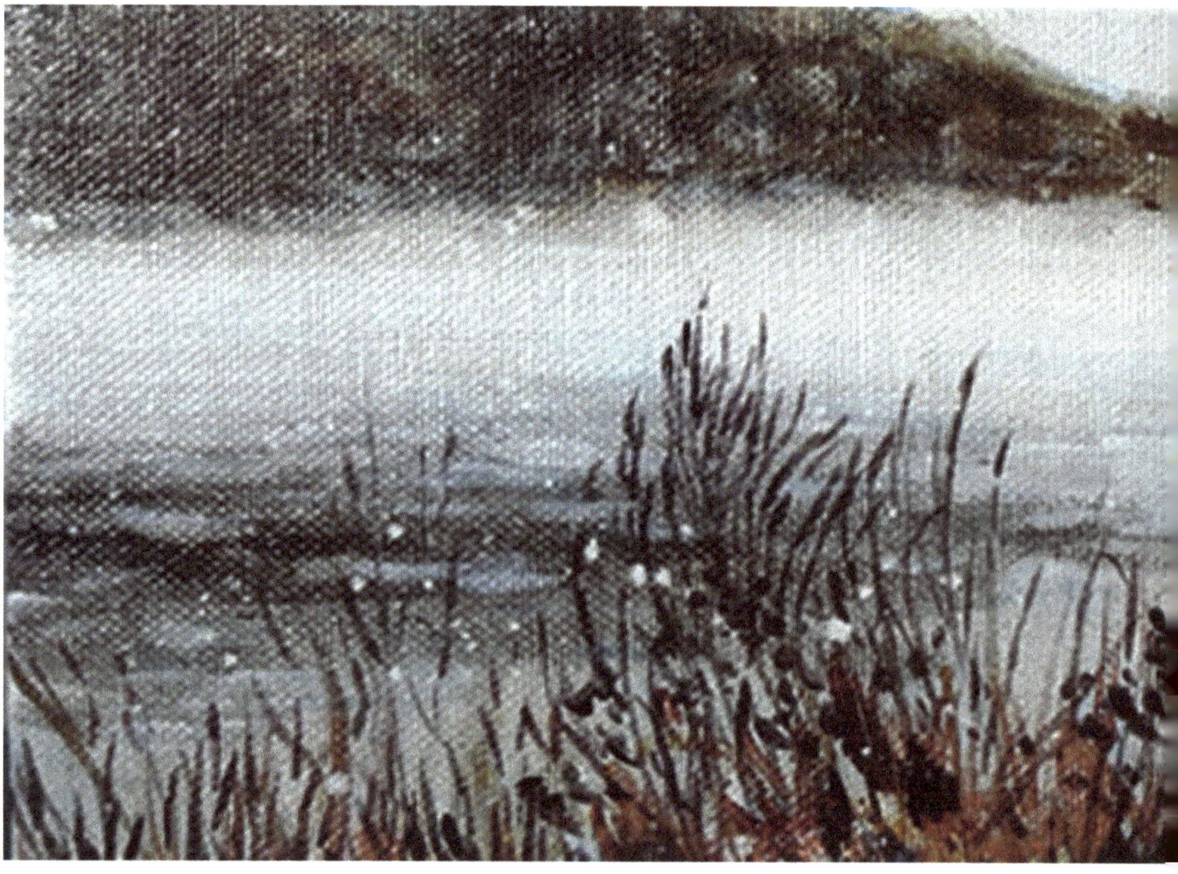

The temperatures have warmed so much that there is a heavy fog rising from the streams and creeks this morning. It is raining on and off, and the river is just gorgeous, veiled like this.

I'm thinking of this children's nursery rhyme:

> One misty, moisty morning,
>
> When cloudy was the weather,
>
> I chanced to meet an old man clothed all in leather.
>
> He began to compliment, and I began to grin,
>
> How do you do, and how do you do?
>
> And how do you do again?

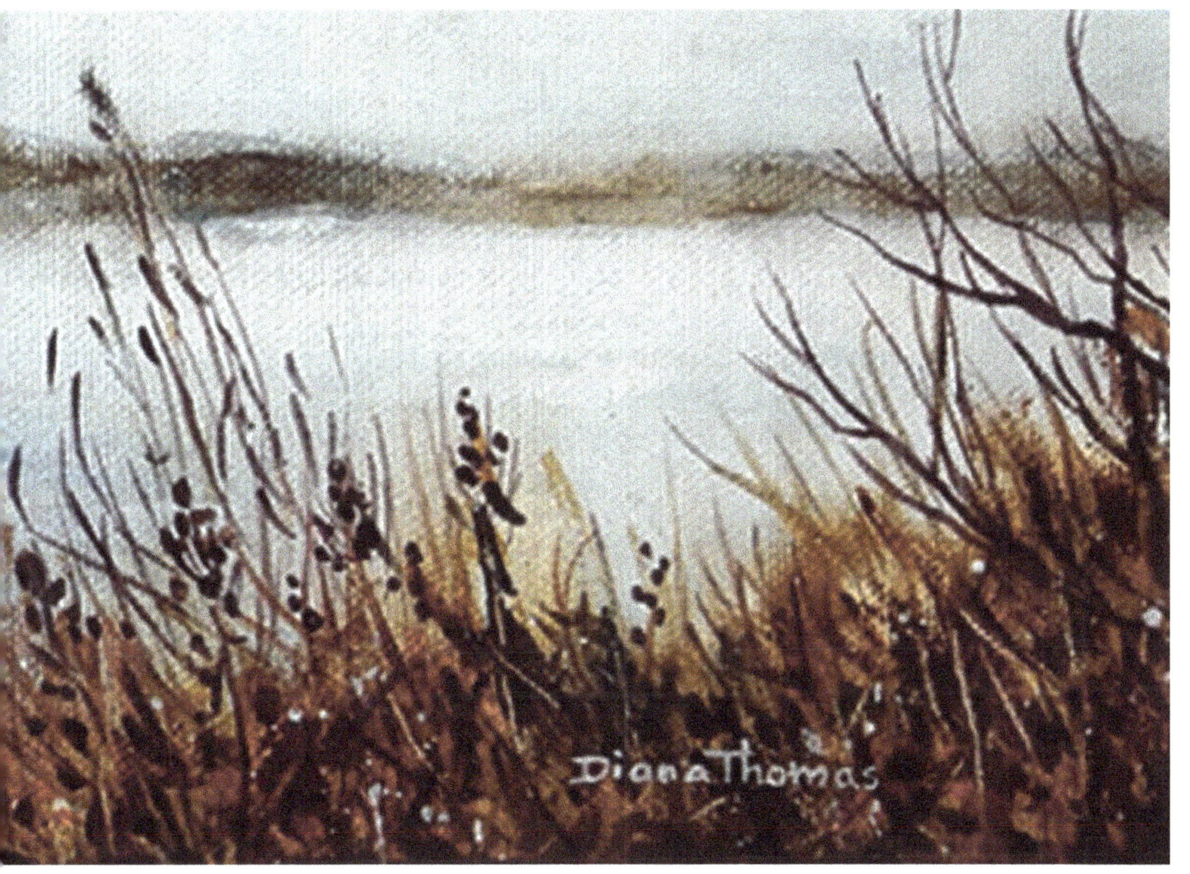

DECEMBER 6–12, 2016

"Come Sit with Me"

Lake Clark Marina, Wrightsville, PA

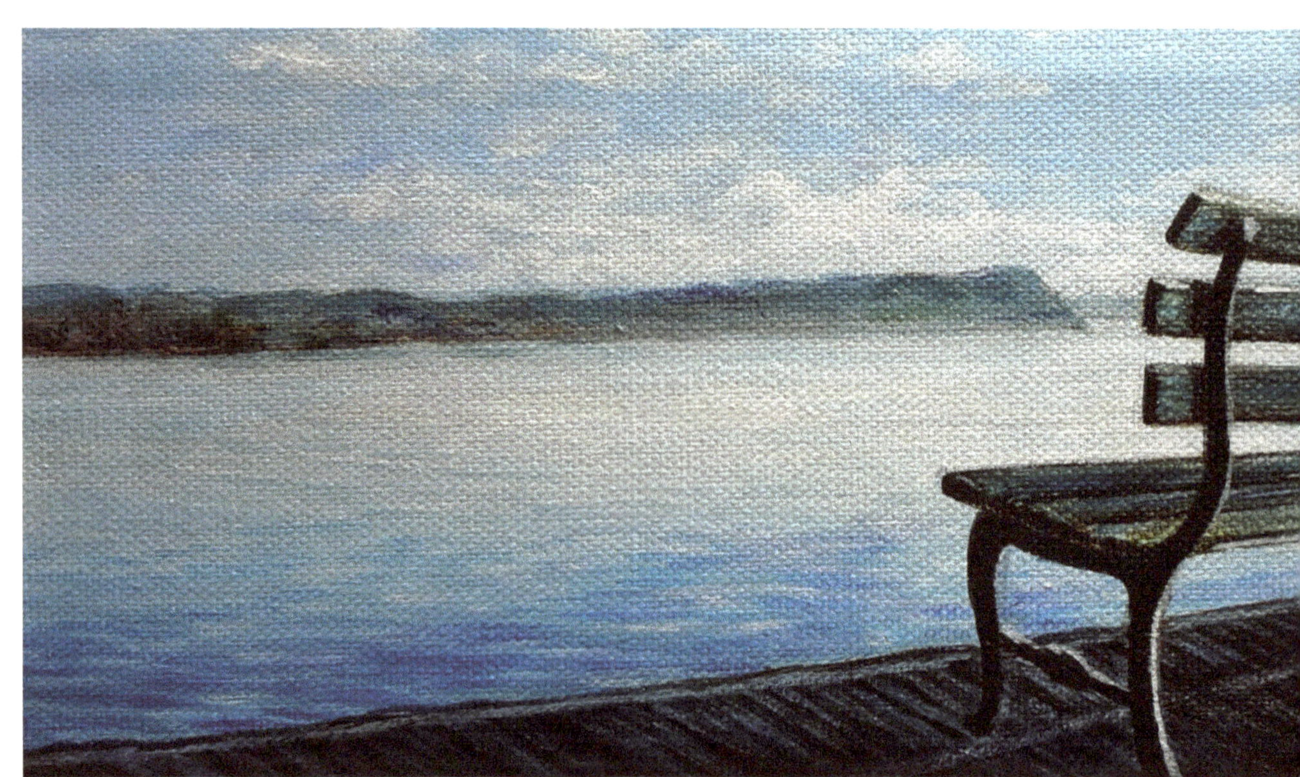

I returned from Haiti around midnight on the 11th. It was a good trip, and of course I need to come to the river for my dose of peace.

It's a hazy morning, as the sun comes out and warms the water. The scene is very still, barely a ripple on the water or current in the air.

This bench is so inviting. Come sit with me, Chrissy. Tell me what heaven is like. Let's sing one of our old favorites:

> "As I went down in the river to pray,
>
> studyin' about that good ole way and
>
> who shall wear the starry crown,
>
> good Lord, show me the way."[7]

Oh, honey, I miss you so much.

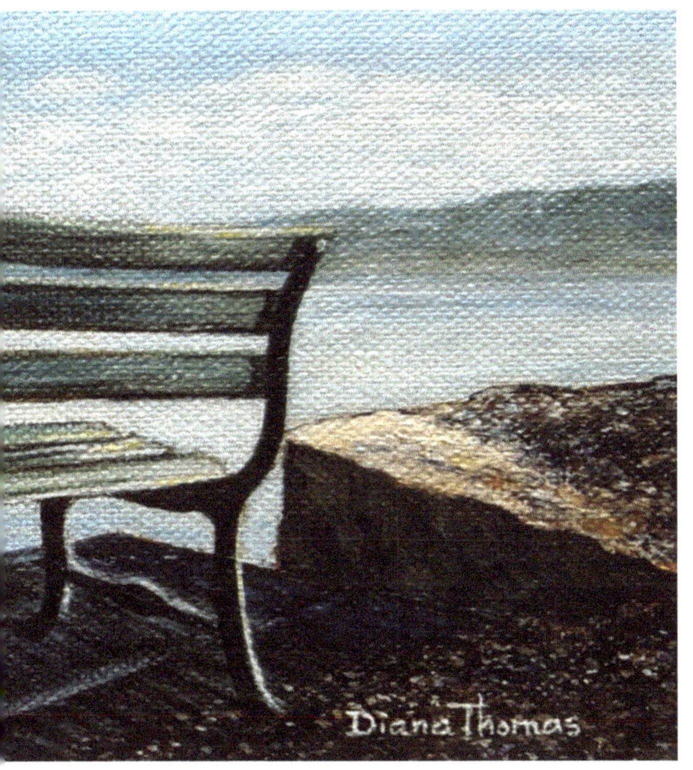

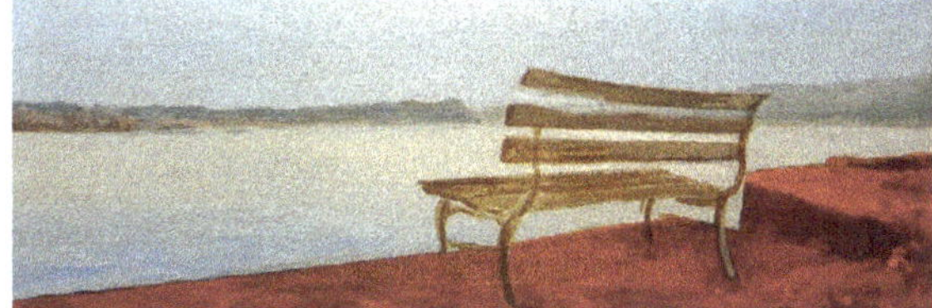

Making the dark area darker by using this complimentary color under the phthalo blue

---

7   African American Spiritual, "Down to the River to Pray." Public domain.

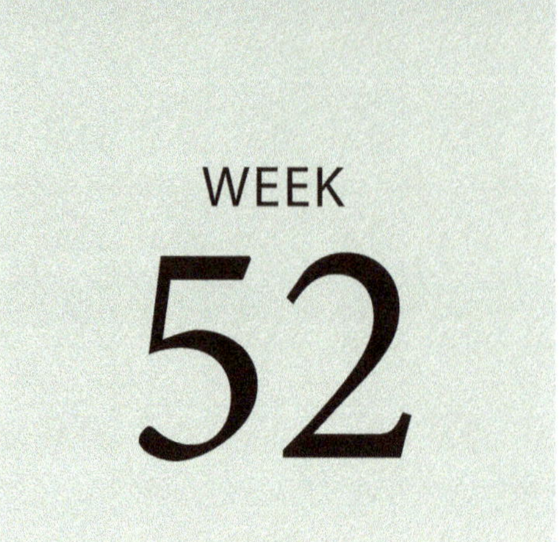

DECEMBER 13–19, 2016

"Full Circle"

Finishing Where I Began

E. Donegal Riverfront Park, Marietta, PA

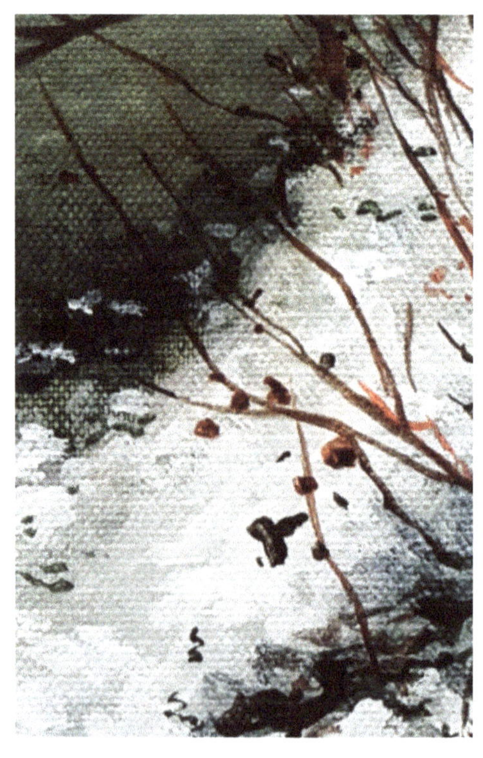

Highs and lows, swifts and slows,
Paddling fast, nose just above water,
Drifting lazy on my back.
You catch me watching you
And listening to your song.

Cold and frosty, frozen hard;
Warm and balmy, sandy shores;
Moonlit, starry, foggy, (froggie), soggy.
What costume will you choose next?
No matter; I adore your every look.

Rippled, white-capped, smooth as glass,
Steely gray or crystal clear,
Reflections cast.
Blue, green, brown and purple dark;
Bronze, gold, silver, gray and white,
Let me guess what shade is next.

Long I've loved you, kept your gifts.
Current colors, constantly drifting,
Moods and phases, going places.
Too soon you take my yesterdays,
Yet promise more tomorrows.

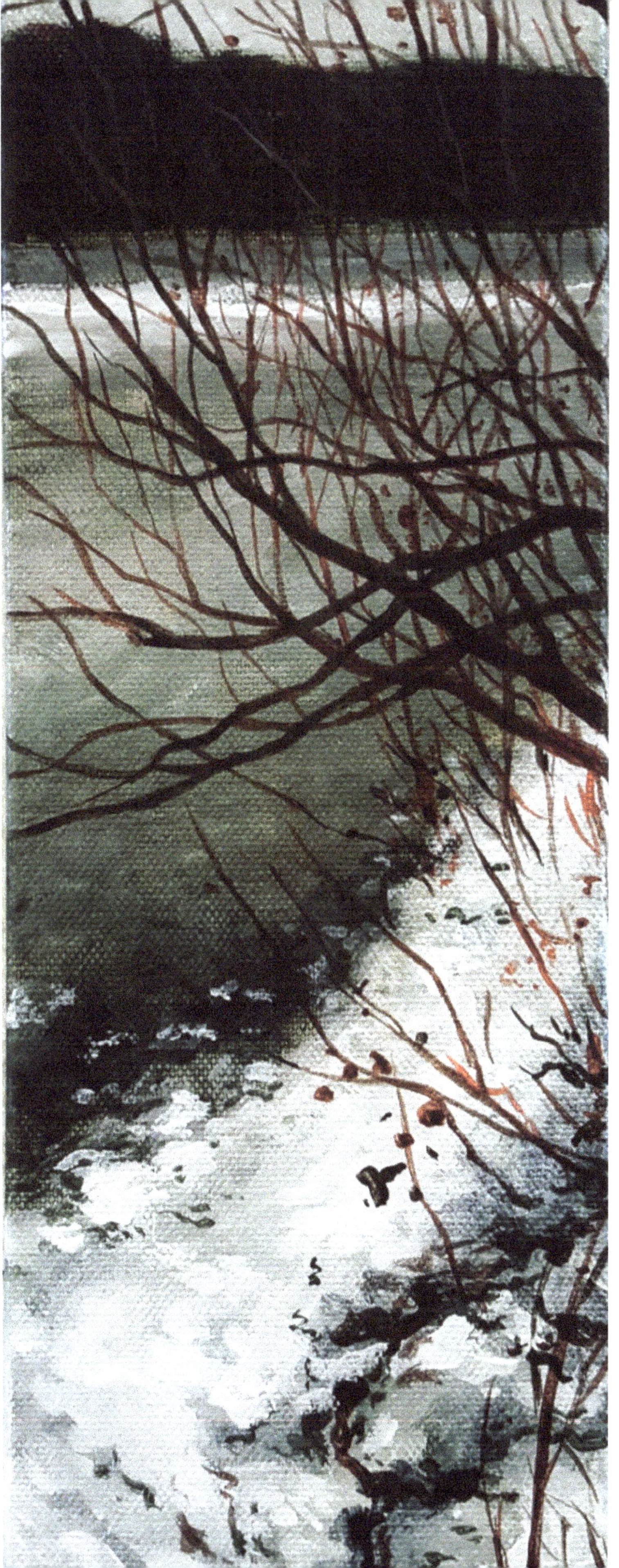

DECEMBER 20–27, 2016

"Black + White + Open Water"

Blue Rock Boat Ramp, Washington Boro, PA

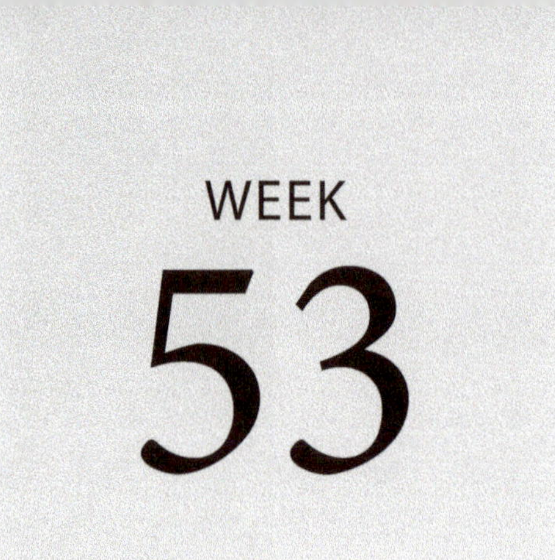

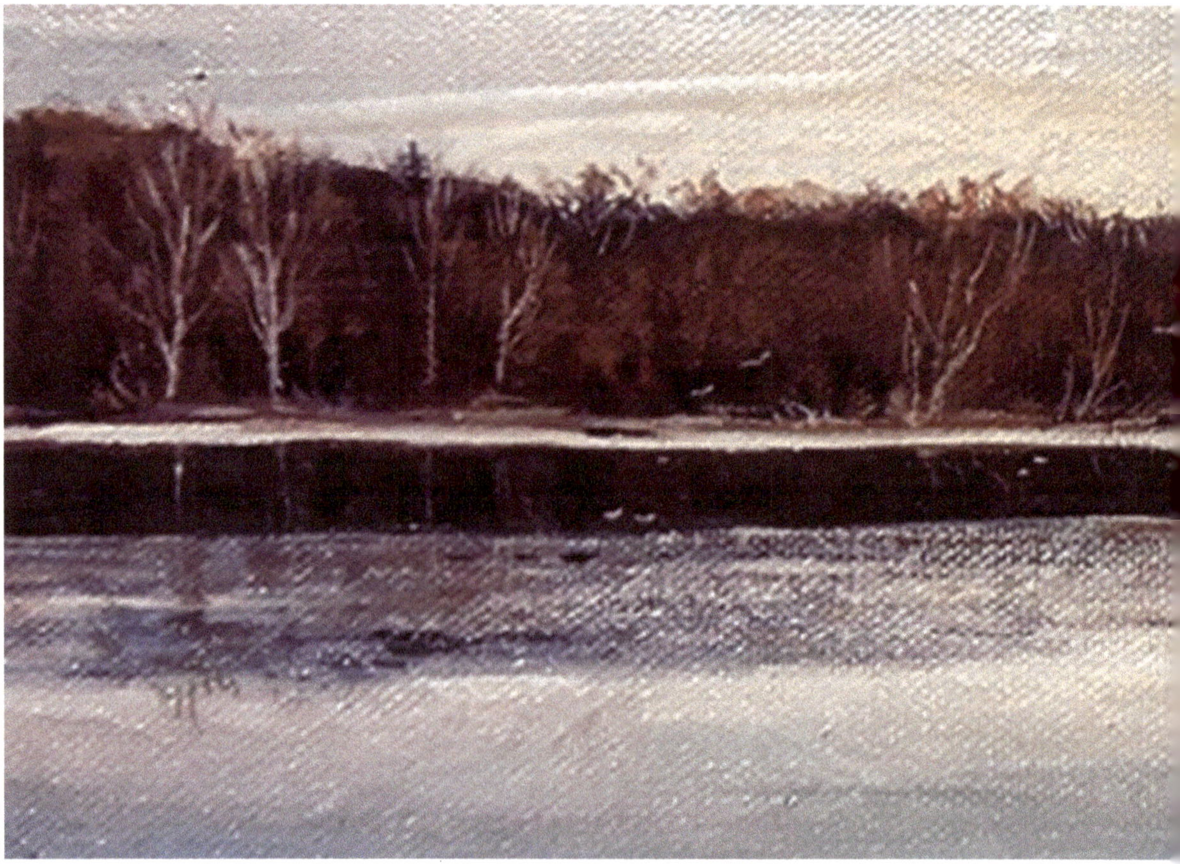

Finishing out the last week of the year, I'm down at the Blue Rock Road boat ramp again. I loved the white sycamores in winter against the dark woods. White seagulls wheel around above a channel of open water, all mysteriously black in the reflection of the island.

The water is shallow here at the "flats," and parts of the river are frozen over early this season. The sky has a pinkish cast, and the highest branches of the trees are a rusty, reddish, sienna brown.

Tranquility—I need it. It soothes the private tumult in my poor head and heart and soul.

Thank you, sweet Susquehanna, dear river that I call "friend." As long as I am able, I will need to visit you. I will probably never stop painting you.

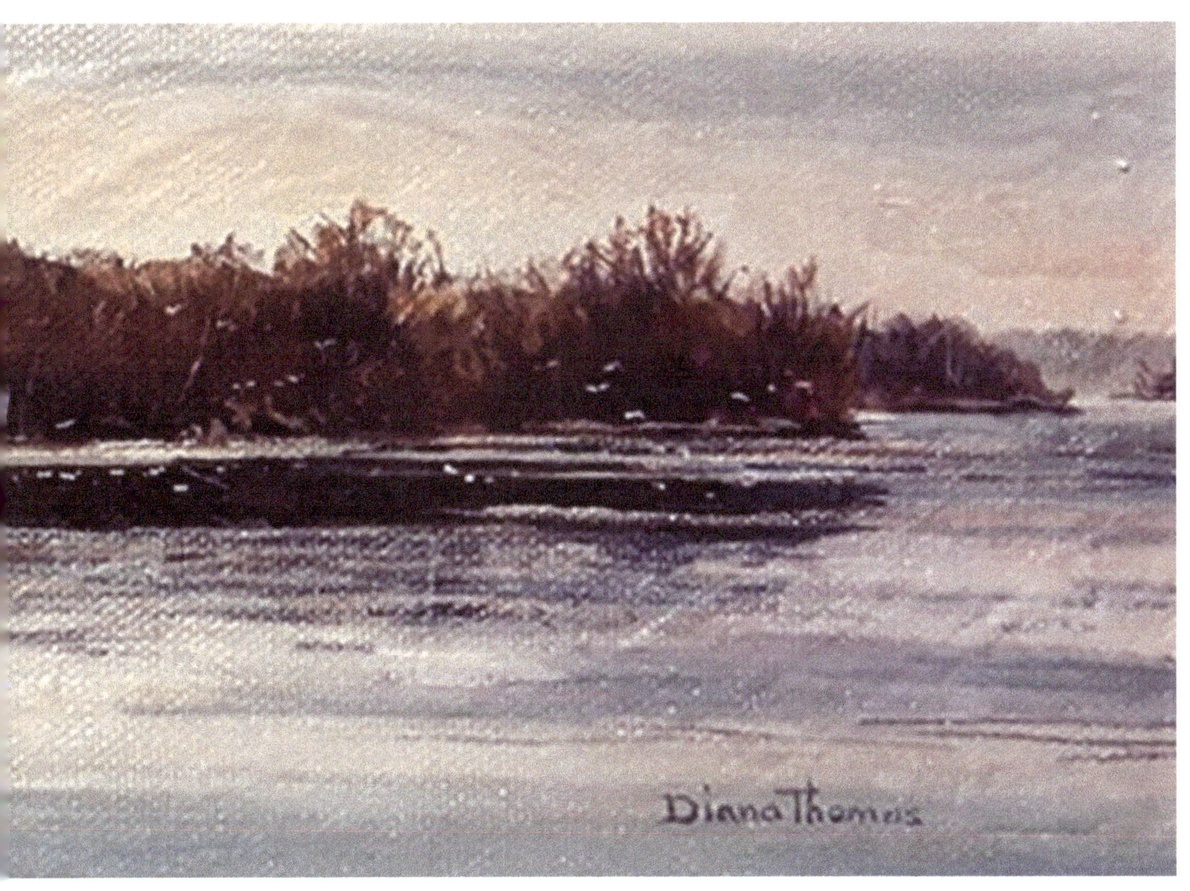

"Chiques View"

Chiques Rock Overlook, Marietta, PA | 2018

These final pages contain works created after the year of "Current Color," but they are not the end by any means. A few of these paintings are taken from photos I took during the initial year of painting. I've only just begun to scratch the surface of the paintings I'd like to do of the wildlife I've observed along the river's banks. New artworks will surely flow from the Susquehanna's amazing story of life as long as I can hold a pencil or paintbrush.

Since I've taken thousands of photos of the river and cherish this repository of images, I have a means of wandering the Susquehanna's shores when the day comes that I'll no longer tread her ancient paths by foot.

I fell in love with the Susquehanna River on my first visit to Lancaster County in 1975. Six years later when I moved to the area, the Susquehanna's siren song soon called me to her banks in every season. She has been my muse, my comfort and my delight since then.

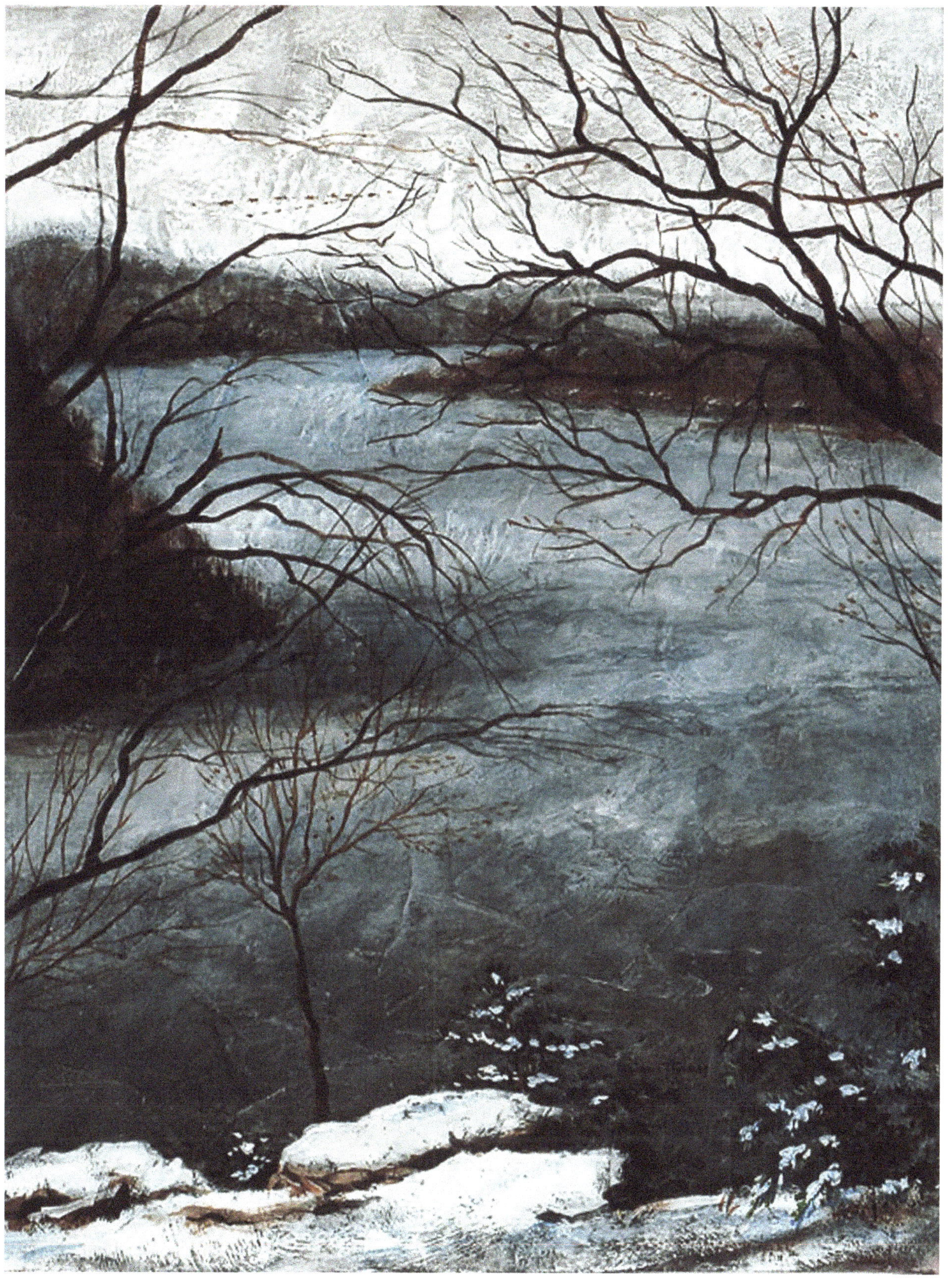

"Mr. and Mrs."

Stolen? Stolen! | December 2017

I loaned 20 of the "Current Color" paintings to a River organization for display in Williamsport, Pennsylvania.

When it was time to make arrangements to return the art, I got a call from one of the young ladies from the organization. Her voice was trembling as

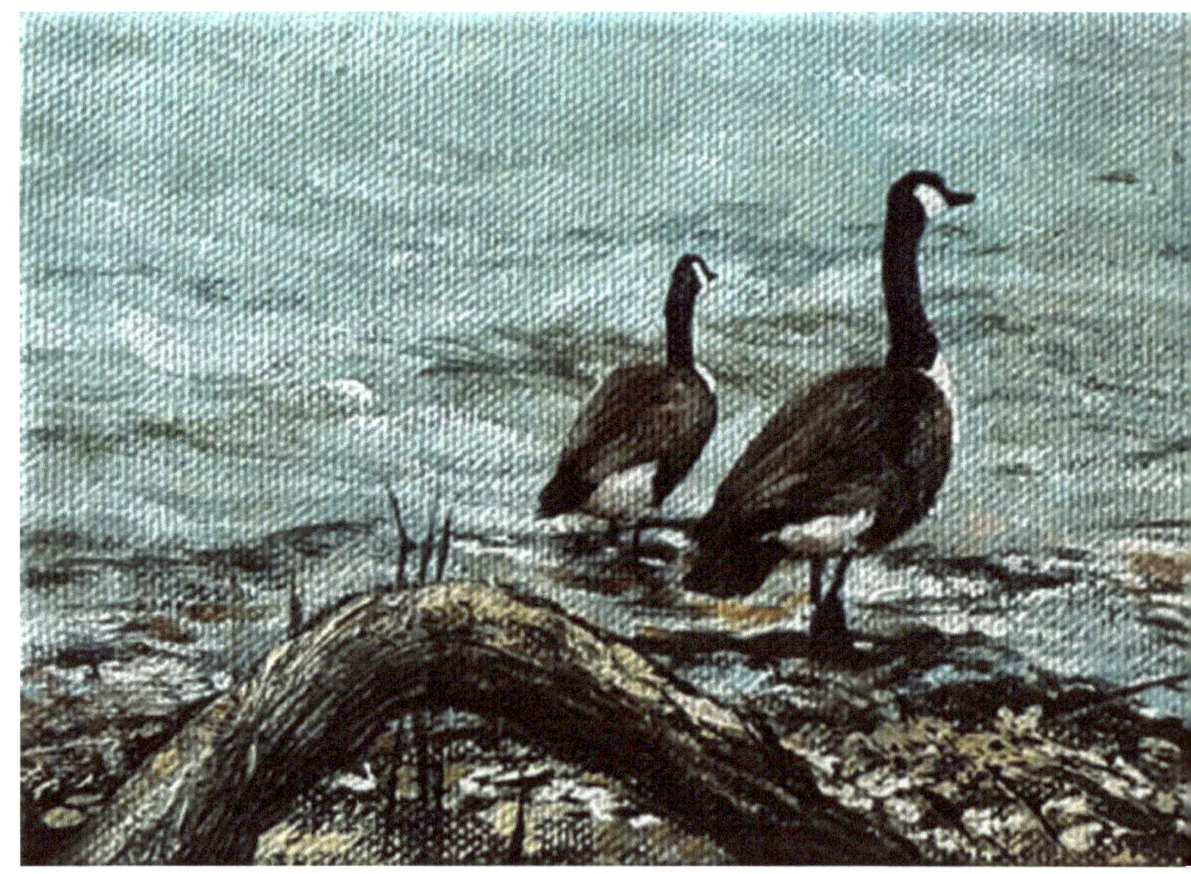

she told me that one of the paintings had been stolen! It took a minute for it all to soak in. Then my main thought was that I would really like to know why the person who took it was so drawn to that piece!

My second thought was that this is a new chapter of the story of "Current Color." A stolen piece fit right in with the lessons I had been learning from the river. Being at the river brought me back to the fact that life goes on. Things come in the flow—both good and bad—that you don't expect. Their beauty shines for a little while; they don't stay forever.

Psalm 103, my favorite psalm, says, "As for man, his days are like grass; as a flower of the field, he flourishes. For the wind passes over it, and it is gone, and its place remembers it no more" (Psalm 103:15–16 NKJV).

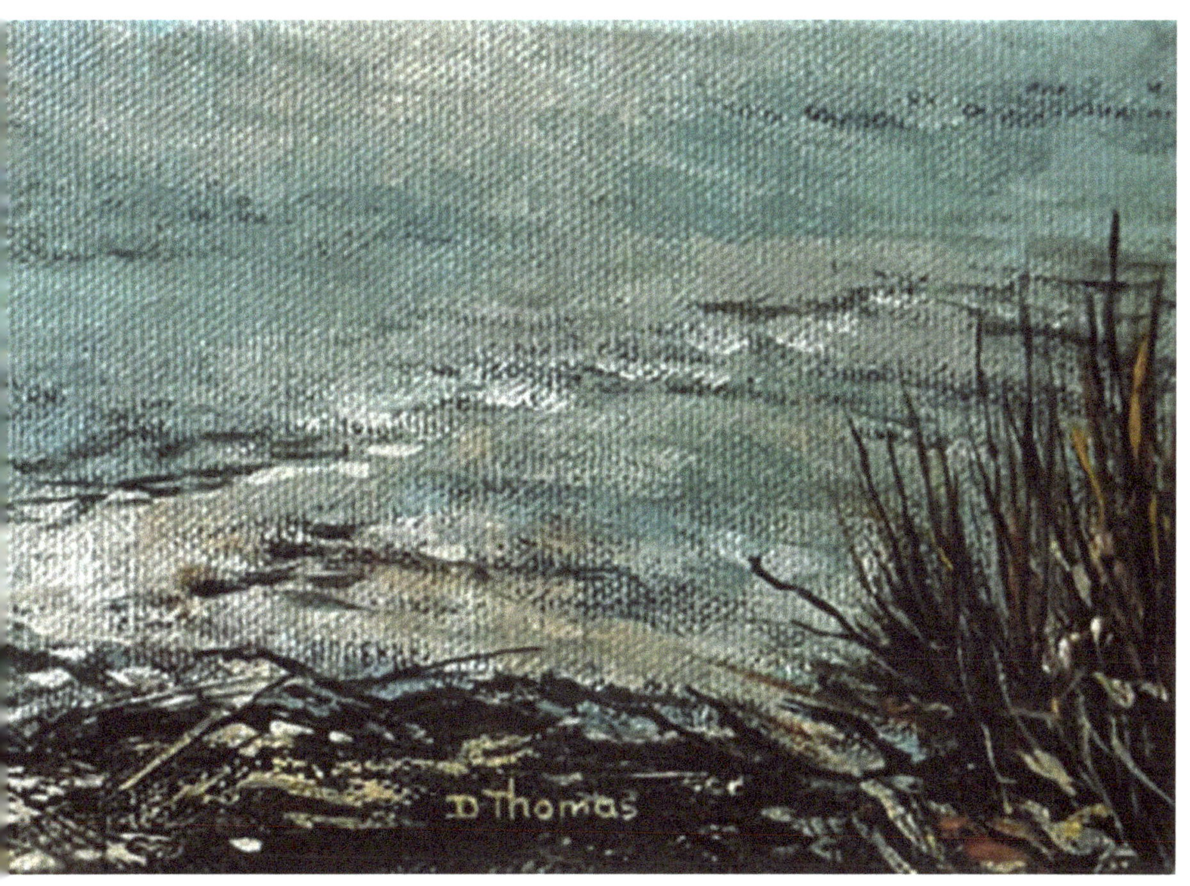

"Lake Clark Light"

Long Level, Wrightsville, PA | January 2018

We have a unique guiding light for the river's boaters and fishermen on the lake formed by Safe Harbor Dam.

As a subject, the light isn't one I was very interested in, but I decided to do it anyway because people like lighthouses.

This one isn't big enough for a "house" in it. It is, however, a recognizable feature of our river at Long Level.

The stormy sky was photographed from the Route 462 bridge on the way to Long Level on the same day I took photos of the light. (Artistic license and good ol' Photoshop combined them.) I can't say I'm at all happy with the lighting on this one, but it's done now.

I hope I am gaining wisdom as I move on through this life. I am glad I have a "lighthouse" in the words of scripture to help me navigate through the storms.

Postscript: Today (April 18, 2019) I met the man who built Lake Clark Light, and we had a good conversation. He built the light "twenty-some years ago as a way to distinguish my marina from Long Level Marina," he said. He described the way he built it; it was made so that it could be easily disassembled in case of flood or ice thaw damage. He said he used a cherry picker to have it painted about every five years and to change the industrial strobe light up top.

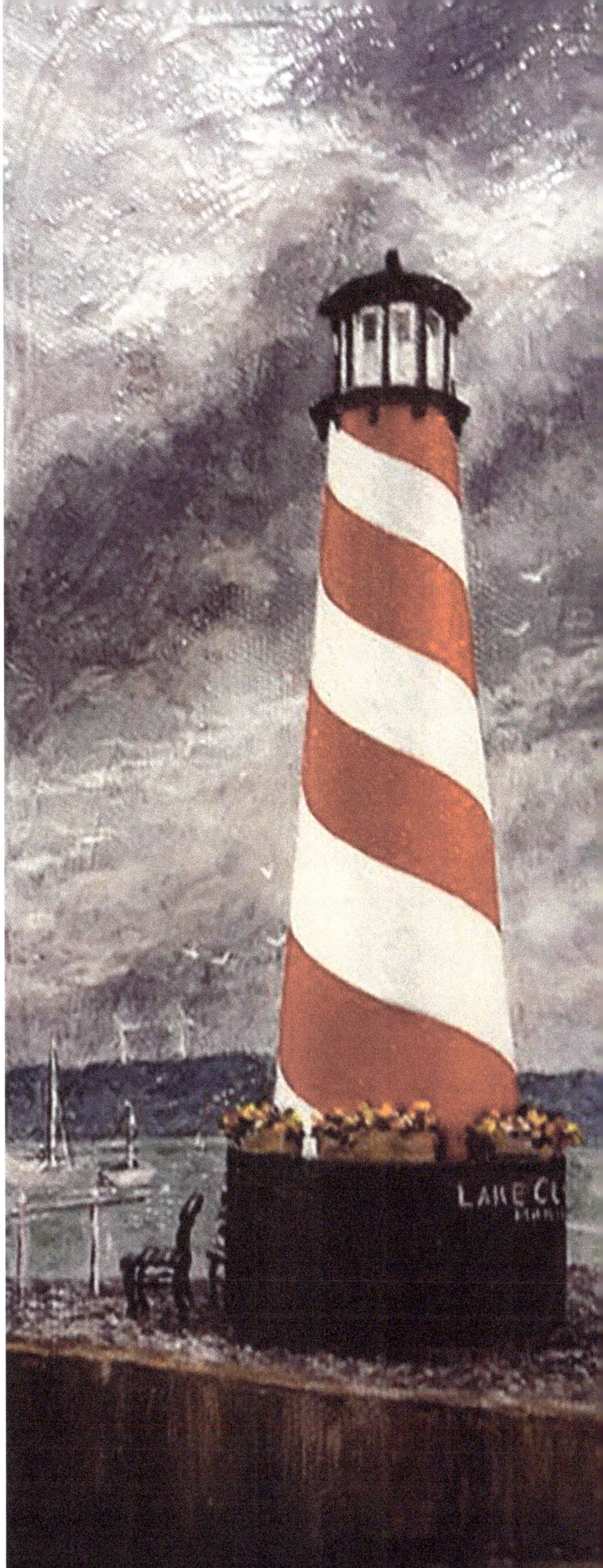

"*Sailboat Cameo*"

Long Level, Wrightsville, PA | March 2018

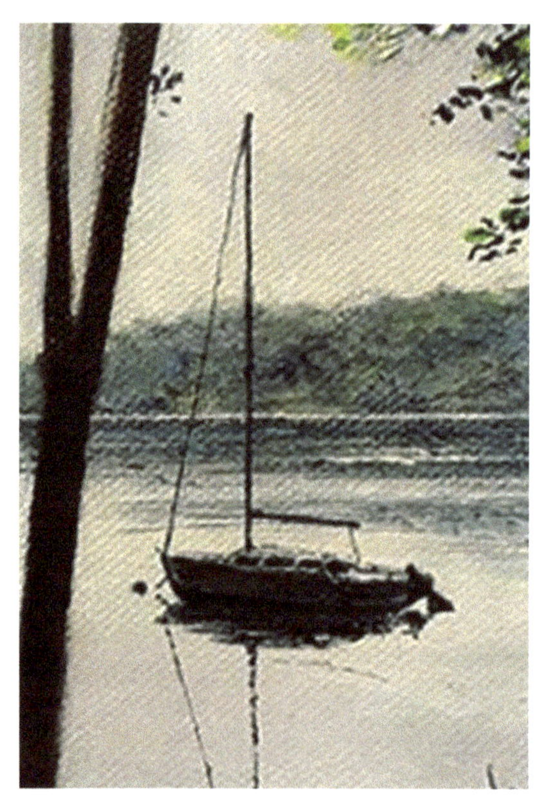

I've wanted to paint this one for a while.

When I took this photo in July 2016, I really loved the contrast of the two dappled greens where the light came through the trees onto the green, green, shady summer grass.

Peace finds me here so often. The still water He leads me beside restores my soul indeed, just like Psalm 23 clearly reminds me.

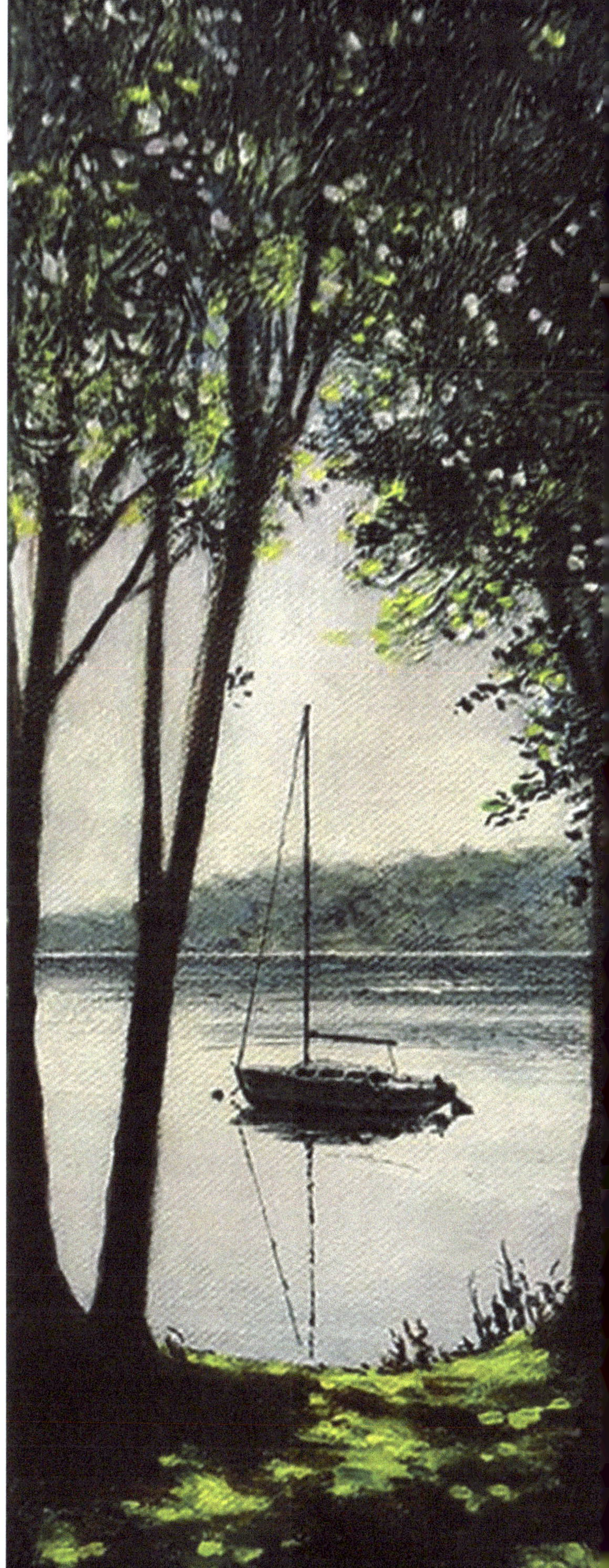

"Mr. and Mrs. 2"

Indian Steps, York County, PA | March 2019

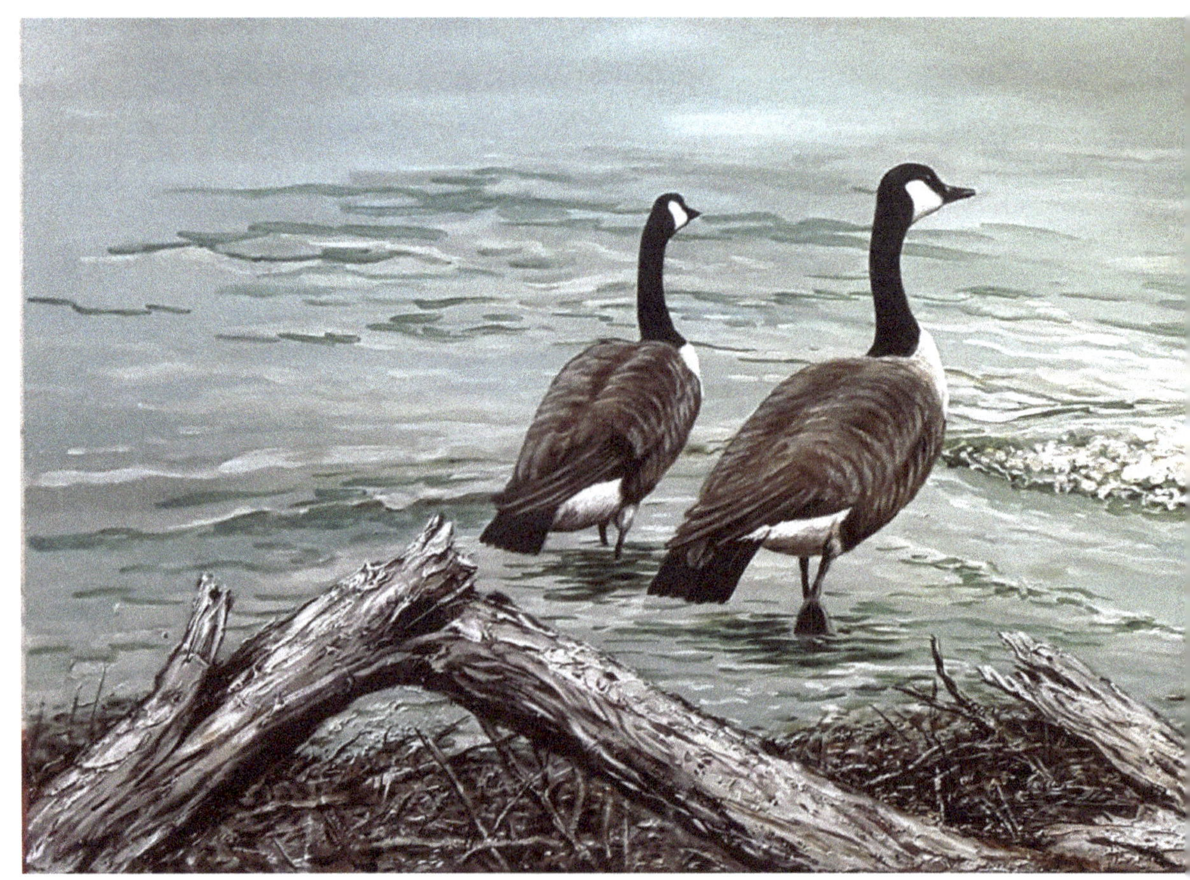

Well, this is interesting. Almost exactly three years after painting the first original for Week 13, I am painting a "new" replacement for this one. I have wanted to paint a few of these at three times the size (12" x 36"), and it seemed perfect to start with this one, since the little original is gone now.

Just painting so much bigger seemed a little frightening, and so was my plan to add the little cresting wave from the original photo.

My first try had some nice features, but I just couldn't live with the first result. There is too much going on; geese are not big enough or dark enough; blah blah blah…. So, I whited out some of it and tried again. I can live with this one. It's much calmer.

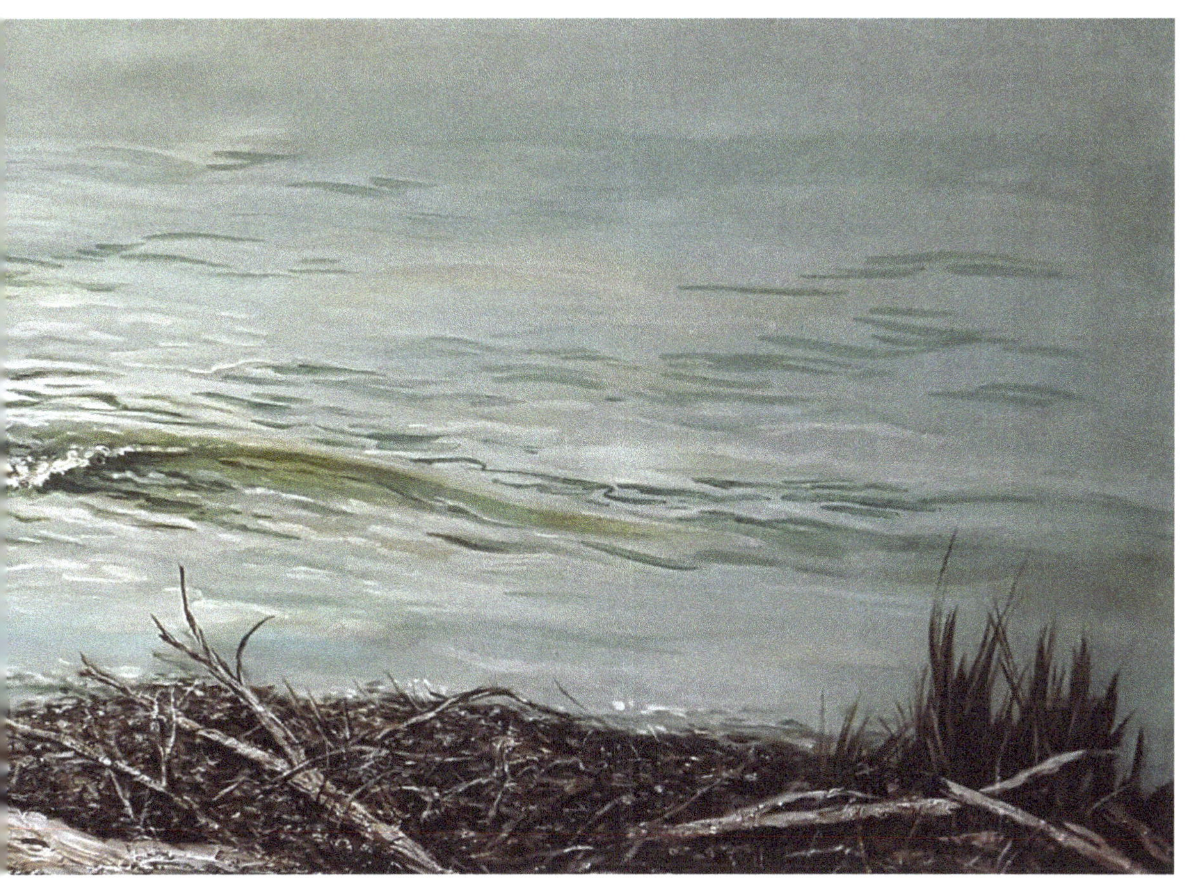

AFTERWORD 6
"Petroglyphs"
April–May 2020

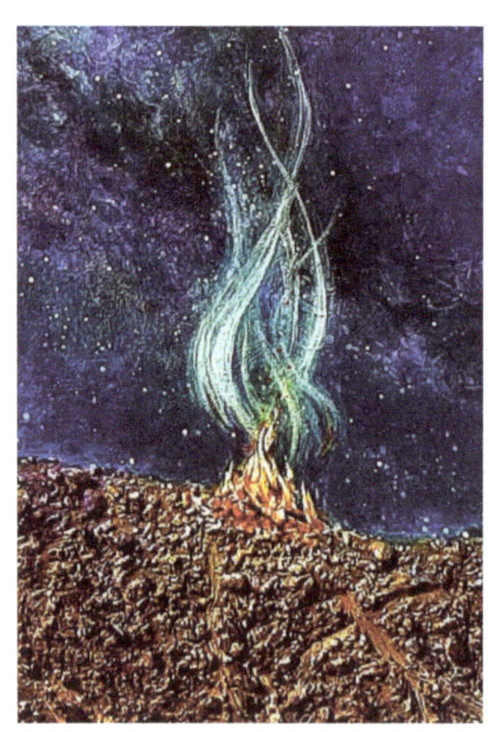

During the year of painting the "Current Color" series, I had wanted to do a scene that included a depiction of the petroglyphs carved into the river's island-like rocks centuries ago by the Susquehannocks, a tribe living along the southern reaches of the Susquehanna River. Their artful markings represented the natural world and the spiritual world.

As an artist, amateur naturalist and contemplative Christian, it wasn't hard to imagine the creators of these works needing to record their grateful awe of the sky above, the majestic river and every part of world in which they lived.

As it turned out, this piece had its own timeline for coming into being and was created a few years after the "Current Color" series, allowing me the time I needed to navigate some deep passages in my own life.

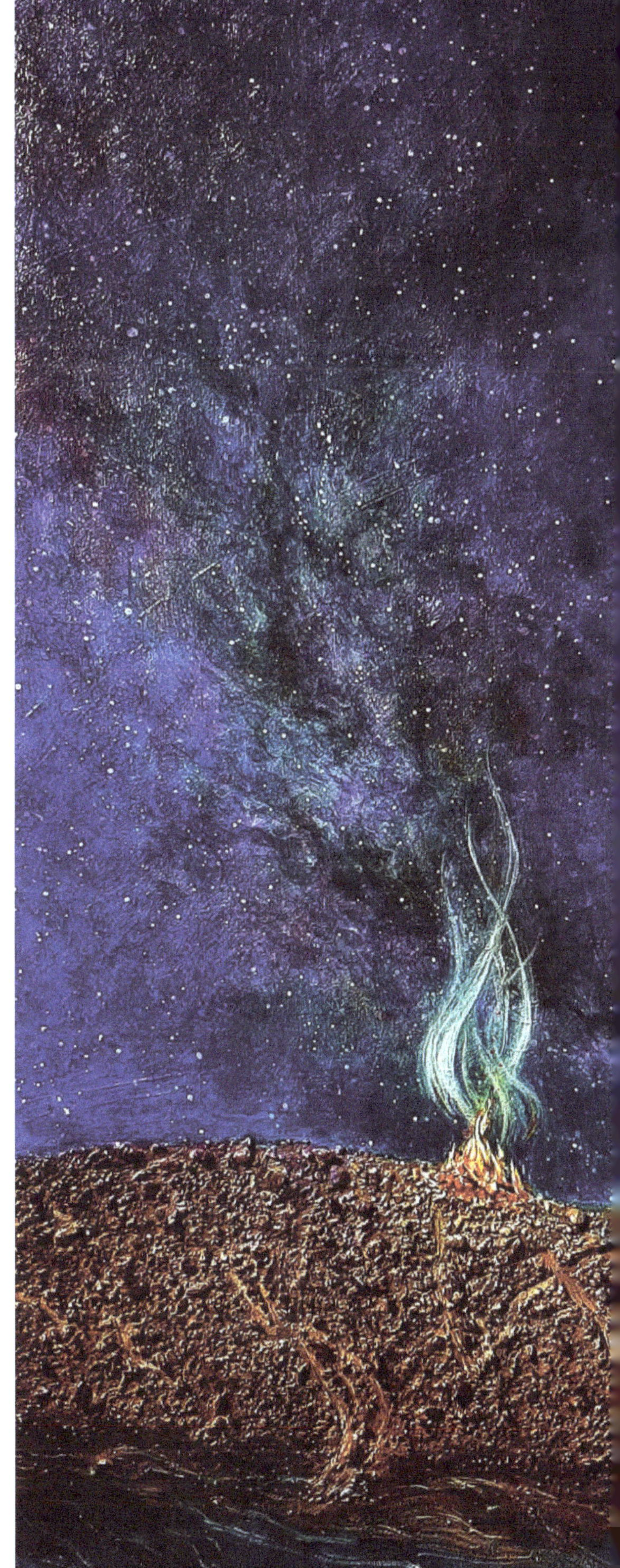

"Havre de Grace Light"

May 2020

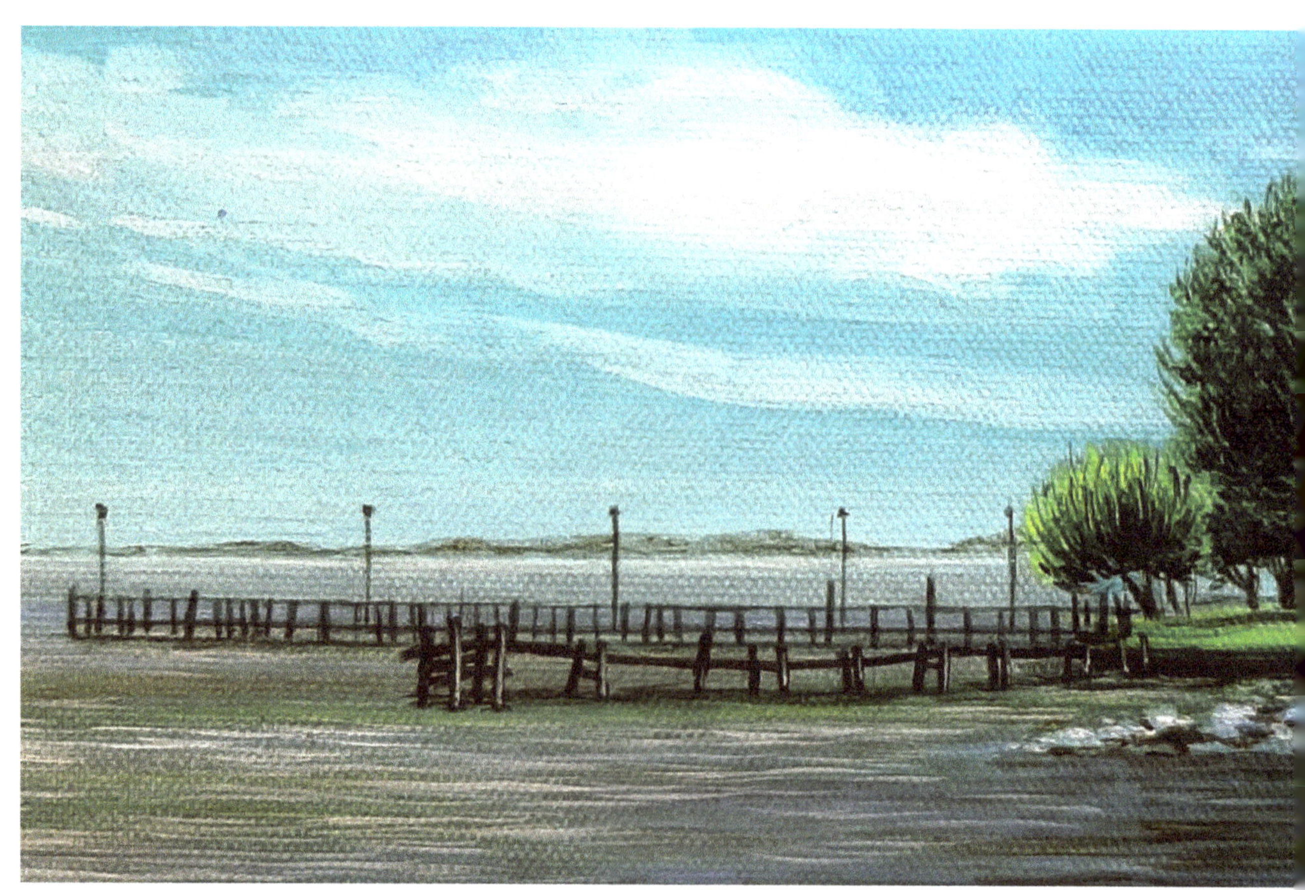

On Mother's Day, all my children sent me cards and flowers and phoned me with sweet and thoughtful messages. Though I tried not to let in the blues, I could feel them creeping into my heart, so I decided to head down to one of my favorite river locations, Havre de Grace, Maryland, for a bit of an artsy change of pace. I spent a pleasant afternoon walking the boardwalk and sketching in the park. Later, I painted this from some of the photos I took. Feeling better, I enjoyed the drive home. Thank you, river. You always bring me peace.

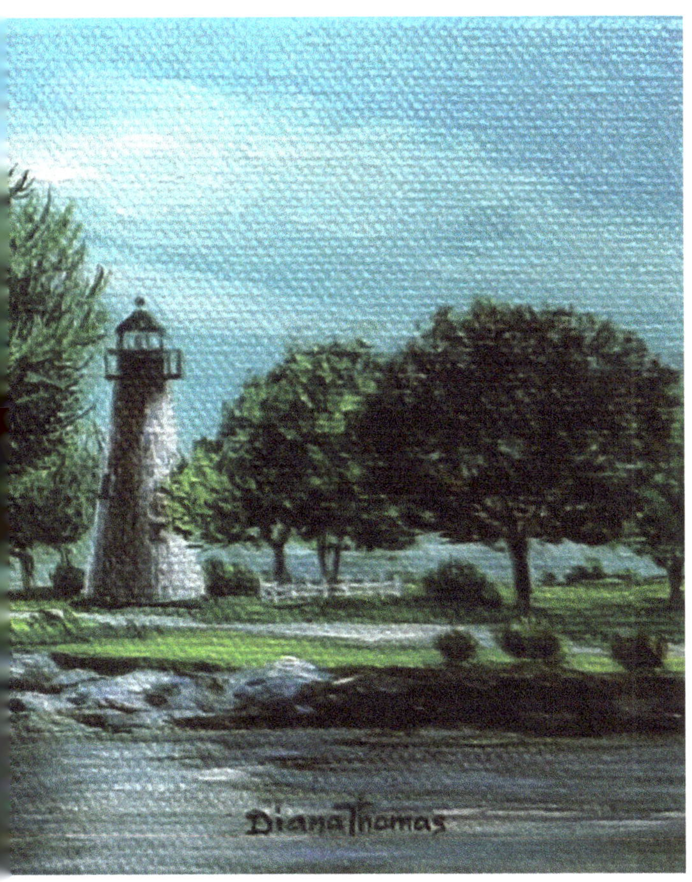

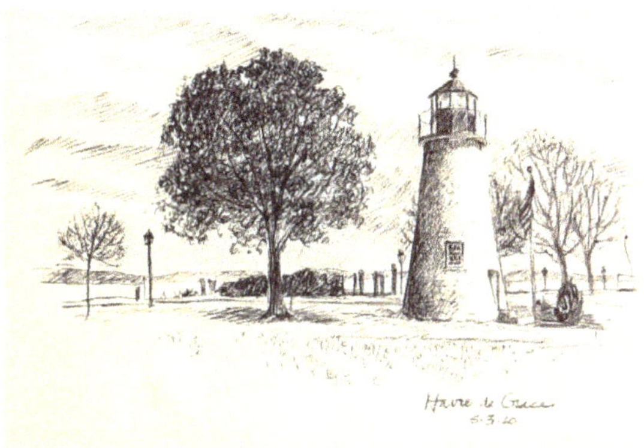

"Great Blue"

Photo reference by Terri Pouliot | June 2020

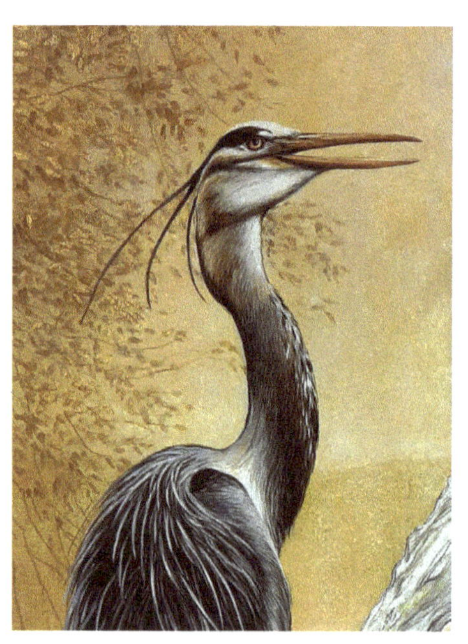

Elegant, tranquil, stately, great blue.
A mystic spirit, you follow your own path.
You wade the river's shores and glide
Slowly overhead in evening croaking a
Raspy "good night."

You carry peace and grace but, oh,
How sharp your eye. How quickly you
Dart your swordlike beak into still
Water for a morning snack.

You are one of the river's sentinels,
Solitary, a keeper of its secrets, a
Knower of its changing ways. A guardian
Of nature's wisdom.

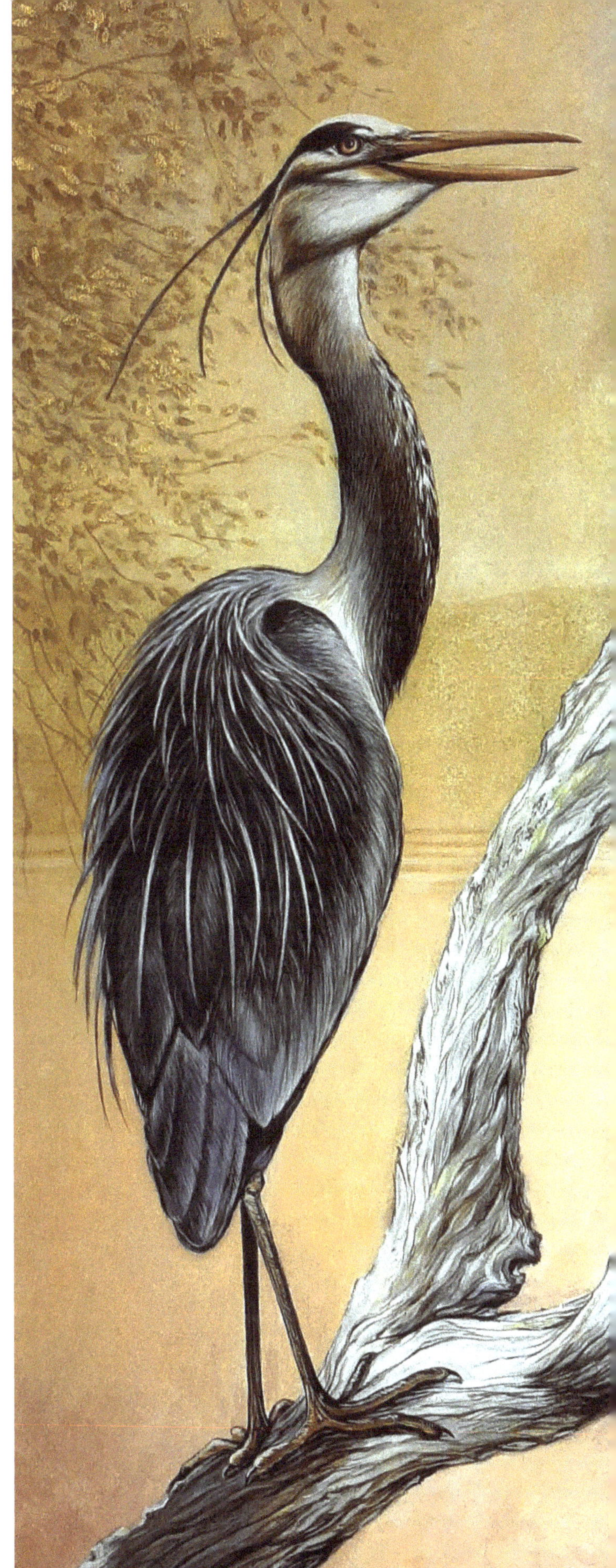

"Peregrine Falcon"

Photo credit: Brad Hepfer | October 2020

The Peregrine falcon, a medium-sized raptor, is one of the fastest animals on earth, able to reach more than 200 miles an hour as it dives for prey, killing it with a sharp blow.

A pair has frequented a high cliff nesting site along the Enola Low Grade Trail for several years. They are fierce sentinels as they search for prey and are not above dive-bombing cyclists riding below on the trail during nesting season or even fighting with a thieving, much larger Bald Eagle to retain their catch.

I marvel that for thousands of years, Peregrines have been captive companions of humans the world over as they work together to hunt small game. Their striking head coloration and speed of flight make them one of my favorite species to spot on the trail.

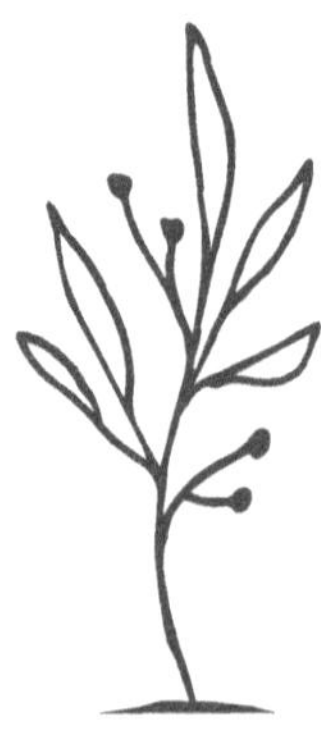

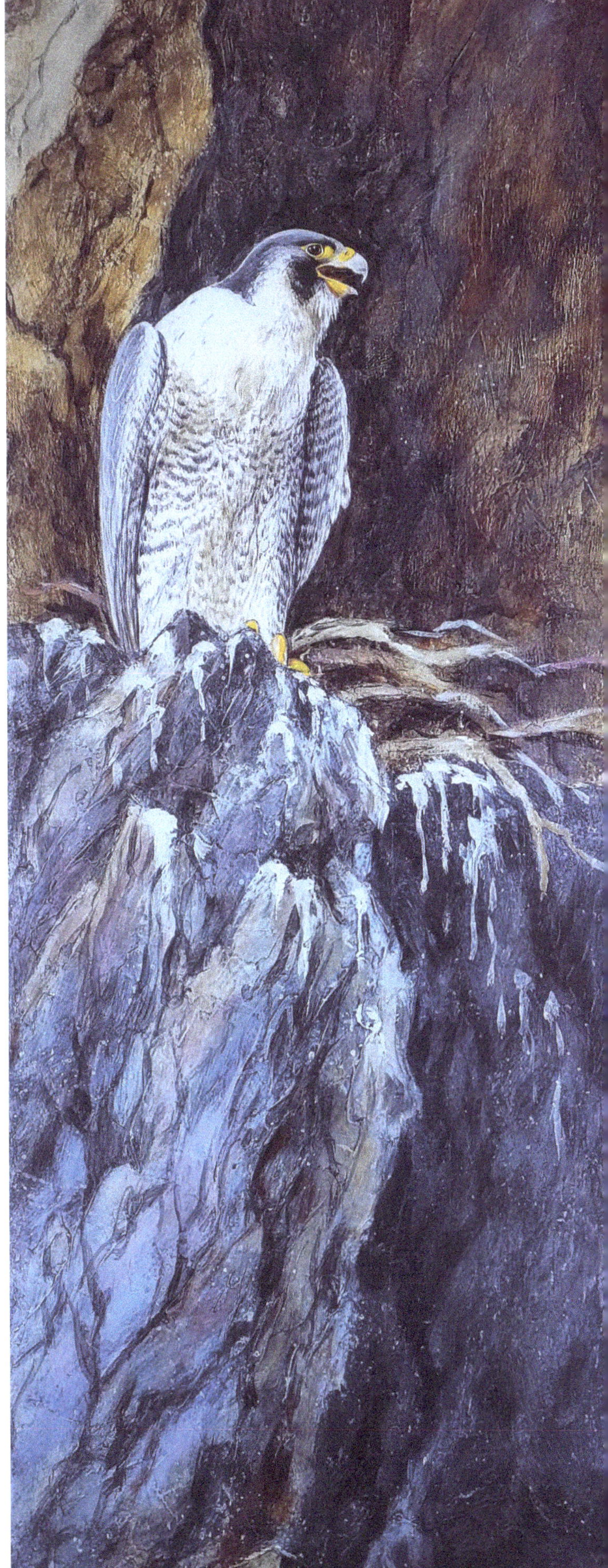

"Does the hawk take flight by
your wisdom and spread its
wings toward the south? Does
the eagle soar at your command
and build its nest on high?
It dwells on a cliff and stays
there at night; a rocky crag is
its stronghold. From there it
looks for food; its eyes detect it
from afar."

(Job 39:26–29)

"Mosaic Sunset"

September 2024

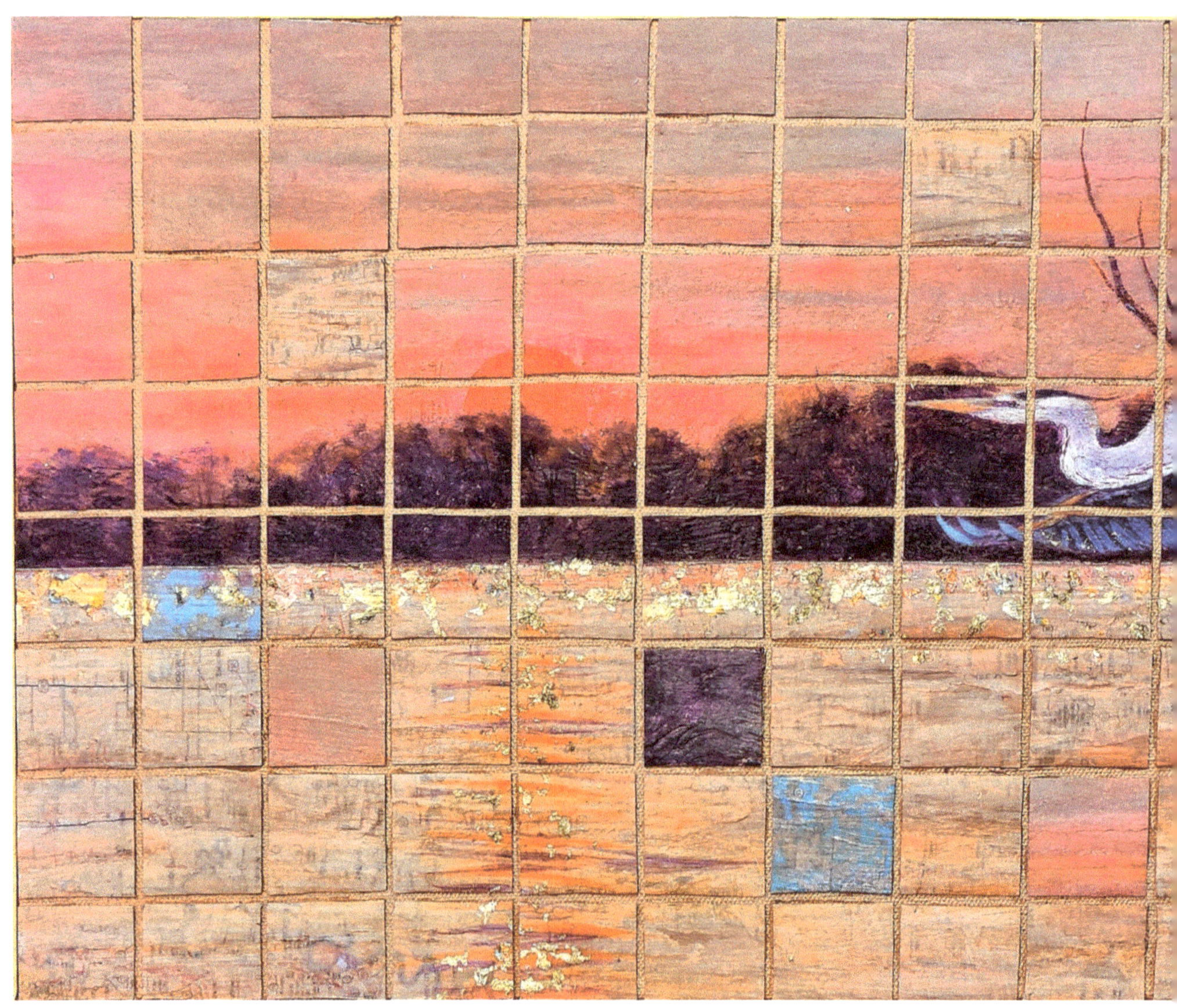

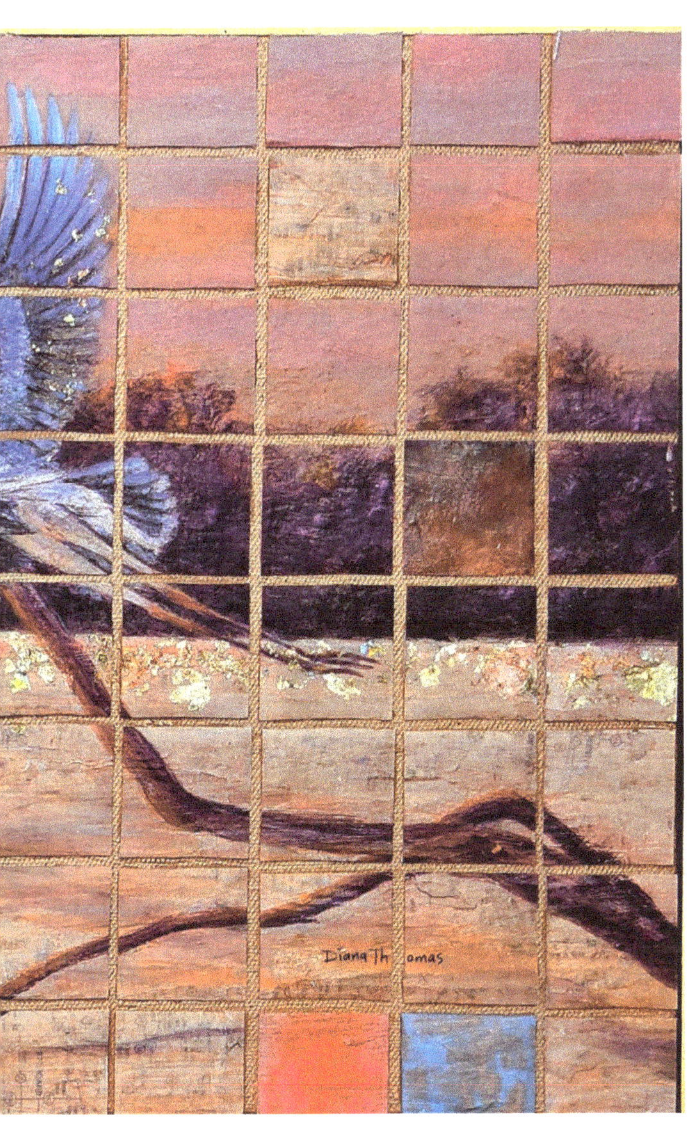

This is a variation on one of my favorite pieces from the "Current Color" series, Week 33, "Evening Commute." I don't really consider it an improvement on the original and definitely not what I'd been shooting for, but it is unique, and experience has shown that's how art works sometimes.

I'd wanted to recreate the original work at a larger size, but after three attempts, I still wasn't happy with the colors or the composition. On the fourth try, I opted for just having fun. The addition of torn pieces of a road map collaged onto the area of the water was an addition I liked, but the composition still left something to be desired.

In an attempt to salvage portions of the piece I did like, I cut the canvas from its frame, shortened the overall size, sliced it into squares, then applied those squares to a new, smaller canvas covered with bronze metallic paint. A few blocks were tinted with colors from elsewhere in the painting, and gold leaf flakes were added. Like some others in the original series, it's not a favorite, but it's interesting, and I can live with it.

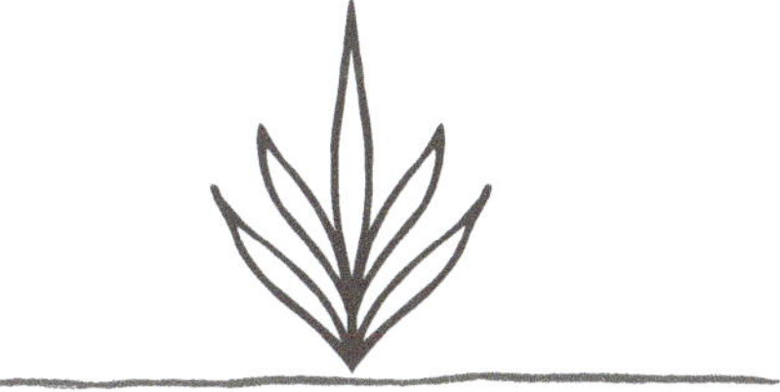

AFTERWORD 11

"River Quilt"

Colors, and currents, seasons and settings,

The River's kaleidoscope of memories

Transport and bring me food for the senses;

Waters lapping on sandy shores,

Musky smell of water and the debris she carries,

Mud, fish, turtles and sun-baked rocks, I hold them all.

An Eagle's piercing cry far overhead,

A Heron, statue still, patient in his fishing spot.

Children at play making little boats of sticks,

Or chasing geese and ducks from their naps,

Old men casting for a big ol' bass,

And lovers walking hand in hand in evening.

Let me find a way to thank you, Susquehanna,

For all you've given me.

"A river watering the garden flowed from Eden; from there it was separated into four headwaters. The name of the first is Pishon; it winds through the entire land of Havilah, where there is gold. (The gold of that land is good; aromatic resin and onyx are also there.)"

(Genesis 2:10–12)

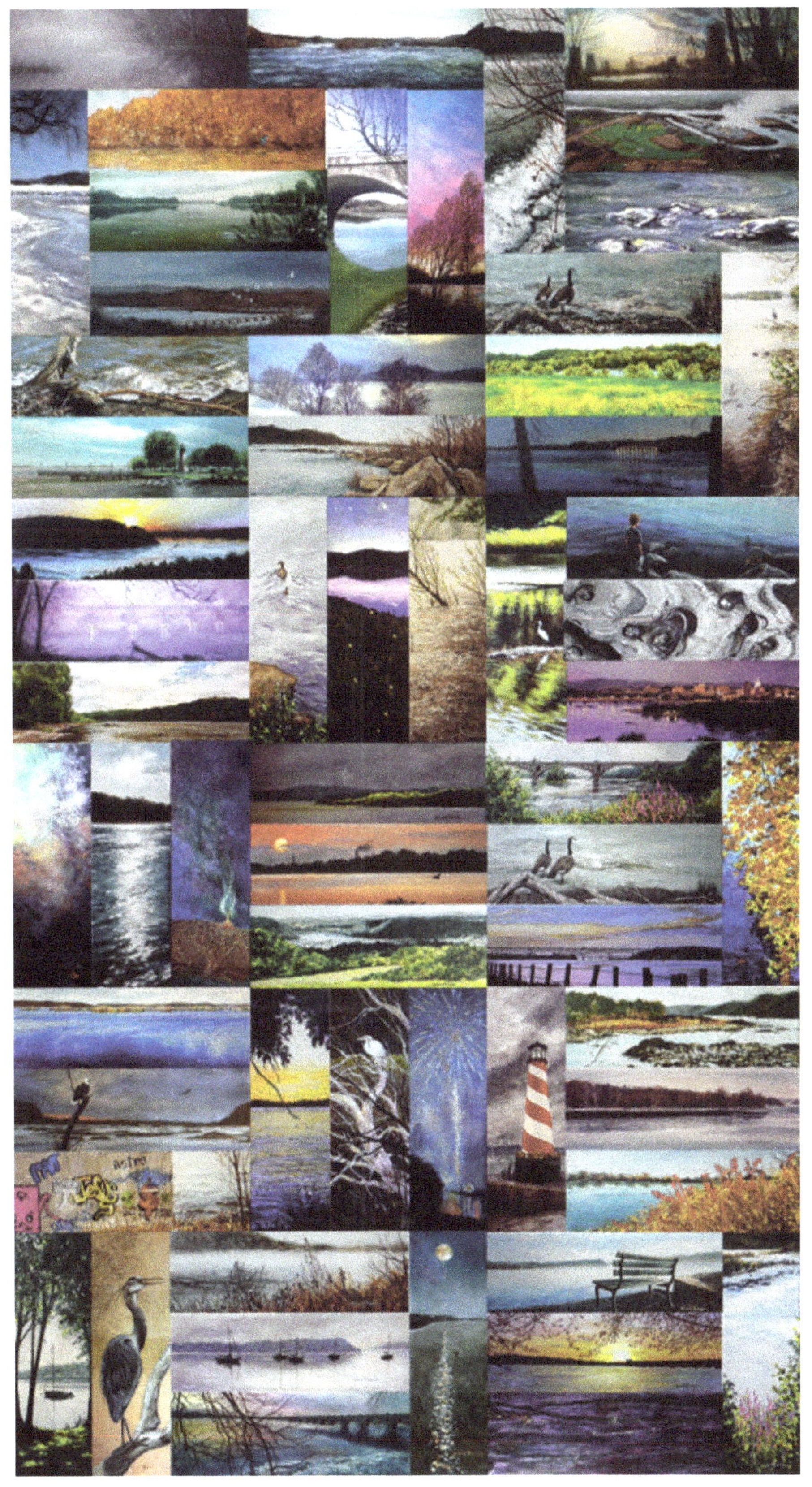